The Elections of 2012

CQ Press, an imprint of SAGE, is the leading publisher of books, periodicals, and electronic products on American government and international affairs. CQ Press consistently ranks among the top commercial publishers in terms of quality, as evidenced by the numerous awards its products have won over the years. CQ Press owes its existence to Nelson Poynter, former publisher of the *St. Petersburg Times,* and his wife Henrietta, with whom he founded Congressional Quarterly in 1945. Poynter established CQ with the mission of promoting democracy through education and in 1975 founded the Modern Media Institute, renamed The Poynter Institute for Media Studies after his death. The Poynter Institute (*www.poynter.org*) is a nonprofit organization dedicated to training journalists and media leaders

In 2008, CQ Press was acquired by SAGE, a leading international publisher of journals, books, and electronic media for academic, educational, and professional markets. Since 1965, SAGE has helped inform and educate a global community of scholars, practitioners, researchers, and students spanning a wide range of subject areas, including business, humanities, social sciences, and science, technology, and medicine. A privately owned corporation, SAGE has offices in Los Angeles, London, New Delhi, and Singapore, in addition to the Washington DC office of CQ Press.

The Elections of 2012

Michael Nelson
EDITOR

Los Angeles | London | New Delhi
Singapore | Washington DC

Los Angeles | London | New Delhi
Singapore | Washington DC

FOR INFORMATION:

CQ Press
An Imprint of SAGE Publications, Inc.
2455 Teller Road
Thousand Oaks, California 91320
E-mail: order@sagepub.com

SAGE Publications Ltd.
1 Oliver's Yard
55 City Road
London, EC1Y 1SP
United Kingdom

SAGE Publications India Pvt. Ltd.
B 1/I 1 Mohan Cooperative Industrial Area
Mathura Road, New Delhi 110 044
India

SAGE Publications Asia-Pacific Pte. Ltd.
3 Church Street
#10-04 Samsung Hub
Singapore 049483

Acquisitions Editor: Charisse Kiino
Production Editor: Veronica Hooper
Copy Editor: Gretchen Treadwell
Typesetter: Hurix Systems Private Ltd.
Proofreader: Dennis W. Webb
Cover Designer: Auburn Associates, Inc.
Marketing Manager: Jonathan Mason
Permissions Editor: Jennifer Barron

Printed in the United States of America

Library of Congress Cataloging-in-Publication Data

A catalog record of this book is available from the Library of Congress.

ISBN: 9781452239934

This book is printed on acid-free paper.

SFI label applies to text stock

13 14 15 16 17 10 9 8 7 6 5 4 3 2 1

Contents

Preface

The Elections of 2012 is the eighth in a series of post-election books by eminent scholars that began in 1984. In four of those elections, a president was reelected to a second term: Ronald Reagan in 1984, Bill Clinton in 1996, George W. Bush in 2004, and Barack Obama in 2012. In all four cases, control of the House of Representatives and the Senate remained in the same political party's hands as before the election. In that sense 2012 was, like its predecessors, an election that affirmed rather than altered the status quo. Both before and after election day, the nation was governed by a Democratic president and Senate and a Republican House.

In another politically important sense, however, 2012 was different. The status quo election was the product of a changing and increasingly more diverse electorate. Voters in 2012 were on average younger than in 1984; they also were more likely to be members of ethnic or racial minorities and less likely to be married or religious. All of these trends favored Obama and other Democratic candidates and caused Republicans to worry that unless their party broadens its appeal to include these growing sectors of the population, its future will be marked by gradual decline.

An awareness of how elections mark both continuity and change animates every chapter of *The Elections of 2012*, all of them by scholars who are accomplished political scientists and engaging writers. In addition to reporting and interpreting the events of 2012, all nine chapters look back in time to place the year's events in historical, institutional, and theoretical contexts. Each chapter also looks forward in assessing the elections' consequences for politics and public policy. Each can be read with profit and pleasure by research scholars, first-year students, and everyone in between.

Understanding why the elections turned out as they did is an important enterprise. Thus, in Chapter 2 Barry C. Burden recounts the presidential nominating process that in 2012 generated the candidacies of the Republican Mitt Romney and the Democrat Barack Obama. In Chapter 3 Marc J. Hetherington carries forward the narrative and analysis through the general election campaign that ended on November 6, 2012. Nicole Mellow assays the regional, demographic, and other bases of voting behavior in Chapter 4. Marjorie Randon Hershey chronicles the rapidly changing role of the media in Chapter 5, and Marian Currinder examines the equally transformed campaign funding landscape in Chapter 6.

Understanding the consequences of the elections for politics and government is also an important task. Gary C. Jacobson in Chapter 7 and Bruce Nesmith and Paul J. Quirk in Chapter 8 write revealingly about the election campaign and results. But their main concerns are for how in coming years the elections will affect the presidency and Congress, respectively. The same is true of the book's first and final chapters: Chapter 1, in which Michael Nelson discusses the historically distinctive and frustrating challenges faced by second-term presidents, and Chapter 9, in which David R. Mayhew assesses the additional challenges confronting President Obama in an era of divided party control and partisan polarization.

On behalf of myself and the other contributors, I offer much-deserved thanks to the outstanding editorial, production, and marketing teams at CQ Press for the assurance, skill, warmth, enthusiasm, and helpfulness with which they worked on this book. We especially thank publisher Charisse Kiino, executive editorial director Brenda Carter, project editor Veronica Hooper, copy editor Gretchen Treadwell, and editorial assistant Davia Grant. As editor of the book, I am also grateful for the reviews of previous works in this series by Rob Boatright, Clark University; Matthew Dickinson, Middlebury College; William Field, Rutgers University; and Veronica Womack, Georgia College and State University.

Michael Nelson
January 2013

About the Contributors

About the Editor

Michael Nelson is Fulmer Professor of Political Science at Rhodes College and a senior fellow at the University of Virginia's Miller Center. A former editor of *The Washington Monthly,* his most recent books include *The Evolving Presidency: Landmark Documents,* 1787–2010 (2012), *The American Presidency: Origins and Development,* 1776–2011 (2012), and *Governing at Home: The White House and Domestic Policymaking* (2011). *The Elections of 2012* is the eighth in a series of postelection books that began in 1984. Nelson has contributed to numerous journals, including the *Journal of Policy History, Journal of Politics,* and *Political Science Quarterly.* He also has written multiple articles on subjects as varied as baseball, Frank Sinatra, and C.S. Lewis. More than fifty of his articles have been anthologized in works of political science, history, and English composition.

About the Contributors

Barry C. Burden is professor of political science at the University of Wisconsin-Madison. His research on U.S. politics emphasizes electoral politics and representation. He is author of *Personal Roots of Representation* (2007), editor of *Uncertainty in American Politics* (2003), and coauthor with David C. Kimball of *Why Americans Split Their Tickets: Campaigns, Competition, and Divided Government* (2002). He has also published articles in journals including the *American Political Science Review, American Journal of Political Science, Legislative Studies Quarterly,* and *Political Science Quarterly.* His current research focuses on election administration.

Marian Currinder is a senior fellow at the Government Affairs Institute at Georgetown University. Previously she was an assistant professor of American politics at the College of Charleston. She was an American Political Science Association Congressional Fellow in 2003–04 and worked for Representative David Price (D-NC). She has published several journal articles and book chapters on congressional politics and campaign finance, and is the author of *Money in the House: Campaign Funds and Congressional Party Politics* (2008). She is currently working on a book about partisan polarization in Congress, *The Great Divide* (2013).

Marjorie Randon Hershey is professor of political science at Indiana University. She specializes in the study of political parties, media coverage of American campaigns, and the construction of explanations for election results. She is the author of *Party Politics in America* (now in its fifteenth edition) as well as other books, and her articles have appeared in the *American Journal of Political Science*, the *Journal of Politics*, *Public Opinion Quarterly*, *Political Communication*, *Polity*, *Social Science Quarterly*, and other professional journals and edited volumes. She is the editor of the forthcoming *CQ Guide to Political Parties*.

Marc J. Hetherington is professor of political science at Vanderbilt University. He specializes in the study of political trust and party polarization in the electorate. He has published two books: *Authoritarianism and Polarization in American Politics* (2009) and *Why Trust Matters: Declining Political Trust and the Demise of American Liberalism* (2006). He has also published numerous articles in a variety of political science journals, including the *American Political Science Review*, *American Journal of Political Science*, and *Journal of Politics*. He received the Emerging Scholar Award from the Elections, Public Opinion, and Voting Behavior of the American Political Science Association in 2004 and has won numerous teaching awards over the years.

Gary C. Jacobson is Distinguished Professor of Political Science at the University of California, San Diego, where he has taught since 1979. He specializes in the study of U.S. elections, parties, interest groups, public opinion, and Congress. He is the author of *The Politics of Congressional Elections* (2009), *The Electoral Origins of Divided Government* (1990), *Money in Congressional Elections* (1980), and coauthor of *The Logic of American Politics* (2009), and *Strategy and Choice in Congressional Elections* (1983), as well as more than ninety research articles. His most recent book is *A Divider, Not a Uniter: George W. Bush and the American People* (2010).

David R. Mayhew has written books on American politics that include *Partisan Balance* (2011), *Parties and Policies* (2008), *Divided We Govern* (2005), *Electoral Realignments* (2002), *America's Congress* (2000), and *Congress: The Electoral Connection* (1974). Recently, he has written about wars and American politics, incumbency advantage in presidential elections, the Senate filibuster, theorizing about Congress, American electoral history, and the "Long 1950s" as a policy era. He is Sterling Professor of Political Science at Yale University, a fellow of the American Academy of Arts and Sciences, and a member of the American Philosophical Society.

Nicole Mellow is associate professor of political science at Williams College, where she teaches classes on American political development, the presidency, political parties, American state-building, and political geography. In addition to articles on parties and partisanship and on political leadership, she is the author of *The State of Disunion: Regional Sources of Modern American Partisanship* (2008). She is currently working with Jeffrey Tulis on a book, *Legacies of Loss in American Politics.*

Bruce Nesmith is Joan and Abbott Lipsky Professor of Political Science at Coe College. He teaches courses on American political institutions, religion and U.S. politics, and political philosophy. He is the author of *The New Republican Coalition: The Reagan Campaigns and White Evangelicals* (1994). His current research deals with policymaking by the president and Congress.

Paul J. Quirk holds the Phil Lind Chair in U.S. Politics and Representation at the University of British Columbia. He earned his PhD at Harvard University and has held faculty appointments at several American universities. He has published widely on the presidency, Congress, public opinion, and public policymaking and has received the Aaron Wildavsky Enduring Contribution Award of the Public Policy Section of the American Political Science Association and the Brownlow Book Award of the National Academy of Public Administration. He is coeditor of *Institutions of American Democracy: The Legislative Branch* (2006) and coauthor of *Deliberative Choices: Debating Public Policy in Congress* (2006). His chapter on presidential competence appears in the tenth edition of *The Presidency and the Political System,* edited by Michael Nelson (2014). He is working with Bruce Nesmith on a book-length study of the presidency and Congress as policymaking institutions.

1

2013 and Beyond

Barack Obama and the Perils of Second-term Presidents

Michael Nelson

President Barack Obama won a narrow victory over former Massachusetts governor Mitt Romney in the 2012 election. Unlike that of every other two-term president since Woodrow Wilson in 1916, Obama's reelection majority was smaller than the majority he won in his initial election four years earlier.[1] Franklin D. Roosevelt went from 57 percent of the national popular vote and 472 electoral votes in 1932 to 61 percent and 523 electoral votes in 1936. Dwight D. Eisenhower's share of the popular vote rose from 56 percent in 1952 to 57 percent in 1956, and the number of electoral votes he received grew from 442 to 457. Richard Nixon won a nail biter in 1968, with 43 percent of the popular vote and 301 electoral votes in a three-candidate race. In 1972 he received 61 percent support from the voters and 520 electoral votes. Ronald Reagan leapt from 51 percent of the popular vote and 489 electoral votes in 1980 to a 59 percent, 525 electoral vote majority in 1984. Both of Bill Clinton's two elections involved a serious third-party challenger, but he rose from 43 percent of the popular vote in 1992 to 49 percent in 1996 and his electoral vote count increased from 370 to 379. Although George W. Bush was elected by a whisker in both 2000 and 2004, his popular vote share rose from 48 percent to 51 percent and his electoral vote count increased from 271 to 286. In contrast to his reelected predecessors, Obama's victory in 2012 with 52 percent of the popular vote and 332 electoral votes lagged his triumph in 2008, when he defeated Sen. John McCain of Arizona with 53 percent and 365 electoral votes.[2]

A narrow victory is a victory nonetheless and not to be gainsaid. Three of Obama's six most recent predecessors in the presidency—Gerald R. Ford in 1976, Jimmy Carter in 1980, and George H. W. Bush in 1992—were defeated at the polls. But Obama, like Reagan in 1984, Clinton in 1996, and Bush in 2004, enjoyed an enormous electoral advantage that the three defeated presidents did not: a united party. Ford had to defeat a serious challenge from a major Republican rival, former governor Reagan of California. Carter had to fight for renomination against an equally impressive Democratic challenger, Sen. Edward M. Kennedy of Massachusetts. George H. W. Bush's opponent was much less formidable but no less distracting: political commentator and former White House aide Patrick Buchanan. In every case these presidents prevailed but only after being attacked for months by their intraparty rivals—diverting time, talent, and money from preparing for the general election campaign in order to fend off the primary challenge, and making concessions on matters such as the party platform and speaking time at the national convention in an effort to reunite the party.

Presidents who have to battle for renomination forfeit much of the electoral advantage of being president because they receive the same kind of hammering that those seeking the other party's nomination encounter. In 2012, for example, Romney was battered and bruised politically and his campaign treasury was almost empty by the time he finally wrapped up the Republican nomination in April. In a seemingly endless series of primary debates, Romney's rivals for the Republican nomination relentlessly attacked him in an effort to bring down the frontrunner. In order to beat them back, he had to run much further to the right than he planned, branding himself as "severely conservative" and urging undocumented Latino immigrants to "self-deport" from the country. Meanwhile, his opponents' charges followed a script that the Obama campaign soon borrowed. For example, former House speaker Newt Gingrich accused Romney of having "looted" companies during his career as a business consultant and branded him a "vulture capitalist." Gov. Rick Perry of Texas said that Romney had gotten rich by "sticking it to someone else."[3]

In contrast, Obama coasted to renomination. To be sure, he had critics within the Democratic Party, most of them liberals who thought that his $787 billion economic stimulus plan in 2009 was too modest, blamed him for allowing his health care reform bill to rely on private insurance and pharmaceutical companies, disapproved of his vigorous prosecution of the war in Afghanistan that he inherited from George W. Bush, believed that he was too pliable on matters of taxing and spending in the face of congressional Republican resistance to Democratic policies, and blamed him for his party's massive defeat in the 2010 midterm elections, in which the Republicans seized control of the House of Representatives, made substantial gains in the Senate, and took command of most of the nation's state governments.

Clinton had been similarly unpopular among Democratic liberals in 1996 as a result of his own tack toward the political center after overseeing the loss of both congressional chambers to the GOP in 1994. Taking a page from Clinton's preelection year playbook, Obama raised so much money from Democratic donors that he scared off any potential challengers to his renomination. By the time the first Republican and Democratic caucus votes were cast in Iowa on January 3, 2012, Obama had already spent tens of millions of dollars building the infrastructure for his general election campaign and still had more than $60 million on hand. Like George W. Bush, Obama's bid for an uncontested renomination also benefited from the increasing polarization that separates Democratic and Republican voters and activists. Rank-and-file Republicans might disapprove mightily of Obama's performance as president, as Democrats had of Bush, but that made his own party's constituencies even more inclined to support him. In the election day national exit poll, all but 6 percent of Republicans said they voted against Obama and all but 8 percent of Democrats said they voted for him.[4]

Narrow as it was, Obama's victory was clear. The television networks were able to call the election for him by 11:10 p.m. Eastern Standard Time. His party gained eight seats in the House, narrowing the Republican majority in that chamber to 234 to 201. Democrats also added two seats in the Senate to expand their majority to fifty-five to forty-five. Remarkably, they achieved this gain even though they had to defend twenty-three seats and the Republicans only ten, an artifact of the Democrats' triumph in the congressional elections six years earlier. These victories, including the president's, came in the face of slow economic growth and an unemployment rate that only dipped below 8 percent a few weeks before the election. No president in the post-World War II era had been reelected with an unemployment rate that high.

Post-election commentators paid particular attention to the exit poll results, which showed that Obama did especially well among those sectors of the electorate that are growing most rapidly. White voters, whom Romney carried with 59 percent (a greater majority than either McCain attained in 2008 or Bush won in 2004), comprised all but 12 percent of the electorate as recently as 1980. By 2012, 28 percent of the voters were nonwhite—African Americans (13 percent), Latinos (10 percent and rising), Asian Americans (3 percent, also rising), and others (2 percent)—with demographers projecting that the nonwhite share of the electorate will continue to grow in coming years at a rate of about 2 percentage points per presidential election. (As for the long term, it bears mentioning that in 2011, for the first time, more nonwhite than white babies were born in the United States.) Obama won 93 percent of the black vote, 71 percent of the Latino vote, and 73 percent of the Asian American vote.

Similarly, although Romney did well among seniors, earning 56 percent support from those aged sixty-five and older, Obama prevailed among younger voters, who presumably will remain in the electorate for a much longer time, earning 60 percent support from eighteen- to twenty-nine-year-olds. Unmarried voters, another expanding demographic constituency, favored Obama by 63 percent to 37 percent. Voters who marked "none" when asked about their religious affiliation—yet another growing sector of the electorate—favored the president by 70 percent to 26 percent. Finally, Obama did well among the substantial and increasing number of people claiming postgraduate degrees—18 percent of all voters. He bested Romney by 55 percent to 42 percent in this largely professional sector of the adult population.

Democrats took heart from these numbers. Ten years before the election, John B. Judis and Ruy Teixeira published *The Emerging Democratic*

Majority, which identified the very population trends that came to fruition in 2012 so advantageously for Obama and his party.[5] Surely, Democratic readers of the book rejoiced, an even better educated, more multiracial electorate that will include even fewer married people and Christians will only make the Democrats still more successful at the polls in the years to come against the shrinking GOP coalition of white, married Christians. Others pointed out the contrast between the six presidential elections that occurred from 1968 to 1988 and the six elections that have occurred since then. Of the first six, the Republican nominees won five, four of them by landslides. Starting in 1992, however, the Democratic candidate for president has won more popular votes than his Republican rival in five of six elections, and no Republican has been elected with an electoral vote margin of more than one state.

Less remarked, however, was that in the quarter-century of Republican dominance of the presidency that preceded Clinton's election in 1992, Democrats controlled the House without interruption and dominated the Senate for all but the first six years of the Reagan administration. Since then, the House has been Republican for sixteen of twenty-two years and the Senate has been Democratic for just twelve of those years, only about half the time. Similarly, state governments, most of which Democrats controlled before Clinton ushered in the era of Democratic dominance in presidential elections, have generally swung to the GOP. As a result of the 2012 elections, Republican governors outnumber Democrats by thirty to twenty and Republicans control twenty-eight state houses of representatives and twenty-eight state senates.

The question these results raise is: Did 2012 mark a new political era characterized by an emerging Democratic majority, or simply the continuation of the old era of divided government, in which voters seldom entrust either political party with control of the presidency and both houses of Congress? Divided government was long the exception in American politics: from 1900 to 1968, the presidency, House, and Senate were all in the same party's hands 80 percent of the time. Since then, divided party control has become the normal governing situation in Washington. United party government has prevailed since 1969 only during the one-term Carter presidency, the first two years of Clinton's presidency, the middle four years of George W. Bush's presidency, and the first two years of the Obama presidency—that is, just 26 percent of the time.

Some wave a different caution flag at those who think the country is becoming relentlessly Democratic. Historically, every new lasting partisan majority has been launched by a president who not only won a second term but also was succeeded in the next election by a president of his own party. Thomas Jefferson was elected in 1800 and 1804, and so was fellow Democratic-Republican James Madison in 1808. Democratic president Andrew Jackson's victories in 1828 and 1832 were followed by Democratic president Martin Van Buren's election in 1836. Ushering in a new Republican majority, Abraham Lincoln was elected in 1860 and 1864, as was fellow partisan Ulysses S. Grant in 1868. Republican William McKinley's victories in 1896 and 1900 set the stage for the election of Theodore Roosevelt, also a Republican, in 1904. Democrat Franklin D. Roosevelt was elected four times—in 1932, 1936, 1940, and 1944—and voters then chose Democrat Harry S. Truman in 1948. After Ronald Reagan, a Republican, won in 1980 and 1984, George H. W. Bush, also a Republican, was elected in 1988. In sum, the path to a new and lasting partisan majority leads through the founding president's second term to his successor's election.

Obama has secured that term and, if it is successful and the Democrats nominate a credible candidate in 2016, their chances of becoming the nation's majority party for years to come will be enhanced. The problem is that a president's second term almost invariably turns out to be less successful than the first term. Historians may argue about whether the second terms of eighteenth- and nineteenth-century presidents George Washington, Thomas Jefferson, James Madison, James Monroe, Andrew Jackson, Ulysses S. Grant, and Grover Cleveland fit this pattern.[6] But in the era of the modern presidency, second terms have been disappointing experiences for all of the presidents who earned them. As noted previously, two modern presidents, Franklin Roosevelt and Reagan, were succeeded by the election of a member of their party. Only one reelected president, Richard Nixon, left office in disgrace. But every two-term president—Woodrow Wilson, Dwight D. Eisenhower, Bill Clinton, George W. Bush, and even FDR and Reagan—found his second term to be less productive than his first term.

The Anomaly of Second-term Disappointment

Why do second terms tend to be disappointing? After all, one might reasonably expect the opposite to be true. The second-term president, who under the two-term limit imposed by the Twenty-second Amendment cannot run again, is free from the cares of reelection politics that many presidents regard as an impediment to doing the best job possible. At least that is what they say when they endorse the proposal for a single, six-year presidential term, as several recent former presidents have done, including Eisenhower, Nixon, Ford, and Carter.[7] Obama himself said in January 2010 that he would "rather be a really good one-term president than a mediocre two-term president."[8]

More important, presidents begin the second term with four years of on-the-job training. They are in the ascending phase of the "cycle of increasing effectiveness" that comes with experience in office. As Paul Light, the inventor of the concept, has written,

> Presidents can be expected to learn over time. The presidential information base should expand; the president's personal expertise should increase. As the president and the staff become more familiar with the working of the office, there will be a learning effect. They will identify

> useful sources of information; they will produce effective strategies for domestic choice. Clearly, prolonged contact with specific policy issues will produce specialization and knowledge.[9]

Even more than in domestic policy, most second-term presidents become increasingly sure-footed in foreign policy. Few presidents enter office with much international experience. They have been either governors consumed with domestic policy or senators focused on it. (The notable exceptions—Richard Nixon and George H. W. Bush—both served for eight years as vice president.) A first-term president's learning curve is steep in the domestic responsibilities of the office but steeper in those involving the nation's role in the world. The president enters the second term better prepared to discover where the opportunities for international progress may be found, as Ronald Reagan did when he negotiated a nuclear arms reduction treaty with the Soviet Union, Bill Clinton did when he brokered a peace agreement in Northern Ireland, and George W. Bush did when he launched the "surge" in Iraq.[10]

Clinton, who was Obama's most recent Democratic predecessor in the White House, grew in most aspects of the presidency, following the pattern of his long tenure as governor of Arkansas. His Arkansas-heavy White House staff, hastily thrown together late in the transition period that followed the 1992 election and correspondingly chaotic during his first two years in office, gradually became more sure-footed after he appointed Washington veteran Leon Panetta as chief of staff. The president himself gained confidence as commander in chief when he discovered that the American people respected him for having the courage to make the unpopular decisions that extended U.S. assistance to Bosnia, Haiti, and Mexico. He learned how to deal with a professional, independent-minded Congress after many years in which his only legislative experience was with Arkansas's part-time amateur legislature. Clinton's deportment mirrored his growth. Out went the much photographed jogging shorts, self-revelations about his preferences in underpants, and limp salutes. In, after hours spent studying videotapes of Reagan, came a straight, shoulders-back posture and, with some coaching, crisp salutes.

Obama was equally unprepared by his pre-presidential experience of public service to hit the deck running. Unlike Clinton, he had been a legislator, but eight years in the Illinois state senate and four years as a U.S. senator scarcely prepared him for the issues or institutions with which a president must deal—especially because most of his time in the Senate was spent running for president. Like Clinton, Obama initially staffed his White House with friends and associates from home, some of whom had serious Washington experience and some of whom did not. It took time for Obama to realize how deeply partisan Congress was and, as a consequence, how immune Republican legislators would be to his efforts to forge bipartisan majorities. He also had much to learn about being an effective commander in chief. In the early months of his presidency, when beribboned generals told him they needed substantially more troops for the war in Afghanistan,

Obama readily acquiesced. In 2010, however, when faced with a similar request, he subjected the military to a painstaking review of what the mission would be, how the troops would be deployed, and how success would be attained by 2014 when, he insisted, they would be withdrawn.[11] Finally, four years of executive experience—which is four more than Obama had at the beginning of his first term—better equipped him to manage the large and complex branch of government he heads.

Offsetting these advantages of the second term, however, are more numerous and significant disadvantages for the president. As David Crockett has written about the second-term president, "When his knowledge and experience are at their highest, his political capital only gets lower."[12] These disadvantages are described in the rest of the chapter roughly in the order that they develop during a president's tenure in office.

Postponed Problems

After George W. Bush was reelected in 2004, his chief political adviser, Karl Rove, commissioned a study of second terms from the White House's in-house think tank, the Office of Strategic Initiatives. According to Rove, the study "argued that second terms were often tarnished by scandal or unpopular wars, or were lackluster because a president pursued a timid agenda or had won reelection by an appeal based on personality rather than ideas."[13] In other words, although Rove did not say so, the study came too late to do President Bush much good. Some of the most important problems that Bush would encounter as a second-term president had already developed by the time the study identified them. In truth, many of the seeds of second-term disappointment for all reelected presidents are planted during the first term—for reasons whose planting makes perfect political sense at the time.

During the second term, problems that were postponed from the first term because they were so controversial or intractable as to jeopardize the president's reelection come back to haunt the administration.[14] During his first term, for example, Franklin Roosevelt downplayed his important constitutional differences with the Supreme Court for fear that he would lose support among voters who approved of his policies but would resent any attack on judicial independence. Reagan blithely allowed his first-term tax cuts and defense spending increases to drive the budget deficit skyward rather than engage in preelection belt tightening that might slow the politically popular economic recovery in 1984. George W. Bush, who talked about the need for Social Security reform when he sought the presidency in 2000, did nothing about it during his first four years in office. As Dan Balz has observed, "Domestically, Social Security rose to the top of his [second-term] agenda because it was too risky and too difficult to deal with in his first term."[15] In every case, the president's strategy of postponement was politically successful. Roosevelt in 1936, Reagan in 1984, and Bush in 2004 were all reelected. But after each election, the postponed problems loomed larger than ever over the second term.

Scandal occupies a special category of recurring second-term problems inherited from the first term. As John Fortier and Norman Ornstein have pointed out, scandals are a common feature of second terms, but typically "second-term scandals began in the first term and were suppressed successfully by the White House, enabling the president to win reelection and avoid embarrassment."[16] Even if the president has done nothing scandalous, observes Reagan administration alumnus Frank Donatelli, "The federal government is this enormous apparatus, and it's just a matter of time before someone somewhere winds up screwing up."[17]

Nixon engaged in a massive cover-up of the Watergate affair hoping to prevent it from sullying his reelection campaign in 1972. Pursuing an unpopular policy in Nicaragua that he cared about deeply, Reagan nonetheless chose not to fight with Congress over the 1984 Boland Amendment, which barred the government from giving military aid to the anticommunist contra rebels in that country. Instead, his administration provided covert aid to the contras funded by the secret sale of American weapons to the hostile government of Iran. The Iran-contra scandal, when it surfaced during Reagan's second term, nearly brought down his presidency. In ways both similar and different, the adulterous first-term affair that Clinton had with Monica Lewinsky, a twenty-one-year-old White House intern, came back to haunt him when it became public during his second term. Like Reagan in 1984, Clinton was reelected in 1996, as was Nixon in 1972. But during the second term, Reagan was nearly undone by a congressional investigation of Iran-contra, the House impeached Clinton for conduct related to the Lewinsky scandal, and Nixon was forced to resign lest he face not only impeachment but also certain conviction and removal from office by the Senate.

Only the pattern of history, not any available evidence, alerts one to the possibility that Obama may have to deal with a second-term scandal rooted in conduct that lay outside public scrutiny during his first term. But on a congeries of policy problems involving taxes, spending, massive entitlement programs such as Medicare, Medicaid, and Social Security, annual budget deficits of about $1 trillion per year, and the national debt (about $16 trillion and growing), first-term avoidance was the rule in Obama's Washington. The fingerprints of senators and representatives, many of them Republicans, are all over the fiscal crime scene, not just the president's. But the accumulated problems of many years of federal profligacy are bound to shadow Obama's second term even if it is scandal-free.

Empty Reelection Campaigns

Short-term political strategy also helps to lay the groundwork for second-term difficulties when presidents wage their reelection campaigns. Understandably, such campaigns tend to be "above party" affairs. The president, after all, is the nation's chief of state as well as its more partisan chief of government. As chief of state, the president embodies in a symbolic way all that unites Americans as a people, much as the monarch does in Great Britain.[18] When George W. Bush stood on the rubble of New York City's World Trade Center gripping a bullhorn in one hand and a firefighter's shoulder with the other, or Barack Obama announced from the White House that Navy SEALs had killed terrorist leader Osama bin Laden, Republicans and Democrats united in celebration of their president's achievement.

Presidents seeking reelection naturally try to drape themselves in the broadly unifying garb of chief of state, which means avoiding controversial or even specific issues as much as possible and distancing themselves to some extent from their party's candidates for Congress and other offices. They are best able to do so when they avoid a bruising intraparty battle for renomination, as Obama did in 2012. But the result, even when presidents win reelection landslides (as Obama did not), is that they are in no position to claim a mandate to accomplish anything in particular during the second term. Nor do the president's fellow party members in Congress feel much personal obligation to help.

In addition to being weak on substance, presidential reelection campaigns tend to be long on announcements in the White House Rose Garden, elaborately staged appearances before mass audiences, and other media events. They typically are short on face-to-face campaigning among the voters and direct encounters with the press. Consequently, the president does not learn much from the campaign (as he did when first elected) about what the voters are thinking. This lack of immersion in the shifting currents of public opinion can lead to serious miscalculations after the election. Ironically, all three of the presidents who won the largest reelection majorities (thus demonstrating the unmatched sensitivity of their political antennae) blundered severely at the beginning of the second term: Roosevelt and his Court-packing scheme in 1937, Nixon and Watergate in 1973, and Reagan and Iran-contra in 1985.[19]

Even George W. Bush, who was only narrowly reelected in 2004, claimed to have "earned capital in the campaign, political capital," and added, "I intend to spend it." He bragged, "I've got the will of the people at my back . . . , and that's what I intend to tell the Congress."[20] Convinced that his bare majority of popular and electoral votes had conferred a mandate to pursue Social Security reform, an issue he barely mentioned during the election, Bush launched a futile and politically damaging campaign to enact new legislation as soon as he was inaugurated for a second term. Self-inflicted political wounds by Bush and his three landslide-winning predecessors ended any hopes for a successful second term.

A final characteristic of presidential campaigns for reelection also creates problems for the second term. Almost by definition, such campaigns affirm the status quo. But it is hard to translate an "aren't things fine?" theme into gains for the president's party in Congress. After all, if the country is on the right track, why should the voters want to turn out any incumbents, whether they are the president's fellow partisans or members of the opposition?

Roosevelt, Eisenhower, Nixon, Reagan, Clinton, and Bush fell prey to most of these syndromes. In every case, the president asked the voters, in effect, to express their approval of the first term or at least to conclude that he was the lesser of two evils compared with his opponent. Little was said about what the second term would bring. Even less was done to help the party's candidates for Congress. The predictable result: the president was reelected, but with a campaign whose significance was undermined by its lack of content and by disappointing results for the president's party in the congressional elections. Indeed, Republicans Eisenhower, Nixon, and Reagan each came out of his reelection with the same wholly or partially Democratic Congress with which he had entered it. The electorate that gave Eisenhower 57 percent of its votes also reelected 95 percent of the incumbent House members and 86 percent of the incumbent senators who were running for an additional term. Nixon's 61 percent victory was undermined by reelection rates of 94 percent in the Democratic House and 85 percent in the Democratic Senate. Similarly, in the same election in which Reagan earned 59 percent of the popular vote, 95 percent of House members and 90 percent of senators also were successful.

Clinton's reelection campaign in 1996 fit the historical pattern. He seldom called on the voters to elect a Democratic Congress—to do so would have jeopardized his efforts to rise above the partisan fray. Instead of pushing a change-oriented agenda, Clinton pointed with pride to the status quo, taking credit for the success of his first-term economic policies. Discussions of the future were shrouded in the gauzy rhetoric of "building a bridge to the twenty-first century." Not surprisingly, as in previous elections that returned a president to power, incumbents did well across the board in 1996: 95 percent of senators and 95 percent of representatives who sought reelection were successful. Democratic leaders in Congress, who had long resented Clinton's "triangulation" strategy for winning a second term (it placed the president as far above and apart from congressional Democrats on the left as from congressional Republicans on the right), understandably felt that they owed little to him. Clinton ended his first term with a Republican Congress and began his second term the same way.

Bush's 2004 reelection campaign offers a mixed case. As noted earlier, his candidacy was no less content-lite about his plans for the second term than those of his predecessors. But Bush was determined not to win a "lonely victory." "I don't want what Nixon had," he told his political strategists. "I don't want what Reagan had."[21] What Bush wanted—and worked hard to get—was coattails in the congressional elections. He was partially successful. To be sure, incumbents were massively reelected at a rate of 99 percent in the House and 96 percent in the Senate. But a string of Republican victories in open-seat Senate elections increased the GOP's majority in that chamber from fifty-one seats to fifty-five. Laying it on the line for his party, however, did little for Bush's programmatic agenda. Neither Republican activists nor Republican candidates for Congress had been asked during the election to support Social Security reform, and many abandoned the cause as soon as they saw how unpopular it was.

Obama could not plausibly campaign in 2012 on the one-word slogan "Hope," as he had in 2008. Instead, he rebranded his appeal with the equally substance-free "Forward." Unexpectedly, the president was able to perform the chief of state role to a tee just days before the election, when Hurricane Sandy did massive damage to densely populated areas of New Jersey and New York. Obama toured the Jersey shore with Republican governor Chris Christie, previously a fierce partisan critic, who now praised the president for their "great working relationship" and said that Obama had "sprung into action immediately" when the hurricane hit.[22] In the national exit poll, 15 percent of voters said that Obama's response to the hurricane was the most important factor in their decision about how to vote, and 73 percent of them voted for the president.

At times during the general election campaign, Obama's aides told reporters that he had a second-term policy agenda that included tackling issues such as climate change and immigration reform. In an unguarded moment, the president was overheard confiding to Russian leader Dmitri Medvedev that "after the election I'll have more flexibility" in scaling down the nation's politically resilient missile defense program.[23] But the president's only substantive public discussion of his second term was almost willfully obscure: it came in an off-the-record interview with the *Des Moines Register* two weeks before the election.[24] The one issue the president talked about emphatically throughout the campaign was his longstanding desire to increase income taxes on high earners—a carryover from 2008 that he still hoped to achieve. He reaped the harvest of this rare act of specificity immediately after the election, when Republican leaders in Congress grudgingly conceded that they had lost the argument and increased taxes on households earning $450,000 or more per year. Unlike Bush—but like Bush's reelection-seeking predecessors—Obama provided little help to his party's congressional candidates. His coattails were short. Only 16 of 215 Republican House members who were on the November ballot were defeated by Democratic opponents, and only one Republican senator.

No Honeymoon

A third reason that presidents experience disappointment during their second terms is that they are not granted the honeymoon that most first-term presidents enjoy.[25] Newly elected presidents usually receive the early approval of millions of voters who opposed them in the election, as Obama did in early 2009 when his 53 percent majority in the 2008 election became a 65 percent approval rating in post-inauguration polls.[26] Yet some crucial ingredients that make up the first-term honeymoon are not present the second time around, notably the general willingness of the public and the Washington community to give the new president a chance and the widespread (and, of course, impossible) hopes of all sectors of the nation that he will govern in their many and often contradictory interests.

The importance of the honeymoon period extends beyond good will and starry-eyed sentimentality. The honeymoon glow, its temporary nature noted ruefully by Lyndon B. Johnson in his remark that "you've got just one year when they treat you right," helps to explain, for example, why presidents make more new legislative requests to Congress in the first year of their administrations than in any other year, most of them during the first five months.[27] It also accounts for why so many of the landmark legislative achievements for which presidents such as Woodrow Wilson, Franklin Roosevelt, Lyndon B. Johnson, and Ronald Reagan are remembered took place during the first year of their first term.[28]

Partisan polarization, both among members of Congress and, increasingly, among voters, has diminished the president's ability to attract support across party lines even in the afterglow of a victorious election. Still, Obama's second-term surge of increased public support was remarkably small. According to data compiled by Micah Cohen, right after the 1996 election Clinton received a 5 percentage point increase in the Gallup Poll's measure of net job approval—that is, the percent of voters who say they approve of the president's performance in office minus the percent who disapprove—the same boost Reagan received after being reelected in 1984. George W. Bush's net approval rating rose 8 points from the poll taken just before the 2004 election to the poll taken just after. Obama's net approval rating increased as well in 2012, but only by 2 points. The percent of voters who approved his performance actually remained flat at 52 percent, and his 2 point improvement came entirely from preelection disapprovers who now expressed no opinion.[29]

Midterm Election

Almost halfway into the second term comes the midterm congressional election and the fabled "six-year itch," the fourth common ingredient of second-term frustration. Midterm elections of any kind seldom provide good news for presidents—the only midterm in history in which the president's party gained ground in both the House and the Senate was in 1934, during Franklin Roosevelt's first term. But a president's first midterm election, which occurs two years into the first term, generally is less punishing than the one that takes place during the second term, at the six-year mark. Roosevelt's Democrats lost seventy-one House members and six senators in 1938, midway through his second term. Congressional Republicans lost forty-eight seats in the House and thirteen in the Senate in 1958, the sixth year of Eisenhower's tenure as president. Republicans lost forty-eight House members and five senators in 1974, six years after Nixon was first elected. Reagan's Republicans lost five seats in the House and eight in the

Senate (along with control of the upper chamber) in 1986, halfway through his second term.

Clinton broke the pattern in 1998, when Democrats ran even in the Senate elections and actually gained five seats in the House. Although this was a remarkable achievement, Colleen Shogan has pointed out that the circumstances that occasioned the result are unlikely to be repeated: a Republican Party set on pursuing an impeachment that the public did not want, and a Democratic Party artificially united behind its president in reaction against a nearly unprecedented partisan overreach by the opposition.[30] Not surprisingly, politics as usual prevailed again in 2006, during the next two-term president's second midterm election. George W. Bush's Republican Party not only lost thirty House seats and six Senate seats, but also surrendered its majority in both chambers to the Democrats.

These losses take their toll on the president's relationship with Congress as the second term wears on. As Michael Grossman, Martha Kumar, and Francis Rourke have shown, the final two years of second-term administrations "have been accompanied by declines in presidential support in Congress on issues where the president took a clear stand."[31] This is especially true when the opposition party controls one or both houses of Congress, which has been the case for nearly every second-term president since the Civil War. Looking ahead to 2014, the small number of competitive districts currently held by Republicans means that Democrats are highly unlikely to win control of the House. (Obama carried only fifteen districts won by House Republicans in 2012.)[32] No midterm election in history has produced even a ten-seat gain for the president's party, much less the seventeen-seat gain that the Democrats would need to secure a majority in that chamber.[33]

In the Senate elections, moreover, the Democrats will have to defend twenty-one seats to the Republicans' fourteen. That is not an insurmountable problem; the Democrats thrived in the face of longer odds in 2012. But some of the Democratic senators whose seats will be on the ballot serve in states that have grown dramatically more Republican since they were last elected in 2008, including Mark Pryor of Arkansas, Mary Landrieu of Louisiana, and Jay Rockefeller of West Virginia, whose seat became open when he announced in January 2013 that he would not seek reelection. Others represent states that Romney carried in 2012, including Kay Hagan of North Carolina, Mark Begich of Alaska, Tim Johnson of South Dakota, and Max Baucus of Montana. In contrast, the only seat the Republicans will be defending in a state carried by Obama is in Maine, where Susan Collins is a strong incumbent and which probably will go Democratic only if she does not run for reelection. Further, Democratic candidates for all offices in 2014 will have to confront the dangers posed by the considerably smaller electorate that participates in midterm elections, especially the reduced presence of the young voters and racial and ethnic minorities who turned out in such large numbers for Obama and, as long as they were in the voting booth anyway, cast ballots for other Democrats in 2012.

Lame-duck President

During Obama's final campaign appearances in 2012, he noted wistfully to crowds that this was the last political campaign he ever would wage. Political observers marked the underlying significance of this statement: at the moment of his reelection, Obama, like all second-term presidents since Eisenhower, became a lame duck, unable to run for another term as president.

One reason for the weakened political condition of the second-term president is the two-term limit imposed by the Twenty-second Amendment, which was passed by Congress in 1947 and ratified by the states in 1951. (The amendment exempted President Harry S. Truman, who was serving at the time, but he chose not to run in 1952.) To be sure, a two-term tradition had existed ever since Thomas Jefferson, willfully misinterpreting George Washington's mainly personal decision not to serve a third term as president, proclaimed in 1807 that no one should violate Washington's "sound precedent."[34] In the years that followed, only Franklin Roosevelt lasted more than two terms, winning a third election in 1940 and a fourth in 1944. But several other presidents, including Ulysses S. Grant and Woodrow Wilson, kept open the possibility of running again, which meant that second-term presidents could not be counted out as lame ducks until late in their tenure. By codifying the two-term tradition, the Twenty-second Amendment removed all doubt that, in beginning the second term, the president also was beginning his last term.

The disempowering effects of lame-duck status are at first subtle, manifested, for example, in the slow disappearance of the president from the evening news and the front pages as the media spotlight gradually shifts to the contest to select a successor. Dana Perino, who was George W. Bush's second-term press secretary, noted toward the end of the 2008 campaign that "if we are on the front page of the paper, [it must be because] we have done something terribly wrong or have a huge problem."[35] In 2012, no sooner were the returns in than cable news channels and political websites and blogs were alive with speculation about 2016. Would Republican vice presidential nominee Paul Ryan of Wisconsin seek his party's presidential nomination? What about Florida senator Marco Rubio or former Florida governor Jeb Bush? Would Secretary of State Hillary Clinton or Vice President Joseph Biden try to become the Democratic nominee—or both of them, or neither?

To the extent that the spotlight continues to shine on the president, its glare becomes harsher. Typically, the proportion of presidential news stories that are favorable declines and the proportion of unfavorable stories increases from the first to the last years of an administration.[36] Perhaps in response, the popularity of most second-term presidents undergoes a steeper descent than during the first term. A certain lassitude may ensue: Paul Brace and Barbara Hinckley find that "a significant drop in energy in second terms occurs," with the president less likely to take to the hustings or even the airwaves to defend the party or administration.[37]

As the end of the second term approaches, the lame-duck effects become more tangible and visible. Members of the president's team, both within the White House and in the departments and agencies of the bureaucracy, begin their exodus to greener pastures in the private sector, fully aware both that their employment with the president is drawing to an inevitable close and that their value in the job market will decline dramatically as soon as the president leaves office. Finding competent and loyal replacements to join the administration, at this late hour and for such a short time, is correspondingly difficult. Richard Schott and Dagmar Hamilton observe that "candidates are less willing to make financial and other sacrifices for an appointment of merely a year or two, and much of the excitement and challenge of being part of a new administration have dissipated." As for members of the career civil service, their sense of commitment to the policies and programs of the administration dwindles steadily as the arrival of a new chief executive draws near.[38]

During the final year of the second term, the Senate takes an especially jaundiced view of the president's judicial nominations. Historically, the rejection rate for final-year nominations to the Supreme Court has been 48 percent, compared with 14 percent for nominations made earlier in the term. When the opposition party controls the Senate, the final-year rejection rate rises to 75 percent.[39] Opposition-party senators are even more likely to resist an outgoing president's nominations to the nation's thirteen courts of appeals, sometimes by bottling up the nominees in committee and at other times by threatening a filibuster. No modern Supreme Court nomination has been filibustered, but it is not hard to imagine that happening if Obama were to nominate a liberal to replace a retiring conservative.

Obama faces a federal court system closely divided between Republican and Democratic appointees. The Supreme Court has five generally conservative justices, all appointed by Republicans presidents, and four generally liberal justices, all appointed by Democrats.[40] The thirteen appeals courts are just as closely divided between judges appointed by Democrats (49 percent) and Republicans (51 percent). Obama was considerably slower than Bill Clinton and George W. Bush to fill vacancies on these courts and on the federal district courts during his first term. He also chose judges who were about four years older, on average, than Bush's, meaning that their presence on the bench probably will not last as long.[41]

Obama's ability to fill any seats on the Supreme Court that become vacant in the next few years will depend greatly on when the vacancies occur. During the president's second term conservative justices Antonin Scalia and Anthony Kennedy will both turn eighty. If their health permits, they may decide to remain on the Court in the hope that a Republican president will be elected in 2016 and become the one to replace them. Meanwhile, liberal justice Ruth Bader Ginsberg will turn eighty-three and fellow liberal Stephen Breyer will turn seventy-eight during Obama's second term. (The next oldest justice, Clarence Thomas, was born ten years after Breyer and at sixty-eight will still be relatively young by Supreme Court standards.) Even if the two older liberals remain healthy, they may decide to time their retirement to assure that Obama will nominate their successor. But if that is their goal they had better do so sooner rather than later. The closer to the 2016 election a vacancy occurs, the more likely it is that Republicans in the Senate will find a way to prevent any Obama nominee from being confirmed. George W. Bush was in this way fortunate that the two vacancies that occurred on the Supreme Court during his second term both appeared in its first year.

To be sure, lame-duck presidents are not without resources. Hoping "to establish a final diplomatic victory as their legacy," they are "much more likely to schedule foreign trips in the final year of their administrations."[42] In addition, the constitutional powers of the presidency remain intact throughout the term, as Clinton's predecessor, George H. W. Bush, showed after losing the election of 1992. During his final two months as president, Bush dispatched 25,000 American troops to Somalia, signed the North American Free Trade Agreement (NAFTA), bombed Iraq, reached an arms control agreement with Russia, and pardoned six high-ranking former Reagan administration officials of any crimes they may have committed in connection with the Iran-contra affair. Clinton also spent much of his final days in office issuing pardons, some of them highly controversial. Clinton's successor, George W. Bush, knowing he would never face the voters again, rejected their verdict in the Democrat-dominated 2006 midterm election that the war in Iraq had been a failure. Instead of withdrawing American troops, Bush deployed an additional 20,000—the surge—under his authority as commander in chief. It turned out to be the most successful decision he made in a generally unsuccessful war.

Conclusion

Pattern is not predestination, at least not in politics. To observe that modern presidents have been less successful in their second terms than in their first terms, even when that observation is adduced by explanations that are deeply grounded in the workings of the political system, is not to say that no second term ever will surpass a first term, or even that Obama's second term will not turn out more successfully than his first term. Historical "what ifs" are of limited value, but who is to say, for example, that John F. Kennedy, a narrowly elected president in 1960 who used his first term mainly to set the agenda for a massive, mandate-giving reelection in 1964, would not have reaped the harvest of his earlier efforts in the form of historic legislative achievements in a second term? Obama was denied an overwhelming reelection in 2012, but four years as president have made him more surefooted in his conduct of the office, including experience at dealing with a Republican-controlled House of Representatives. He also began his second term with a historical sensitivity to the new challenges he faced. "I don't presume that because I won an election that suddenly everybody agrees with me on everything," he said in a post-election news conference. "I'm more than familiar with all the literature about presidential overreach in second terms. We are very cautious about that."[43]

Still, the historical pattern and the explanations that underlie it do not augur well for Obama's second term: the postponement of thorny problems until after the election, the lack of substance in his 2012 reelection campaign, the absence of a postelection honeymoon period, the midterm election in 2014, the coming exodus of talented and experienced presidential lieutenants and the difficulty of replacing them, and the growing problems attendant with advanced lame-duck status during the waning years of the term.

Underlying most of these problems is the Twenty-second Amendment. No constitutional amendment has undone the Framers' intentions more completely than the two-term limit. The delegates to the Constitutional Convention of 1787 designed all of their provisions for the term and election of the executive around the central goal of allowing the president to be always eligible for reelection. They believed strongly that presidential reeligibility was good for the president, who would have every incentive to do the best possible job, and good for the country, which would have the option of keeping a president it liked in office. Nor has any amendment been rushed to enactment by Congress in such haste and with such disregard for the original constitutional design. Briefly restored to power in the 1946 congressional election after a long absence, Republicans passed the amendment in posthumous resentment of Franklin Roosevelt's four victories. An argument could have been made, after careful consideration of the debates at the Constitutional Convention, that the Framers had been wrong not to impose a presidential term limit in the first place or that the times had changed since 1787 in ways that made such a limit necessary. But the enactors of the Twenty-second Amendment were uninterested in serious constitutional argument and unwilling to take the time to construct one.[44]

Most Americans support the two-term limit on presidents. If anything, they want to extend the constitutional term-limit principle to members of Congress. One can only hope that at some point, putting fervor aside, they will pause to consider what they have done to the second-term presidents whom they have elected.

Notes

1. Wilson won a three-way contest in 1912 with 42 percent of the popular vote and 435 electoral votes. In 1916, facing only one rival, his share of the popular vote rose to 49 percent but he received only 277 electoral votes.
2. Presidents who were elected to at least two terms are the focus of this chapter. This criterion deemphasizes the experiences of successor presidents, even those who were later elected to one full term, such as Theodore Roosevelt, Calvin Coolidge, Harry S. Truman, and Lyndon B. Johnson.
3. Karen Tumulty, "Mitt Romney's Road to Tampa," *Washington Post,* August 25, 2012.
4. The exit poll data cited in this chapter may be found at www.cnn.com/election/2012/results/race/president#exit-polls.
5. John B. Judis and Ruy Teixeira, *The Emerging Democratic Majority* (New York: Scribner, 2002).
6. Although not comparing second-term to first-term success, one scholar rates Washington, Madison, and Jackson as having had "successful second terms," Jefferson and Monroe as having had "troubled second terms," and Grant and Cleveland as having had "failed second terms." Alfred J. Zacher, *Trial and Triumph: Presidential Power in the Second Term* (Fort Wayne, Ind.: Presidential Press, 1996), 333.
7. Jackson proposed the single, six-year term during his first term as president. In 1913, Republican senator Miles Poindexter of Washington stated the case against such proposals with unsurpassed succinctness: "Six years is entirely too long for a bad man, and it is too short for a good man." James L. Sundquist, *Constitutional Reform and Effective Government,* rev. ed. (Washington, D.C.: Brookings Institution, 1992), 46–54.
8. Quoted in Robert W. Merry, *Where They Stand: The American Presidents in the Eyes of Voters and Historians* (New York: Simon & Schuster, 2012), xv.
9. Paul C. Light, *The President's Agenda: Domestic Policy Choice from Kennedy to Reagan* (Baltimore: Johns Hopkins University Press, 1991), 37.
10. David Greenberg, "The Myth of Second-term Failure," *New Republic,* December 6, 2012.
11. See Jonathan Alter, *The Promise: President Obama, Year One* (New York: Simon & Schuster, 2010; and Bob Woodward, *Obama's Wars* (New York: Simon & Schuster, 2010).
12. David A. Crockett, "'An Excess of Refinement': Lame Duck Presidents in Constitutional and Historical Context," *Presidential Studies Quarterly* 38 (December 2004): 713.
13. Karl Rove, *Courage and Consequences: My Life as a Conservative in the Fight* (New York: Simon & Schuster, 2010), 404.
14. In their study of the Eisenhower, Nixon, and Reagan presidencies, Brace and Hinckley found that "the ratio of negative to positive events was much larger during the second terms," mostly because of "things set in motion [by these presidents] during their first terms." Paul Brace and Barbara Hinckley, *Follow the Leader: Opinion Polls and the Modern Presidency* (New York: Basic Books, 1992), 40, 41.
15. Dan Balz, "Bush's Ambitious Second-term Agenda Hits Reality," in *Second-Term Blues: How George W. Bush Has Governed*, eds. John C. Fortier and Norman J. Ornstein (Washington, D.C.: Brookings Institution Press, 2007), 23.
16. John C. Fortier and Norman J. Ornstein, "Introduction," in ibid., 4.
17. Susan Page, "Beware of Second-Term Disasters," *USA Today*, January 15, 2013.

18. Erwin C. Hargrove and Michael Nelson, *Presidents, Politics, and Policy* (Baltimore: Johns Hopkins University Press, 1982), 20–24.
19. One could add Johnson and his massive escalation of the Vietnam War after winning a landslide election in 1964 to this list.
20. Quoted in Michael Nelson, "George W. Bush, Majority President," in *The Elections of 2004* (Washington, D.C.: CQ Press, 2005), 1.
21. Quoted in ibid., 2.
22. Jason Horowitz, "Gov. Chris Christie, an Obama Critic, Praises the President amid N.J. Storm Damage," *Washington Post*, October 31, 2012.
23. J. David Goodman, "Microphone Catches a Candid Obama," New York Times, March 26, 2012.
24. Rachel Weiner, "Obama's 'Blunt' Interview with Des Moines Register Now Public," *PostPolitics*, October 24, 2012, www.washingtonpost.com/blogs/post-politics/wp/2012/10/24/obama-if-i-win-gop-relationship-with-latinos-will-be-big-reason/.
25. Light, *The President's Agenda*, 39.
26. Nate Silver, "For Second-term Presidents, a Shorter Honeymoon," *Five Thirty Eight*, Jan. 19, 2013, http://fivethirtyeight.blogs.nytimes.com/2013/01/19/for-second-term-presidents-a-shorter-honeymoon/#more-38279.
27. Light, *The President's Agenda*, 41–45, 241. Johnson is quoted in Harry McPherson, *A Political Education* (Boston: Little, Brown, 1972), 268.
28. William Lammers, "Domestic Policy Leadership in the First Year," in *Understanding the Presidency*, eds. James P. Pfiffner and Roger H. Davidson (New York: Longman, 1997), 215–232.
29. Micah Cohen, "Polls Show Below-average Post-election Approval Bounce for Obama," *Five Thirty Eight*, Nov. 30, 2012, http://fivethirtyeight.blogs.nytimes.com/2012/11/30/polls-show-below-average-post-election-approval-bounce-for-obama/.
30. Colleen J. Shogan, "The Sixth-year Curse," *Presidential Studies Quarterly* 36 (March 2006): 89–101.
31. Michael B. Grossman, Martha Joynt Kumar, and Francis E. Rourke, "Second-term Presidencies: The Aging of Administrations," in *The Presidency and the Political System*, 2nd ed., ed. Michael Nelson (Washington, D.C.: CQ Press, 1988), 217–219.
32. Chris Cillizza, "As 'Fiscal Cliff' Looms, Republicans Have No Political Incentive to Make Deal with Obama," *Washington Post*, December 30, 2012.
33. The Democrats gained nine seats in 1934, a second-year-term midterm and five seats in 1998, a sixth-year midterm.
34. For an account of the enactment of the Twenty-second Amendment, see Sidney M. Milkis and Michael Nelson, *The American Presidency: Origins and Development*, 1776–2011 (Washington, D.C.: CQ Press, 2012); Jefferson is quoted in "Thomas Jefferson's Letter to the Vermont Legislature (1807)," in *The Evolving Presidency: Landmark Documents, 1787–2010* (Washington, D.C.: CQ Press, 2012), 317–320.
35. Page, "Beware of Second-term Disasters."
36. Michael Baruch Grossman and Martha Joynt Kumar, *Portraying the President* (Baltimore: Johns Hopkins University Press, 1981), 262.
37. Brace and Hinckley, *Follow the Leader*, 41–43, 60–61, 194–197.
38. Richard L. Schott and Dagmar S. Hamilton, *People, Positions, and Power* (Chicago: University of Chicago Press, 1983), 27.
39. Calculated from data presented in John Anthony Maltese, *The Selling of Supreme Court Nominees* (Baltimore: Johns Hopkins University Press, 1995), 2–8. Updated by the author.

40. According to Lee Epstein, William M. Landes, and Richard Posner, "Justices appointed by Republican presidents vote more conservatively on average than justices appointed by Democratic ones." Similarly, "Like Supreme Court justices, court of appeals judges appointed by Republican presidents are more likely, other things being equal, to vote for conservative than for liberal outcomes." See Epstein, Landes, and Posner, *The Behavioral of Federal Judges: A Theoretical and Empirical Study of Rational Choice* (Cambridge, Mass.: Harvard University Press, 2013), 8, 68.
41. Charlie Savage, "Obama Lags on Judicial Picks, Limiting His Mark on Courts," *New York Times*, August 17, 2012.
42. Brace and Hinckley, *Follow the Leader,* 61, 196–197.
43. Glenn Thrush and Reid J. Epstein, "Can Obama Defy the Second-term Curse?" *Politico*, Jan. 19, 2013, www.politico.com/story/2013/01/4-pitfalls-president-obama-faces-86428.html.
44. Milkis and Nelson, *The American Presidency,* 32–36.

2

The Nominations

Ideology, Timing, and Organization

Barry C. Burden

The 2012 Republican presidential nomination was a roller coaster of events and changing fortunes. Seemingly random elements played a significant role in shaping the contours of the race, making the nomination process appear capricious. Mitt Romney's eventual success in winning the Republican nomination reflects well on his campaign but was also a product of dynamic, unanticipated aspects of the electoral environment in which he ran.

Three major factors contributed to Romney's selection as the Republican presidential nominee. First, ideology emerged as a defining feature of the party's field of contenders. While his competitors took advantage of their connections to ideologically extreme elements within the party, Romney had to prove his conservative credentials to a party that included groups such as Tea Party supporters, Christian evangelicals, foreign policy hawks, and free-market libertarians. In the end Romney won this battle because many Republicans opted for electability over ideological purity, and also because the conservative vote did not coalesce behind a single anti-Romney candidate. Second, Romney's competitors failed to align the dynamics of their campaigns with the calendar of primaries and caucuses. Herman Cain, Rick Perry, and Newt Gingrich each led Romney in the polls at some point in the campaign. Yet all of them peaked too early and then fell from grace, leaving a relatively weak Rick Santorum as Romney's main rival by the time the primaries and caucuses began. Third, Romney had a superior campaign organization that allowed him to take maximum advantage of his ideological position and timing. As the only candidate other than Ron Paul who had run for president before, Romney raised far more money than his opponents, had a more extensive field operation, and better managed essential campaign activities. These advantages allowed him to weather periods when his frontrunner status was in doubt and to emerge at the national convention in Tampa in August 2012 as the nominee of the Republican Party.

The Backdrop

Entering the 2012 presidential contest, the electoral environment was framed by both President Barack Obama, who was running for reelection, and the newly energized conservative opposition to his presidency. After an impressive victory over John McCain in 2008, Obama entered office with high expectations and even higher job approval ratings. But as the economy remained stagnated, opponents began to vocalize their concerns. These complaints targeted Obama as a person (centering on such things as his associations with controversial figures and his heritage), his performance in office (namely the growing national debt and uncomfortably high unemployment levels), and his key policy enactments (particularly his $787 billion economic stimulus package, support for American automobile companies, and the health care reforms known as Obamacare).

By the summer of 2010 a loose network of conservative, evangelical, and libertarian activists had coalesced into the Tea Party movement. Its public protests were driven by anger about taxes, wasteful spending, and the size of government, or what rank-and-file activists believed was a march toward "socialism" in the United States. Later the Tea Party movement came to encompass social issues including abortion and immigration, thereby crystallizing hatred of Obama and becoming a key element of the Republican coalition.[1] In the 2010 midterm election, buoyed by high turnout among Tea Party supporters, Republicans regained majority control of the House of Representatives, picked up seats in the Senate, and won governorships in important states such as Ohio and Wisconsin. The elections marked the same kind of defeat for Obama that the 1994 midterms had for Bill Clinton when the GOP's "Contract with America" captured popular discontent with the administration.

Victory in 2010 motivated Republican activists to pursue even bigger ideological gains in 2012 against a vulnerable President Obama. Rather than settle for an acceptable nominee with a decent chance of victory in the general election, many conservatives adopted a more stringent ideological standard, holding out for a top-to-bottom conservative who would roll back Obamacare, cut taxes, crack down on illegal immigration, outlaw abortion, and prevent any additional domestic government spending. Their strict ideological standards have been likened to those of the anti-Vietnam protesters of the early 1970s who pushed the Democratic Party toward the nomination of liberal George McGovern in 1972.[2]

Some potential candidates fit into the Tea Party mold nicely: 2008 vice presidential candidate Sarah Palin, who frequently spoke at their rallies; former House Speaker Newt Gingrich, who described himself a conservative revolutionary; representative Michele Bachmann, who founded the congressional Tea Party Caucus; and libertarian representative Ron Paul.[3] Governor Mitt Romney was not a natural fit. Romney, who had enacted a health insurance mandate as governor of Massachusetts and taken moderate positions on key social issues such as abortion and same sex marriage, faced continual questions about his conservative commitments.

This unusual confluence of forces produced a field of candidates that was surprisingly weak given the electoral vulnerability of the incumbent president. One Republican strategist called it "the weakest Republican field since Wendell Wilkie won the nomination on the sixth ballot in 1940."[4] Republican governors and members of Congress were slower to endorse candidates than they had been in the previous five open nomination years.[5] Their hesitation is noteworthy because endorsements are some of the best indicators of party's support for a candidate.[6] Candidates also had difficulty raising money because donors were reluctant to make early contributions.[7] Despite being a stronger candidate this time around than when he first sought the Republican nomination in 2008, Romney raised less in the second quarter of 2011 than he did in the second quarter of 2007.

This highlights another major development for the 2012 election: the birth of the so-called super PAC. As Marian Currinder's chapter in this volume documents, these "independent-expenditure only" political action committees can spend directly on campaign advertising as long as they do not coordinate their activities with the candidates' campaign organizations.[8] Many of these groups also spawned related 501(c)4 committees, which were not even required to disclose their donors. Because they are not officially connected to the campaigns, these independent groups do not fear public backlash for harsh attacks in the way that a candidate or party might.[9] Accordingly, their advertising efforts are more negative; attack ads comprised 6 percent of television spots in the 2008 Republican nomination but half of those aired in the 2012 contest.[10] Super PACs played a key role in keeping some underfunded campaigns alive. Winning Our Future, funded primarily by developer Sheldon Adelson, provided Gingrich with roughly $12 million in support. Because the 2012 campaign had an unsettled field with less money initially flowing to candidates than in other years, super PACs were even more important than they otherwise would have been.

Super PACs and "(c)4" committees may have also come to supplant the traditional public matching funds provided by the Federal Elections Commission (FEC). As late as 2008, many of the primary candidates were still abiding by the FEC's fundraising guidelines to get matching funds from the government. That system became nearly irrelevant in 2012. All of the major candidates eschewed public funding, betting that their campaigns and supportive independent groups would more than make up the difference.

The Field of Contenders

The 2012 Republican nomination was shaped by the notable figures who chose *not* to run. It is true that every presidential election features appealing candidates who decline to run; prominent examples include New York governor Mario Cuomo in 1992 and army general Colin Powell in 1996. But 2012 was unique for the number of significant figures who sat on the sidelines. Perhaps these candidates assumed that Obama would be reelected, and that it would be less risky to launch presidential campaigns in 2016. For others the rise of super PACs and 501(c)4 groups made the fundraising challenges too steep. Still others were repelled by the prospect of having to please a demanding set of conservative party activists.

The no-shows would themselves have made a formidable field of Republican contenders. Chris Christie, the straight-talking governor of New Jersey, traveled the country giving speeches much as an early presidential candidate would. Christie continued to flirt with the idea of running until the fall of 2011, when he finally declared that he would not run. Mitch Daniels, governor of Indiana and former director of the Office of Management and Budget under George W. Bush, was wooed by fiscal conservatives. He made his intentions clear about staying in Indiana in the spring of 2011. Former Arkansas governor Mike Huckabee, who finished second in the delegate count behind John McCain in 2008, was on the short list of frontrunners for the 2012 nomination. Early polls showed him with higher levels of favorability than any of the other candidates, but he chose to focus on his Fox News television program. Budget Committee chair Paul Ryan of Wisconsin drew attention because of his proposals for Medicaid and Medicare reform, but he also opted not to run. Perhaps of greatest popular interest was former Alaska governor and McCain running mate Sarah Palin. A hero of the Tea Party movement, Palin had resigned the governorship in the summer of 2009 and spent the next two years raising funds for her PAC, appearing on Fox News, giving speeches, endorsing candidates, and even staring in her own cable reality show. She opted out of a presidential run in the fall of 2011 to continue focus on these activities.

Table 2.1 identifies the significant candidates who did decide to run for the Republican nomination in 2012. The list shows that while the field of significant contenders was no smaller than in recent nomination contests, it was unique. These candidates lacked experience on the national stage. Between 1960 and 2008, about 40 percent of presidential contenders had run for president before; in 2012 only two of the eventual candidates had. Moreover, three of those who ran were sitting or former members of the House of Representatives, an unusual perch from which to launch a successful presidential campaign.[11] Between 1960 and 2012, more than a third of all contenders had come from the Senate and another 22 percent from governorships, with just 13 percent coming from the House. The field was also unique in terms of the range of issue positions represented. Aside from Romney and Utahan Jon Huntsman, all of the candidates were hard-core conservatives on social, fiscal, and international issues.[12]

Mitt Romney entered the race early and as its frontrunner. No longer in office or actively working in business, he was free to devote much of his time since his last run to developing an effective campaign. Romney raised funds continuously, assembled a professional staff, traveled the country making connections with fellow Republicans, collected endorsements, and honed his message to make the strongest possible argument for his candidacy. This groundwork did not exactly generate excitement among Republican activists, but it gave him credibility and placed him in the top tier of candidates.

Table 2.1 Significant Republican Contenders

Candidate	Experience	Delegates	Exit Date
Mitt Romney	Presidential candidate (2007–08) Governor of Massachusetts (2003–07) CEO of Salt Lake Olympics (1999–2002) Management and private equity executive (1977–9)	1,575	—
Rick Santorum	U.S. senator from Pennsylvania (1995–2007)	245	April 10
Newt Gingrich	Author, lecturer, and consultant (1999–) U.S. representative from Georgia (1979–99) Speaker of the House (1995–99)	138	May 2
Ron Paul	Presidential candidate (2007–08) U.S. representative from Texas (1976–77, 1979–85, 1997–) Libertarian Party candidate for president (1988)	177	—
Jon Huntsman	U.S. ambassador to China (2009–11) Governor of Utah (2005–09)	2	January 16
Michele Bachmann	U.S. representative from Minnesota (2007–)	0	January 4
Herman Cain	Restaurant executive (1985–99)	0	December 3
Tim Pawlenty	Governor of Minnesota (1999–2003)	0	September 12
Rick Perry	Governor of Texas (2000–)	0	January 19

Notes: Totals are taken from the *Wall Street Journal* (projects.wsj.com/campaign2012/delegates) and *New York Times* (elections.nytimes.com/2012/primaries/delegates). Some other media outlets disagree on the numbers of delegates won by each candidate.

Source: Compiled by the author.

Rick Santorum was nothing like Romney but ended up being his most substantial competition. As a senator from Pennsylvania, Santorum had been a conservative firebrand, known at the end of his legislative career for controversial positions on cultural issues such as abortion and same sex marriage, but also for his stinging defeat in the 2006 midterm elections. He entered the campaign with one of the purest conservative records but little money, organization, or staff. Initially the media did not take him seriously, and for months he traveled in relative anonymity around Iowa.

Newt Gingrich lived several political lives, from the heyday of the Contract with America and his ascension to Speaker of the House in 1995 to his embarrassing departure from Congress just four years later. His volatile career played out in miniature during the nomination campaign. Gingrich's initial entry into the race was greeted with apprehension due to the baggage of time in Washington, a complicated marital history, and a haughty personal style. He also alienated some conservative allies when in May 2011 he called representative Paul Ryan's proposal for Medicare reform "right-wing social engineering."

The following month a group of top Gingrich aides, including his campaign manager and spokesperson, resigned en masse. They were apparently displeased with his decision to take a two-week Greek cruise in the middle of the campaign and a scandal over the purchase of several hundred thousand dollars of jewelry at Tiffany's. The early implosion of his campaign sent conservatives searching for a different alternative to Romney. Yet resignations were not unusual; a similar staff departure from John McCain's campaign occurred in the summer of 2007. Like McCain, Gingrich benefited from the newly lowered expectations and slowly climbed his way back to contention.

Tim Pawlenty brought several assets to the campaign: experience as governor of Minnesota, likability, a common touch with blue-collar voters, and the ability to win in a Democratic state. For these reasons he had been on McCain's short list of potential running mates in 2008. Yet Pawlenty's campaign raised little money and generated even less enthusiasm among Republican activists. He departed the race early after losing the August 2011 straw poll in Iowa, a state where he had invested time and money. As "everybody's second choice," he brought back memories of Democratic candidates such as New Mexico governor Bill Richardson in 2004 and Arizona governor Bruce Babbitt in 1988.

Representative Michele Bachmann was the archetypical Tea Party activist. Her roots were in evangelical Christianity and opposition to anything done by the federal government other than national security. Bachmann was active in movements against abortion and same-sex marriage, and she had founded the congressional Tea Party Caucus. Bachmann announced her candidacy in Iowa in June 2011 and devoted much of her time to the Iowa straw poll, which she narrowly won.

Against this unimpressive field, Texas governor Rick Perry was cast as the white knight who would salvage the nomination for conservatives. He was the only one of the cadre of desirables who, unlike Christie, Daniels, and Palin, was successfully recruited into the race. In theory Perry was the ideal Republican candidate. He had governed the influential state of Texas since George W. Bush's departure in 2000. He easily won three statewide elections, and demonstrated an ability to win the votes of Latinos. He appealed to evangelicals and presided over the creation of many new jobs in an otherwise weak national economy. His entrance into the presidential field—which was timed to rob Michele Bachmann of much bounce coming out of the Iowa straw poll—created an immediate buzz that put him near the top of the late-summer polls. But Perry, as noted subsequently, stumbled badly in the debates with his Republican opponents.

The least likely candidate was restaurant executive Herman Cain. Generally ignored when he entered the race in May, Cain later benefitted from a conservative vacuum left by Rick Perry's missteps in the GOP debates. Cain had no real political experience, lacked many connections within the party, and as an African American did not fit the typical Republican profile. Yet he too benefitted from conservative discontent and a fragmented field.

He vaulted into the first tier of candidates when he pulled off a surprising and sizable win in the Florida straw poll in late September. His economic message revolved around his "9-9-9 plan" to impose a flat 9 percent tax rate on corporate income, personal income, and sales. By the time of the Republican candidate debate in New Hampshire on October 11, Cain was polling nearly as well as Romney.

Jon Huntsman bore little resemblance to the rest of field. Anathema to many conservatives, his most recent job was in the Obama administration as ambassador to China, although he had earlier been in business and served as governor of Utah. Huntsman was the most moderate candidate in the race, defending such things as climate change science that his peers dismissed. Because of his policy positions and similarity to Romney as a Mormon with business credentials, Huntsman's candidacy never took off. He began unprepared and suffered from a thin and contentious staff that launched a sloppy campaign.[13]

There are two ways to sort out the Republican field. The first is the traditional divide between *insiders* and *outsiders*. Insiders are politicians with long records in office and policymaking experience in Washington. This group includes House members Bachmann, Santorum, Paul, and especially Gingrich. Outsiders have experiences rooted in their states or in business outside of Washington: Romney, Pawlenty, Perry, and especially Cain. But in the wake of the Tea Party's ascendance, the insider-outsider distinction overlapped with a different cleavage. This division was between the GOP establishment, embodied in Romney, and the rest of the field, which was less conventional.[14] The antiestablishment profile gave an opening to Gingrich and Santorum, who might otherwise have been discounted as part of the Washington crowd. To succeed, they would need to cast themselves as ideologically purer and more passionate than Romney.

The Not-So-Invisible Primary

The *invisible primary*—the lengthy preliminary stage of the campaign that predates the actual primaries and caucuses—facilitated the winnowing of the field in 2012 as it always does, driving out candidates who lagged in poll standing, experience, and fundraising.[15] But the rise and fall of individual candidates in 2012 was far more fluid and unpredictable than in previous years. The many debates and the attention paid to the fates of individual candidates made the prevoting period far from invisible. Except for Perry's later entrance, the field was set by the end of the spring 2011, leaving nine months of not-so-invisible primary before the first real nominating events in Iowa and New Hampshire. During this phase of the campaign Romney remained a steady second choice among Republicans while a series of his conservative opponents jumped ahead of him on brief waves of excitement and then crashed in a trough of disappointment. The source of much of this fluctuation was the prolonged series of Republican candidate debates.

The 2012 nomination contest expanded a trend from recent presidential elections by increasing the number of debates, forums, and other candidate events during the invisible primary. More than twenty of these events were held between May 2011 and March 2012. Their frequency and good television ratings certainly helped Gingrich, who was running low on campaign funds but excelled at sharp debate repartee. Perry was the main debate victim. In his first appearance, at the Reagan Presidential Library debate in early September, he took some flak for calling Social Security a "Ponzi scheme." Several days later at a CNN/Tea Party debate in Tampa he was booed for having mandated the human papillomavirus (HPV) vaccine for preteen girls in Texas. The vaccine is intended to protect girls from a sexually transmitted disease that contributes to cervical cancer. His fellow candidates continued to attack the frontrunner ten days later in Orlando where his erratic style and unconvincing defense of benefits provided to immigrants in Texas did not help.

The debates displayed how central the Tea Party movement had become to Republican nomination politics. With negotiations over how to deal with the approaching "debt ceiling" dominating politics in Washington, the Republican presidential candidates were asked in an Iowa debate if they would accept a federal budget agreement in which every dollar in tax increases was matched by ten dollars in spending reductions. All eight candidates refused such a deal. On several occasions debate audiences shocked viewers with their extreme reactions to what was happening on stage. At one event the crowd cheered when Ron Paul suggested that an uninsured person with a serious condition should be allowed to die; in another instance the audience cheered when Perry discussed how many people the state of Texas executed.

It was difficult for Romney to outflank his opponents in this environment. Consider the view of the *Wall Street Journal* opinion page, which often acts as a mouthpiece for Republican conservatives. After Romney entered the race, the newspaper's editors called the individual health care mandate he implemented in Massachusetts a "fatal flaw" that left him "compromised and not credible."[16] Pawlenty seized on the link between Obama and Romney's policies, calling the law "Obamneycare." Gingrich later began calling Romney the "Massachusetts moderate."

To gird himself for what initially appeared to be a lengthy nomination season, Romney pursued a "Rose Garden" strategy typical of incumbents and frontrunners. Although he participated in nearly all of the debates, he skipped the Iowa straw poll out of concern that he might fare poorly. He spent most of the invisible primary season raising money at private events rather than fielding questions at public events.[17] With only one exception, no Republican outraised Romney in any quarterly reporting period.[18] Candidates such as Santorum lacked the luxury of running an under-the-radar campaign. To avoid being forgotten altogether, they needed to earn free media to grab attention that they could transform into better fundraising, poll numbers, and perceptions of viability. The debates became a vital source of attention for second-tier and resource-poor contenders who could deliver the red meat the party activists desired.

The polls indicated that Republican voters were shopping for an unambiguously conservative candidate to take on Romney. Figure 2.1 shows the poll standings of five Republican candidates, using a smoothing curve to summarize the many individual surveys taken during the nomination contest. The graph shows that Republican voters considered and then discarded Perry, Cain, and Gingrich. Each candidate experienced what Sides and Vavreck call a "boomlet," a quick spike in public excitement followed by an equally fast fall.[19] This occurred because as each candidate-of-the-day rose to prominence, voters, the media, and their opponents began to target them, scrutinizing their records and pointing out their failings on the campaign trail. Romney, in contrast, had already been vetted during his first run for the presidency in 2008 and was never the darling of hard-core conservatives. His campaign brought few moments of exhilaration but remained competitive; in fact, Romney slowly increased his standing in the polls as the campaign wore on. As a result of the splintered campaign, Romney did not establish himself as a leader in national polls of Republican voters until about March of 2012, just as he began to wrap up the necessary delegates to make his nomination inevitable.

Figure 2.1 Republican Candidate Standings in the Polls (August 2011 to April 2012)

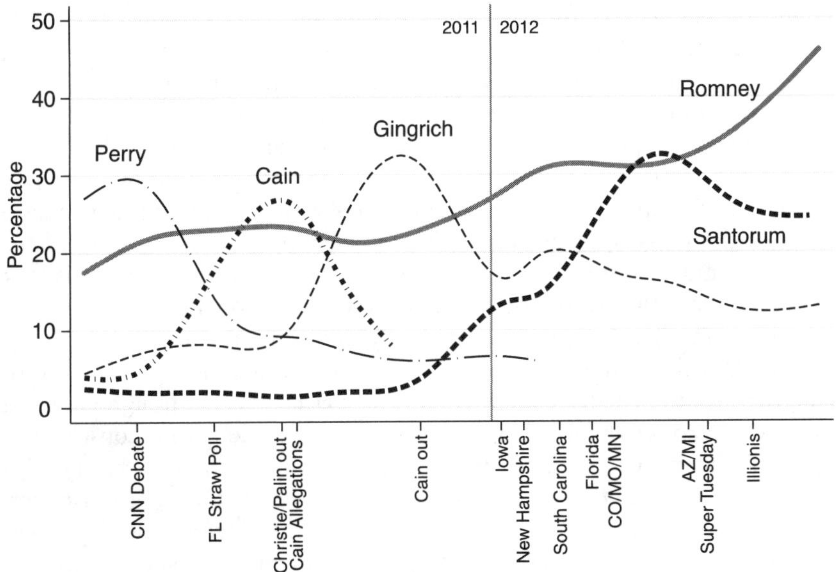

Notes: Lines are median splines representing the 145 surveys reported by Pollster.com and RealClearPolitics that were fielded between August 17, 2011, and April 23, 2012.

Source: Compiled by the author.

Aside from Romney, the only Republican not to experience a boomlet was Paul, who held steady with a dedicated core of about 10 percent of Republican voters. He appears not to have been hurt by a controversy that emerged in December 2011 about racist statements in a newsletter his organization had once issued. But he also never threatened to run away with the nomination. Paul's support came from a highly committed group but his libertarian positions on some social and foreign policies were unacceptable to many Republicans. His support rose marginally over time, from 8 or 9 percent during the not-so-invisible primary period to 12 or 13 percent once voting got underway and other candidates withdrew from the race.

Rick Perry's debate performances undermined his campaign. Most damning was the November 9 debate in Michigan. Answering a question about how to spur job creation with fewer regulations, he spontaneously stated that "it's three agencies of government, when I get there, that are gone: Commerce, Education, and . . . the . . . ," simply forgetting the third. As Paul and Romney offered to help him with suggestions, questioner John Harwood asked, "but you can't name the third one?" Perry continued to stumble and concluded, "I can't. The third one, I can't. Sorry. Oops" Later in the debate he remembered "by the way, that was the Department of Energy I was reaching for a while ago," but this was a gaffe that invited further scrutiny of his record and competence.

Perry's implosion paved the way for Herman Cain. Like Romney, Cain's background appealed to business-friendly Republicans. His tax plan resonated with Tea Party voters, and his conservative credentials were never in doubt. Cain quickly rose to the top of the field despite little organization, political experience, or funding. The Cain boomlet unraveled just as quickly when allegations of sexual harassment and extramarital affairs emerged in October. Several women had received financial settlements from the restaurant association that Cain led. He denied the allegations in November as his campaign was imploding. The end of his campaign was cemented when he gave a disastrous interview in which he did not appear to know anything about the crisis in Libya. When asked for his views on the president's handling of the mass uprising there, Cain seemed confused and fumbled for several minutes without producing a real answer to the question. This lack of familiarity with foreign policy issues and further revelations about sexual affairs assured that he would not be the Republican nominee in 2012.

With Cain's rapid decline the anti-Romney mantle passed back to Gingrich, who opened a sizable lead in early December. Although Gingrich claimed the conservative label, he too faced opposition from conservative opinion-makers. Columnist David Brooks complained about his lack of "the right temperament and character" and his desire for big government. George Will opined that Gingrich "embodies almost everything disagreeable about modern Washington" through his paid work for special interests advocating for programs such as support for ethanol. Other conservative critics focused on Gingrich's hypocrisy, consulting gig with Freddie Mac, and lack of personal appeal.[20] His support ebbed somewhat, but the zingers he delivered in debates helped keep Gingrich viable.

In an unsettled field, as late as mid-December the important evangelical voting bloc in Iowa had yet to coalesce behind a candidate.[21] In 2008 a network of home school parents and other religious conservatives had lifted Mike Huckabee to victory in the caucuses.[22] Whoever captured that rather late, organized support in 2012 would almost certainly become the conservative standard-bearer to challenge Romney. Had Cain, Gingrich, Perry, or even Bachmann peaked later, they might have won the Iowa caucuses and taken on the role of the main alternative to Romney. Surprisingly, that person turned out to be Santorum.

Santorum had the most skeletal operation in Iowa, but devoted himself to the state and traveled to hundreds of town hall meetings in an effort to visit every one of Iowa's ninety-nine counties. He often traveled alone in a single pickup truck, whereas most other candidates had buses, teams of staff, and in Romney's case a plane.[23] Romney's super PAC viewed Gingrich as the main threat to victory in Iowa and used heavy television advertising in the Hawkeye State to raise questions about the former Speaker of the House. This provided more of an opening for Santorum to score well by peaking near the night of the caucuses. Santorum's success in the Iowa caucus occurred not despite but because his campaign had for so long been under the radar. Two Iowa evangelical leaders endorsed him in the weeks before the caucus. This was not the stuff of significant media coverage, but their influence was significant in the intimate caucus environment. His rise in the final days before the caucus from single to double digits went mostly unnoticed.

Rules, Rules, Rules

As the invisible primary season transitioned into real primary and caucus events in early 2012, the rules governing Republican nominations became paramount. The effects of rules are difficult to assess in advance because they depend on the field of candidates, their regional strengths, and how they divide up the vote. All told, the rules probably disadvantaged Romney slightly.

It is worth noting that the two major parties continue to use somewhat different rules to settle presidential nominations. Democrats select twice as many convention delegates: 5,552 compared with 2,286 for the Republicans. The Democratic Party also makes greater use of *superdelegates,* party leaders who are automatic delegates and need not pledge themselves to any candidate. Superdelegates make up about 14 percent of the Democratic convention but only 6 percent of the Republican convention. Democrats also impose stronger requirements that state delegations' demographic profiles mirror those of the broader electorate. The Democratic rules ask states to give priority to racial and ethnic minorities when selecting at-large delegates, and to seek gender balance in district-chosen delegates. In the Iowa caucuses, Republicans use the secret ballot while Democratic caucus-goers must state their candidate preferences publicly. Finally, Republicans allow winner-take-all rules for allocating delegates while Democrats rely almost exclusively on proportional representation, although that distinction has been overdrawn. Just a handful of states used true winner-take-all, or even a hybrid system in which the leading candidate won a bonus allocation of statewide delegates.[24]

What set 2012 apart in terms of rules was the remarkable amount of cooperation between the two major parties. As the new Republican rules stated, their purpose was to "facilitate a more orderly process in 2012 in contrast to the chaotic schedule experienced in 2008."[25] This was a goal both parties shared. The new parameters gave special status to four "carve out" states: Iowa, New Hampshire, South Carolina, and Nevada. The rules penalized states that violated timing rules, and worked against "frontloading" by pushing events in all the other states later into the campaign season. Eighteen states needed to change statutes to come into compliance with the new rules.[26]

The new Republican National Committee (RNC) rules required states to use a form of proportional representation if they held their contests before April 1. This would prevent a small number of early states from deciding the nomination through winner-take-all rules. Only the "carve out" states of Iowa, New Hampshire, South Carolina, and Nevada were permitted to schedule their delegate-selection events before the first Tuesday in March and use winner-take-all, but even they had to wait until after February 1. Others needed to wait until the first Tuesday in March.[27] But that did not stop Arizona, Florida, Michigan, New Hampshire, and South Carolina, each of which was docked half of their delegates for holding their primaries too early. While Gingrich suffered from getting half of what he might have won in a later South Carolina primary, the penalties hurt Romney most because it limited his delegate hauls in Florida and Arizona. In that sense the rules worked as intended because they limited the influence of early states.

Super Tuesday was far less super in 2012. Only ten states and 437 Republican delegates were at stake on March 6, in sharp contrast with 2008, when Super Tuesday was held a month earlier, featured nineteen states, and awarded 963 delegates. While 45 percent of Republican delegates were picked on Super Tuesday in 2008, less than 20 percent were chosen in 2012. The 2012 Super Tuesday looked more like 2004, when Super Tuesday occurred on March 2 and included ten states. The dispersion of states from a single primary day probably disadvantaged Romney, who would have picked up significant steam from more victories early in the season.

Caucuses displayed troubling pathologies in the 2012 contest. Problems in the Iowa caucuses, as detailed below, were only the first sign of trouble. In Nevada the Republican Party appeared not to be in full control of the process. One prominent voting site there allowed voting on Saturday for religious reasons, and another county took longer than others to report final results. The process was also chaotic in Maine, where turnout reached just 3 percent of registered Republicans. Caucus voting there stretched over a week, or even longer in some counties. The Maine Republican Party announced results, in which Romney narrowly beat Paul, before all communities had voted. This report was updated as later caucus results came in, but in the end it appears that at least one county was not included in the totals.[28] To this day it is not clear what the official, final results were. These are the symptoms of an event staffed by party activists rather than professional election administrators.

Voting Begins

Romney's strongest argument heading into the first primaries and caucuses was his electability. In head-to-head trial heat polls in the summer of 2011 between various Republican candidates and President Obama, only Romney came close to running even. Through much of the spring of 2012 Romney ran a few points behind Obama in most polls while the other Republicans were much further behind the President. The decision for GOP primary voters was whether to focus more on "anyone but Romney" now or "anyone but Obama" later. This kept him in contention in Iowa as other candidates rose and fell.

The initial results from the Iowa caucuses suggested that Romney had narrowly won the argument between electability and ideological purity. On the night of January 3 Romney was credited with a razor-thin victory over Santorum, winning by 8 votes out of more than 120,000 cast, the closest race in Iowa caucus history. As Table 2.2 shows, each had 25 percent of the vote, with Paul at 21 percent and Gingrich well behind at 13 percent. The result provided Santorum with his first moment in the spotlight. Gingrich vowed revenge against Romney, who he believed gave Santorum an opening in Iowa by derailing Gingrich's campaign with negative ads.

Romney's win in Iowa helped him build momentum going into the New Hampshire primary one week later. The Iowa victory set up the possibility that he would sweep the first four states and become unstoppable. But in the days that followed Iowa it was revealed that several caucus sites had problematic counting and reporting processes. At a site in Appanoose County, the handwritten results were erroneous, crediting Romney with too many votes. After more than two weeks of investigation and reconsideration, the Iowa Republican Party officially declared Santorum the winner by thirty-four votes. Unfortunately for Santorum, this announcement came too late to provide him with a boost in New Hampshire.

Romney may not have been beatable in New Hampshire anyway. He had lost the primary narrowly to John McCain four years earlier. He was a familiar figure to the two-thirds of the Granite State that lives in the greater

Table 2.2 Republican Caucus Results

State	Date	Gingrich (%)	Paul (%)	Perry (%)	Romney (%)	Santorum (%)
Iowa	January 3	13	21	10	25	**25**
Nevada	February 4	21	7		**50**	10
Colorado	February 7	13	12	0	35	**40**
Minnesota	February 7	11	27		17	**45**
Maine	(see Notes)	6	36		**38**	18
Wyoming	(see Notes)	8	21		**39**	32
Washington	March 3	10	25		**38**	24
Alaska	March 6	14	24		**32**	29
Idaho	March 6	2	18		**62**	18
North Dakota	March 6	8	28		24	**40**
Guam	March 10	0	0		**96**	0
Kansas	March 10	14	13	0	21	**51**
Northern Mariana Islands	March 10	3	3		**87**	6
U.S. Virgin Islands	March 10	5	**29**		27	6
American Samoa	March 13					
Hawaii	March 13	11	19		**44**	25

Notes: Bold entries indicate which candidate won the popular vote in the state. Blank cells indicate the candidate was not on the ballot. Maine's caucuses were held on a rolling basis across municipalities, with most taking places between February 4 and 11. Wyoming's precinct caucuses, which are technically nonbinding straw polls, were held between February 9 and 29. County conventions then took place between March 6 and 10. A formal vote did not take place in American Samoa, although records indicate that a majority of participants favored Romney.

Source: Compiled by the author.

Boston media market. He also spent significant time in the state and maintained a home on Lake Winnipesaukee. Unsurprisingly, Romney led the balloting on primary day with 39 percent of the vote, as shown in Table 2.3. Paul finished second at 23 percent with Huntsman third and Santorum and Gingrich further back. The media coverage after the primary highlighted that Romney was the first nonincumbent Republican ever to win both Iowa and New Hampshire, setting him up as an all but inevitable nominee.

This naturally alarmed the most conservative elements in the party. A group of leading social conservatives quickly met in Texas to coordinate their support behind a single candidate who could stop Romney.[29] They chose Santorum, but this decision may have come too late, especially because the candidate leading in the South Carolina polls was Gingrich. The next week saw hard-hitting attacks by other candidates against Romney. He was criticized for revealing that he paid only about 15 percent in federal tax on his large income and for claiming that the nearly $375,000 he earned in speaking fees in 2011 was "not very much." Perry referred to Romney's work with Bain Capital as "vulture capitalism," and Gingrich asserted that Romney's practices at Bain were not capitalism at all.

Table 2.3 Republican Primary Results

State	Date	Gingrich (%)	Paul (%)	Perry (%)	Romney (%)	Santorum (%)
New Hampshire	January 10	9	23	1	**39**	9
South Carolina	January 21	**40**	13	0	28	17
Florida	January 31	32	7	0	**46**	13
Missouri	February 7		12	1	25	**55**
Arizona	February 28	16	9	0	**47**	27
Michigan	February 28	7	12	0	**41**	38
Georgia	March 6	**47**	7	0	26	20
Massachusetts	March 6	5	10	0	**72**	12
Ohio	March 6	15	9	1	**38**	37
Oklahoma	March 6	27	10	0	28	**34**
Tennessee	March 6	24	9	0	28	**37**
Vermont	March 6	8	25	1	**39**	24
Virginia	March 6		40		**60**	
Alabama	March 13	29	5	0	29	**35**
Mississippi	March 13	31	4	0	31	**33**
Puerto Rico	March 18	2	1		**83**	8
Illinois	March 20	8	9	1	**47**	35
Louisiana	March 24	16	6	1	27	**49**
Maryland	April 3	11	10	0	**49**	29
Washington, DC	April 3	11	12		**68**	
Wisconsin	April 3	6	11		**44**	37
Connecticut	April 24	10	13		**67**	7
Delaware	April 24	27	11		**56**	6
New York	April 24	13	15		**62**	10
Pennsylvania	April 24	10	13		**58**	18
Rhode Island	April 24	6	24		**63**	6
Indiana	May 8	6	16		**65**	13
North Carolina	May 8	8	11		**66**	10
West Virginia	May 8	6	11		**70**	12
Nebraska	May 15	5	10		**71**	14
Oregon	May 15	5	13		**71**	9
Arkansas	May 22	5	13		**68**	13
Kentucky	May 22	6	13		**67**	9
Texas	May 29	5	12		**69**	8
California	June 5	4	10		**80**	5

(Continued)

Table 2.3 Continued

State	Date	Gingrich (%)	Paul (%)	Perry (%)	Romney (%)	Santorum (%)
Montana	June 5	4	14		**68**	9
New Jersey	June 5	8	10		**81**	5
New Mexico	June 5	6	10		**73**	10
South Dakota	June 5	4	13		**66**	11
Utah	June 26	0	5		**93**	2

Notes: Bold entries indicate which candidate won the popular vote in the state. Blank cells indicate the candidate was not on the ballot. Missouri's primary preceded its county caucuses held between March 15 and 24, and did not lead directly to delegate selection.

Source: Compiled by the author.

Romney had difficulties winning over southern voters. In contrast, Gingrich had represented a district in Georgia for many years and Sarah Palin helped his cause by recommending a vote for Gingrich just before primary day. Rick Perry added yet more fuel to the former Speaker's campaign when he dropped from the race two days before South Carolina and gave Gingrich his endorsement. Finally, Gingrich had a valuable ally in billionaire Sheldon Adelson. A casino magnate and advocate for Israel, Adelson dumped two dollops of $5 million each into the pro-Gingrich super PAC, Winning Our Future. The group quickly secured $3.4 million in airtime on South Carolina television and produced a film calling Romney a "corporate raider." On election night Gingrich handed Romney his first defeat, 40 percent to 28 percent. Santorum and Paul trailed with 17 percent and 13 percent of the vote, respectively.

Despite finishing second in South Carolina, Romney remained the frontrunner in the primary scheduled for January 31 in Florida, a more cosmopolitan state where he led in the polls and had outspent opponents. Romney held off Gingrich on primary day and won the Sunshine State by 14 percentage points. That night he tried to draw a connection between his victory in the primary and the party's convention that would also be held in Florida, a key swing state in the general election. In his victory speech Romney declared, "A competitive primary does not divide us. It prepares us. And when we gather here in Tampa seven months from now for our convention, ours will be a united party with a winning ticket for America." But Gingrich remained defiant, attempting to redefine the race as a two-person contest and declaring that he would battle Romney in all of the forty-six remaining states.

Gingrich's claim was undone when Santorum finished first in three states on February 7. Two of these states used the caucus, a format that suited Santorum's more ideologically committed supporters. Those wins set back Gingrich, but also hurt Romney, especially in Colorado where the governor had easily won in 2008. Romney did appear to narrowly edge out Paul in the Maine caucuses that same week, but the surprising showings by Santorum remained the dominant news story while the candidates awaited the next round of events on February 28. As Figure 2.1 shows, Santorum ran ahead of Romney in the polls through this period.

That changed when Romney scored victories in the Arizona and Michigan primaries on February 28. His margin of victory in Michigan was not large—just 3 percentage points over Santorum—despite it being his birth state and the state where his father had been governor. But the two wins were enough to change the media narrative in Romney's favor. He then moved into the lead in the polls, a lead he would not relinquish again.

The next major event was Super Tuesday on March 6. Although less "super" than in recent elections, it still featured contests in important general election states such as Ohio and Virginia. The day yielded a split verdict, albeit one that favored Romney. He won by a hair over Santorum in Ohio, and was victorious in Virginia because neither Santorum nor Gingrich had failed to deliver enough petition signatures required by state law to get on the ballot. Gingrich's only Super Tuesday victory came in his home state of Georgia, further suggesting the limits of his appeal. Santorum was victorious in the South (Oklahoma and Tennessee) as well as in the North Dakota caucuses, while Romney won Alaska, Idaho, Massachusetts, and Vermont.

Santorum continued to pick up wins in the South, with victories in Alabama and Mississippi on March 13 and Louisiana on March 24. In between, Romney won the delegate-rich Illinois primary on March 20. As a big state that stood alone on that day's primary calendar, Illinois took on added symbolic value. Romney's defeat of Santorum there by 12 percentage points was enhanced two days later when Tea Party stalwart and southern senator Jim DeMint (R-SC) suggested that Gingrich and Santorum leave the race so that the party could unite behind Romney. Soon after, Romney also won Maryland, Washington, DC, and Wisconsin, all on April 3. For the first time his poll standing among Republicans broke the 40 percent threshold. Doubts that Romney would win the nomination were finally put to bed.

Yet the truth was that at several points during the campaign Romney had failed to wrap up a nomination that seemed his for the taking. On multiple occasions good news for the campaign was offset by simultaneous bad news that gave his opponents ammunition. The most jarring of these were comments from Romney aide Eric Fehrnstrom that distracted attention from Romney's big win in the Illinois primary and the endorsement of former Florida governor Jeb Bush. In an interview about the general election, Fehrnstrom said, "I think you hit a reset button for the fall campaign. Everything changes. It's almost like an Etch A Sketch. You can kind of shake it up and restart all over again."[30] This reference to a child's toy in which images can be replaced with a simple shake played into activists' fears that

Romney would abandon conservative positions after winning the nomination. Santorum made the most of the error, campaigning with an Etch A Sketch toy in hand to remind voters that his conservative credentials were less malleable than Romney's.

With less cash and organization than Romney, Santorum needed debates and primary wins to keep his campaign viable, but there would be no more voting until five states held their primaries on April 24. In one of those contests, in Santorum's home state of Pennsylvania, he was merely running even with Romney in the polls. In addition, he was diverted from the campaigning by his young daughter's hospitalization for pneumonia. Santorum had little choice but to fold his campaign on April 10.

Santorum did not formally endorse Romney for another month. In the meantime, Gingrich held a press conference to "suspend" his campaign, reneging on his promise of "going all the way to Tampa." His lengthy withdrawal speech was classic Newt: recounting his accomplishments and offering only faint praise for his competitors. "I am asked sometimes, is Mitt Romney conservative enough?" said Gingrich, "And my answer is simple. Compared to Barack Obama? You know this is not a choice between Mitt Romney and Ronald Reagan. This is a choice between Mitt Romney and the most radical leftist president in American history." Like other conservatives, Gingrich had shifted from "anyone but Romney" to "anyone but Obama."

According to most media counts, Romney officially clinched a majority of convention delegates in the Texas primary on May 29. With no viable opponents still in the race, Romney won two-thirds of the Texas primary vote. The 105 delegates he earned put him over the 1,144 threshold, all but guaranteeing his nomination in Tampa.

As the 2012 primary and caucus results rolled in, a surprising parallel emerged with the Democratic Party results from four years earlier. In 2012 Romney did better in states where Hillary Clinton also had good showings in 2008. Some of the overlap has to do with whether a state was holding a primary or a caucus, events in which both Romney and Clinton struggled. Both candidates also had trouble winning many votes in the South. Surprisingly there is no correlation between Romney's own vote shares in 2008 and 2012. This reflects changes in the field of candidates that Romney faced. Whereas the 2012 contest was defined mainly as a confrontation between the establishment candidate Romney and his more conservative challengers, in 2008 he was one of several moderate candidates along with Rudolph Giuliani and John McCain. This lack of correlation demonstrates how important the field of candidates is to defining a particular candidate's appeal. Finishing third in the 2008 delegate count and then preparing during the next four years for another campaign transformed Romney, as did the fact that his 2012 opponents were drawn primarily from the Tea Party ranks of the party.

Establishment candidates such as Clinton and Romney are generally more moderate, have more resources, are more cautious, have worked their way up through the party hierarchy, and tend to emphasize electability over ideological purity. In contrast, insurgent candidates such as Obama in 2008 and Santorum in 2012 tend to stake out more positions, appeal mainly to activists, and operate on the margins of the party structure. As a result, mainstream candidates such as Clinton and Romney do better in primaries, which encourage broad participation, rather than in caucuses, which cater to more intensive involvement by a smaller number of ideological party activists.[31] This might also explain why Clinton and Romney fared better outside the more traditional South.[32]

Organizational Advantages

Even in the era of online fundraising and social media, the 2012 campaign demonstrated that old-fashioned organizing is still helpful, if not necessary, to victory. Romney began the nomination contest with numerous endorsements from party leaders, plenty of money, and a superior state field operation. This organizational advantage allowed him to gain the most leverage from rules ranging from ballot access to delegate nominations, as well as to weather temporary setbacks.

Late to the race and underfunded, Santorum struggled even to gain ballot access in some states. His lack of professional trappings was part of his charm, but it cost him. When he lost Illinois to Romney by 47 percent to 35 percent, he only earned ten delegates to Romney's forty-one in part because he failed to nominate slates in some districts. Huntsman's organizational troubles were never resolved, and Herman Cain had almost no field operation with which to leverage his moment as frontrunner.[33] None of the Republicans except for Romney and Paul managed to get the necessary signatures to appear on the ballot in the Virginia primary. Paul's fundraising success and dedicated core of volunteers allowed him to win many delegates in later rounds of caucuses.

The 2012 nomination made clear that caucuses reward candidates with enthusiastic and persistent supporters. Most caucuses are multiround events. The media tend to focus on the first round, when voting takes place at the precinct level. But those early rounds do not actually select delegates. This occurs later through a series of telescoping events at which representatives chosen in one round select representatives to move on to the next, higher round, typically from precincts to counties or congressional districts, and then to the state level. After several weeks or months, the process often culminates in a state convention where delegates to the national convention are chosen. Unlike other campaigns, Paul's stepped up its efforts in these later rounds, often at Romney's expense. One startling example was the Iowa Republican State Convention in June. Although delegates are officially unbound, Paul backers managed to elect twenty-three of the state's twenty-eight delegates, a far cry from the opening event on January 3 in which Paul finished third. Paul supporters also used a "scorched earth" policy to pick up most of the delegates in Nevada, Maine, and Idaho.[34]

Predictably, the delegate votes on the floor of the Republican convention bore little resemblance to the more fractured primary and caucus results. Following standard practice, Gingrich and Santorum released their delegates just before the convention so that they could vote for Romney in a show of unity. Ron Paul, however, remained an inconvenient gadfly who provided the only tangible threat to convention unity. Mitt Romney was easily nominated with 2,061 votes out of 2,286. The most significant opposition came from Ron Paul supporters, who cheered his appearance in the convention hall and gave the congressman 185 votes in Tampa. No other candidate earned more than a smattering of support.[35]

The Republican National Convention was cut short by a day due to concerns about Hurricane Isaac, forcing some reshuffling of speakers including Ann Romney. Ron Paul declined an offer to speak because he refused to have his speech approved in advance and to endorse Romney. The convention also did not include George W. Bush or Dick Cheney, who had left the White House just less than four years earlier. Prime time slots were reserved for governors such as Chris Christie and Nikki Haley rather than Republican leaders in Congress. Most memorable was an unscripted, rambling routine by actor Clint Eastwood just before Romney's acceptance speech on the final night of the convention. Eastwood addressed an empty chair in which Obama was imagined to be sitting, a gimmick that did not go over well with most viewers. To help personalize the candidate, Romney's background as a church and community leader was also highlighted at the convention in various testimonials. His speech, which focused almost entirely on economy and federal budget, was highlighted by the assertion that while Obama "promised to begin to slow the rise of the oceans and heal the planet . . . my promise . . . is to help you and your family." Aside from the Eastwood distraction, it was hailed a successful convention that portrayed both Romney and his running mate, Paul Ryan, in a positive light and made direct appeals to moderate voters.

Pivot to the General Election

In some ways the Romney campaign was always focused on the general election matchup with Obama. It had operated largely as an incumbent campaign, focusing on fundraising, staying on message, and avoiding entanglements with his Republican opponents. In most of his primary- and caucus-night victory speeches, Romney criticized the president rather than drawing distinctions with other Republicans. For example, in his address on Super Tuesday, he only briefly acknowledged Gingrich, Paul, and Santorum. Much more of the speech was a list of complaints about

Obamacare, the nation's credit rating, the president's rejection of the Keystone oil pipeline, the nation's high unemployment rate, and Obama's interest in raising taxes.

Although Romney won his party's nomination by a wider margin than Obama won his in 2008, he nonetheless limped into the general election. Romney was viewed less positively than other recent presumptive nominees had been. Gallup surveys showed that in mid-May Romney had a favorability rating of 50 percent among all respondents. This put him well below John McCain's rating of 67 percent at a similar point four years earlier, as well as below Obama, George W. Bush, John Kerry, Al Gore, and Bob Dole.[36]

This in part explains why Ryan was chosen as Romney's vice presidential running mate. Ryan provided a crucial connection to the Tea Party wing of the Republican Party and its stronghold, the House of Representatives. Ryan's selection also pacified conservative opinion leaders writing for publications such as the *Wall Street Journal* and *Weekly Standard*.[37] Adding Ryan to the ticket crystallized differences between the two parties on budgets, entitlements, and health care policy in way that Romney alone could not. Ryan had also demonstrated an ability to perform on national stage when elevated to House Budget Committee chair in 2010 and when he delivered the official Republican Party response to President's Obama's 2011 State of the Union address. He was widely viewed as a serious policymaker with a vision for the nation; he was young and could help widen the party's generational appeal; he was from a midwestern battleground state; and he was a white Catholic, thus representing a key bloc of swing voters. Ryan and Romney hit it off personally on the campaign trail when they teamed up earlier in the year.

Perhaps reflecting the flawed nature of the field in which he competed, Romney did not pick one of his primary opponents as a running mate. This runs against a common pattern: Bill Clinton selected also-ran Al Gore, Ronald Reagan picked George H. W. Bush, and Barack Obama chose Joe Biden. Romney also did not select any of the many governors such as Chris Christie, Scott Walker, Nikki Haley, Bobby Jindal, or Mitch Daniels who were seen as rising stars in the party. Scattered reporting suggests that among those being vetted seriously were senator Marco Rubio of Florida, Ohio senator Rob Portman, and Tim Pawlenty. Rubio had special appeal because he represented a large swing state and because of his connection to Latino voters. Portman and Pawlenty would both have been safe picks who offered connections to the Midwest and sound conservative credentials, but neither would have brought as much excitement to the ticket as Ryan. The Romney campaign announced Ryan's selection on August 11 via a mobile phone application. The next day the ticket appeared together in front of the *U.S.S. Wisconsin,* a battleship stationed along the Virginia coast. This gave the candidates two weeks to campaign, both together and separately, and to prepare for the upcoming Republican convention.

Minor Stumbles on the Way to Charlotte, and Elsewhere

When television became the most important medium for reporting on politics, the major party nominating conventions transformed from raucous battles among state delegations to promotional affairs designed to show unity heading into the general election. Whereas some earlier presidents faced significant challenges for renomination, incumbents have exerted more control over conventions in recent years. As was to be expected, President Obama did not face any notable obstacles for renomination at the Democratic convention in Charlotte. The lack of opposition was a good omen. Incumbents who face serious challenge for renomination are more likely to fare poorly in the general election. George H. W. Bush learned this the hard way in 1992 when conservative commentator Patrick Buchanan did well against him in the New Hampshire primary. Jimmy Carter's fate in the 1980 general election was similarly foreshadowed by the difficulty he had in quelling the movement to nominate senator Edward Kennedy. Much like President George W. Bush's reelection effort in 2004 and President Bill Clinton's in 1996, Obama put little effort into the primaries and caucuses. Instead, he began building his general election campaign machine early and developing arguments against likely Republican nominees Romney and Perry.

Obama breezed through the early primaries and caucuses with little hint of longing among Democratic activists for an alternative nominee. Surveys in the spring of 2011 showed more support for his renomination than for Bill Clinton's in 1996. But cracks in that facade appeared beginning in May 2012. In Democratic primaries in several southern and border states, a substantial percentage of voters selected fringe candidates or options such as "uncommitted" and "no preference." Most embarrassing was Obama losing 41 percent of the West Virginia primary vote to a vanity candidate who, unbeknownst to most voters, was an inmate in federal prison. Although Obama would easily clinch the nomination and retain full control over the party's unified convention in Charlotte, his lower vote shares in several late season primaries highlighted the modest levels of enthusiasm among traditional Democratic voters for the president's reelection bid.

The Obama campaign was designed to reconnect the president with the party's base voters who had lost some enthusiasm for him during his first term in office, while also building a campaign war chest and organization for a high-powered general election campaign. The Obama campaign not only raised but also spent large sums during the nomination season. In addition to what the Democratic National Committee and friendly super PACs spent, Obama's campaign alone spent $49 million during the invisible primary season of 2011. The biggest chunks of that spending were used to raise more money, a strategy that had worked for Obama in his first presidential run.[38]

The Democratic convention in Charlotte also made some weather-induced changes, moving the president's acceptance speech from an outdoor racetrack to the convention hall. The nation heard an adequate acceptance speech by Obama, a helpful one by Vice President Joseph Biden, and especially effective addresses from Bill Clinton and Michelle Obama. Clinton's heavily ad-libbed performance contrasted the surpluses generated during his second term with the incorrect budgetary "arithmetic" Romney offered. Polls indicated that the Democrats got a more sizable and durable "bounce" from their convention than did the Republicans.

During the spring and summer, minor political parties also quietly drafted platforms and identified nominees. The Green Party chose physician Jill Stein as its nominee. Stein had run as a third-party candidate for governor of Massachusetts in 2002 and thus had already debated and campaigned against Romney in a general election. The Greens picked her over controversial celebrity comedian Roseanne Barr. Barr was later selected as nominee of the Peace and Freedom Party, announcing that her running mate would be Iraq War protester Cindy Sheehan. The other minor party candidate of note was former New Mexico governor Gary Johnson running under the Libertarian Party banner. Johnson actually sought the Republican nomination, but got little notice. He withdrew in late 2011 and focused his attention instead on the Libertarian nomination. Meanwhile former Virginia representative Virgil Goode earned the nomination of the Constitution Party. Reflecting divisions among conservatives, the media began to speculate about whether Goode and Johnson might hurt the Romney campaign, especially in Virginia and New Mexico, but paid little attention to how Barr and Stein might cut into Obama's vote totals.[39] Johnson and Goode, unlike Barr and Stein, had a record of winning elections in their home states.

Conclusion

The 2012 Republican nomination is a story of ideology, timing, and organization. Mitt Romney won the GOP nomination both because of and despite his campaign's strengths. Romney surely benefitted from superior funding and organization. These structural advantages allowed him to weather setbacks and remain formidable as the nomination contest moved from one set of states to another. Unlike all of his Republican opponents, Romney had been vetted in an earlier presidential campaign. He avoided the embarrassing revelations, disappointments, and gaffes that hurt his opponents in 2012. He also ran better in trial heats against Obama. All of this gave him an air of electability that none of the other Republican contenders could match. Although many voters in his party doubted his commitment to conservative principles, he survived because primary and caucus voters also care about electability.[40] In this respect his organization, early entry into the race, and even his policy positions allowed him to compensate for dissatisfaction among party activists.

But other elements of Romney's victory lay outside his control. The fragmented field of Republican candidates allowed him to avoid a head-to-head confrontation with a single more conservative opponent. In settling for Romney as it had for McCain four years earlier, the party eventually opted for the electable over the ideologically pure. The difference between the two nominations is that the 2010 election had intervened, bringing with it the Tea Party movement. The emergence of the Tea Party wing of the Republican Party brought out unconventional, and extreme, candidates such as Bachmann and Cain while it scared off moderates such as Christie and Giuliani. This left Romney facing a collection of extremely conservative opponents. Although concerned about his moderate record on issues ranging from abortion to health insurance, Republican insiders never coalesced behind a single conservative alternative to Romney, in part because of imperfect timing. Instead, the party courted and then dumped a series of also-rans who did not meet their exacting standards. Bachmann, Cain, Gingrich, Perry, and Santorum all experienced a short season of giddy enthusiasm followed by disappointment. This left Romney as the proverbial tortoise who outlasted a band of hares who did not complete the race.

Notes

1. Theda Skocpol and Vanessa Williamson, *The Tea Party and the Remaking of Republican Conservatism* (New York: Oxford University Press, 2011).
2. David E. Campbell and Robert D. Putnam, "Crashing the Tea Party," *New York Times,* August 16, 2011.
3. Paul probably deserves credit for early branding of the Tea Party movement. His failed 2008 campaign transformed into the "taxed enough already" effort and matched with the acronym TEA, which conveniently invoked images of early American patriots resisting efforts at taxation by an unaccountable executive.
4. Melinda Henneberger, "Jon Hunstman: The Potential Republican Presidential Candidate Democrats Most Fear," *Time,* May 12, 2011.
5. John Sides and Lynn Vavreck, *The Gamble: Choice and Chance in the 2012 Presidential Election* (Princeton, N.J.: Princeton University Press, 2012).
6. Marty Cohen, David Karol, Hans Noel, and John Zaller, *The Party Decides: Presidential Nominations Before and After Reform* (Chicago: University of Chicago Press, 2008).
7. Kristin Jensen and Jonathan D. Salant, "Cheapest Primary in Decade Defies Forecast," *Bloomberg,* December 1, 2011, www.bloomberg.com/news/2011-12-01/cheapest-primary-in-a-decade-defies-campaign-spending-prediction.html.
8. Many have attributed the rise of super PACs to the 2010 Supreme Court opinions in *Citizens United v. Federal Elections Commission,* but that case only verified that direct campaign expenditures by corporations and unions were permissible. *Citizens United* built upon earlier decisions such as *Federal Elections Commission v. Wisconsin Right to Life* and rulings by the FEC itself. More relevant is *SpeechNow v. Federal Elections Commission,* a Court of Appeals case that allowed independent groups to accept unlimited contributions. The court found that such spending would not lead to corruption as long as the expenditures were uncoordinated with candidates.

9. Deborah Jordan Brooks and Michael Murov, "Assessing Accountability in a Post–*Citizens United* Era: The Effects of Attack Ad Sponsorship by Unknown Independent Groups," *American Politics Research* 40 (2012): 383–418; Conor M. Dowling and Amber Wichowsky, "Attack without Consequence? Anonymity, Disclosure, and Effectiveness of Negative Advertising," presented at the 2012 meeting of the Midwest Political Science Association, Chicago.
10. T. W. Farnam, "Study: Negative Campaign Ads Much More Frequent, Vicious than in Primaries Past," *Washington Post,* February 20, 2012.
11. Barry C. Burden, "United States Senators as Presidential Candidates," *Political Science Quarterly* 117 (2002): 81–102.
12. A partial exception is Ron Paul, who adopted a largely libertarian stance that steered toward an isolationist foreign policy and less government intervention in policing of illegal drugs.
13. Jonathan Martin, "Inside the Huntsman 'Drama,'" *Politico*, August 4, 2011, www.politico.com/news/stories/0811/60641.html.
14. For an analysis that equates "insiders" with the "establishment," see Melvin J. Hinich, Daron R. Shaw, and Taofang Huang, "Insiders, Outsiders, and Voters in the 2000 U.S. Presidential Election," *Presidential Studies Quarterly* 40 (2010): 264–285.
15. Barbara Norrander, "The Attrition Game: Initial Resources, Initial Contests and the Exit of Candidates During the U.S. Presidential Season," *British Journal of Political Science* 36 (2006): 487–507.
16. "Obama's Running Mate: Mitt Romney's ObamaCare Problem," *Wall Street Journal,* May 12, 2011.
17. Seema Mehta, "Mitt Romney's Under-the-Radar Approach to Iowa," *Los Angeles Times,* July 21, 2011.
18. Rick Perry outraised Romney in the third quarter of 2011, $17 million to $14 million. Romney did not use personal funds in his campaign as he had in 2007.
19. Sides and Vavreck, *The Gamble.*
20. Alexander Burns, "Conservative Pundits Turn Down Newt," Politico.com, December 8, 2011.
21. Susan Saulny, "Iowa Evangelicals Split over Caucus Endorsement," *New York Times,* December 12, 2011.
22. Barry C. Burden, "The Nominations: Rules, Strategy, and Uncertainty," in *The Elections of 2008,* ed. Michael Nelson (Washington, D.C.: CQ Press, 2009).
23. "How the Candidates Roll," *New York Times,* December 29, 2011.
24. "The Myth of Republican Presidential Primary Proportionality Revisited," http://frontloading.blogspot.com/2011/09/myth-of-republican-presidential-primary.html.
25. Memorandum from the RNC Counsel's Office, February 11, 2011.
26. Molly Ball, "Pols Hope to Push Back Primaries," *Politico,* December 19, 2010, http://www.politico.com/news/stories/1210/46567.html.
27. Note that RNC penalties for violating the "window" only applied to primaries, so caucus states such as Colorado and Minnesota held their events in February without paying a price in delegates.
28. Eric Russell, "Pressure Mounting for GOP Caucus Reconsideration," *Bangor Daily News,* February 14, 2012.
29. Jonathan Martin, "Social Conservatives Back Rick Santorum," *Politico,* January 14, 2011, http://www.politico.com/blogs/burns-haberman/2012/01/social-conservatives-back-santorum-110869.html.
30. Quoted in Tom Cohen, "Romney's Big Day Marred by Etch A Sketch Remark, *CNN,* March 21, 2012, http://articles.cnn.com/2012-03-21/politics/politics_campaign-wrap_1_mitt-romney-eric-fehrnstrom-general-election?_s=PM:POLITICS.

31. Barbara Norrander, "Nomination Choices: Caucus and Primary Outcomes, 1976–1988," *American Journal of Political Science* 37 (1993): 343–364.
32. Obama also fared better in the South because of the larger black populations there. See Todd Donovan, "Obama and the White Vote," *Political Research Quarterly* 63 (2010): 863–874; Simon Jackman and Lynn Vavreck,"Primary Politics: Race, Gender, and Age in the 2008 Democratic Primary," *Journal of Elections, Public Opinion, and Parties* 20 (2012): 153–186.
33. Mark Benjamin, "The Mystery of the Missing Presidential Campaign: Cain Operation MIA in Key States," *Time* Swampland blog, October 24, 2011.
34. Kim Geiger, "Ron Paul Continues Delegate Offensive, Wins Big in Nevada, Maine," *Los Angeles Times,* May 7, 2012.
35. These totals are taken from www.thegreenpapers.com/P12/R. The website notes that five votes for Paul Ryan were probably intended for Ron Paul, but it appears that the delegation chair misspoke.
36. "Romney Registers Personal Best 50% Favorable Rating," www.gallup.com/poll/154703/Romney-Registers-Personal-Best-Favorable-Rating.aspx.
37. Dan Balz, "Romney Shakes the Race with Pick of Ryan," *Washington Post,* August 11, 2012.
38. Corwin Smidt and Dino Christenson, "More Bang for the Buck: Campaign Spending and Fundraising Success," *American Politics Research,* forthcoming.
39. Julie Hirschfield Davis, "Presidential Race May Hinge on Third Party Candidates," *Bloomberg,* September 13, 2012, http://www.bloomberg.com/news/2012-09-14/presidential-race-may-hinge-on-third-party-candidates.html.
40. Alan I. Abramowitz, "Viability, Electability, and Candidate Choice in a Presidential Primary Election: A Test of Competing Models," *Journal of Politics* 51 (1983): 977–992.

3

The Election

How the Campaign Mattered

Marc J. Hetherington

The media need new stories every day. As a result, they often overstate the effects that political campaigns have on election outcomes. Because each new advertisement or appearance is news that they must cover, the people who give us political information frame their stories to suggest all the twists and turns of the race are critical. In their post-election retrospectives, pundits often argue that this advertisement or that gaffe proved decisive in determining the election's outcome. Such daily episodes are rarely important, as much as pundits would like us to believe otherwise. That, however, is not to say the campaigns do not matter. They do. But how do they matter?

The election of 2012 provides an excellent illustration that it is the long-run strategies of the campaigns, rather than their day-to-day tactics, that have a profound influence on who wins and who loses and by how much. To understand why, we must consider the range of things campaigns do. Their decisions rarely change the dynamics of the race with a stunning advertisement or appeal. Rather political observers can better see a campaign's effects by examining who came out to vote, who stayed home, and what issue stands the candidates decided to take. With these criteria in mind, much evidence suggests that Mitt Romney's campaign contributed to his loss, while Barack Obama's snatched victory from what, perhaps, should have been the jaws of defeat.

The seeds of Romney's setback in 2012 were sown in 2008. That is when the formerly moderate Massachusetts governor began to lurch to the political right. Only a few years before his first run for the presidency in 2008 Romney publicly championed gay rights, abortion rights, and universal access to health care for all citizens. These were popular positions in Massachusetts, one of the nation's most liberal states. However, he and his advisers decided that those positions would be liabilities with the much more conservative Republican presidential primary electorate. Moreover, they viewed other relative moderates who were also vying for the nomination, namely John McCain and Rudy Giuliani, as his toughest foes in 2008. Rather than tangle with them for the few moderate voters in Republican primaries, Romney staked out staunchly conservative positions on the entire range of issues in an effort to appeal to the conservative base of the

Republican Party. Although the gambit did not work in 2008, he managed to stagger through a very weak field in 2012 to secure the nomination.

Changing issue positions in this way may sound cynical at first, but strategic positioning to help win votes is nothing new. To some extent, all candidates attempt to balance their more ideological primary election constituency's wishes with those of the more moderate mass of Americans who vote for president in November. But Governor Romney's problem was more acute than for most candidates for two reasons. First, the positions of key groups within his party base, particularly religious conservatives, were particularly extreme, putting him in direct conflict with critical emerging forces within the electorate. Most notably, the Republican base has little sympathy for immigrants, legal or otherwise. To satisfy this group in the primaries, Romney took a very conservative position on immigration throughout the primaries, going as far at one point to suggest that the millions in the country illegally ought to deport themselves. For obvious reasons, his positions alienated Latino voters, the nation's fastest growing ethnic minority. Similarly, religious conservatives' disdain for gay rights caused Romney to believe that he needed to change his positions on gay marriage and gay adoption to satisfy them. This, in turn, alienated socially liberal younger voters who, in 2012, increased their turnout share to its highest point in recent general elections.

Romney's second problem with his primary election constituency probably explains why he did so much to try to accommodate it on the issues. Specifically, a large swath of the Republican base was uncomfortable with the fact that Mitt Romney is a Mormon. Although Mitt's father, George, encountered little resistance to his religious denomination when he ran for president in 1968, the emergence of white evangelical Protestants as a force in American party politics has changed the political dynamics fundamentally. America is a more tolerant country racially and religiously than it was decades ago, but many evangelical religious groups classify Mormonism as a cult rather than a Christian religion. In fact, election analyst Harry Enten found during the Republican primary campaign that the percentage vote for candidates other than Romney in a county very strongly correlated with the percentage of evangelical Christians living in the county.[1] Knowing that they did not consider him "one of them," Romney apparently felt a particularly acute need to satisfy this constituency where he could. As illustrated subsequently, Romney's decision to position himself far to the right contributed to his defeat, as people who consider themselves moderates abandoned his candidacy in droves.

Even as Romney may have cost himself the election in the prenomination process, Obama plotted a strategy that proved a winner. Without any primary challengers, Barack Obama's campaign only needed to prepare for the general election. And prepare it did. The vaunted turnout machine that produced near record voter participation in 2008 got the job done again in 2012. Although absolute levels of turnout were down, Obama succeeded in turning out people from the demographic groups that the campaign targeted. Generally, campaigns find it hard to get young people and racial and ethnic minorities to the polls on election day, but these groups made up a larger than usual slice of the electorate in 2012. Young people (those aged 18–29) increased their share of the electorate to 19 percent, its highest percentage since exit poll data have been gathered. In addition, nonwhites made up fully 28 percent of the total electorate, an increase of 2 percentage points over 2008.[2] That the Obama campaign boosted minority turnout even with a sluggish economy that was particularly unforgiving to racial and ethnic minorities is a testament to its get-out-the-vote campaign's success.

Also indicative of the Obama campaign's relative strength, it achieved a near sweep of the battleground states, winning nine of the ten states that both campaigns targeted. Going into election day, Ohio was viewed as the lynchpin. Whoever won there would win in the election. Not only did Obama win Ohio by 1.9 percentage points, he also narrowly won toss-up states like Virginia and Florida that many thought Romney would carry and, in fact, needed in order for Ohio to be important. In the end, Obama retained all the states that he won in 2008 except Indiana, which had been a fluke victory the last time around, and North Carolina, which he won in 2008 by a mere 14,000 votes.

In retrospect, Republicans will likely view 2012 as an opportunity missed. In 2010, Republican House and Senate candidates took advantage of widespread voter discontent to make sweeping gains. With unemployment still hovering around 8 percent, the GOP had every reason to expect a victory. Mitt Romney failed to take advantage of the type of sluggish economy that usually leads to a change in president. This chapter explains why.

The Basics

The 2012 election was reasonably close by historical standards. Barack Obama won 50.9 percent of the popular vote, while Mitt Romney garnered 47.4 percent.[3] Only six elections since the dawning of the twentieth century have been closer as far as the popular vote is concerned. Obama's electoral vote margin was somewhat more impressive. He totaled 332 electoral votes compared with Mitt Romney's 206, or about 62 percent of the overall number. This makes it the eighth closest electoral vote election of the post–nineteenth century.[4]

Figure 3.1 displays the 2012 electoral map. States Obama won are shaded. Romney states are white. Table 3.1 shows the percentages of the vote the major party candidates won in each state. Consistent with recent voting patterns, the regional differences cannot be ignored. Every northeastern state, from Maryland in the south to Maine in the north, voted for Obama. The entire Pacific Coast was also strong Democratic territory. Not only did the Democratic ticket win these states, they often won with large margins. For example, New York in the East and California in the

Figure 3.1 2012 Electoral Map

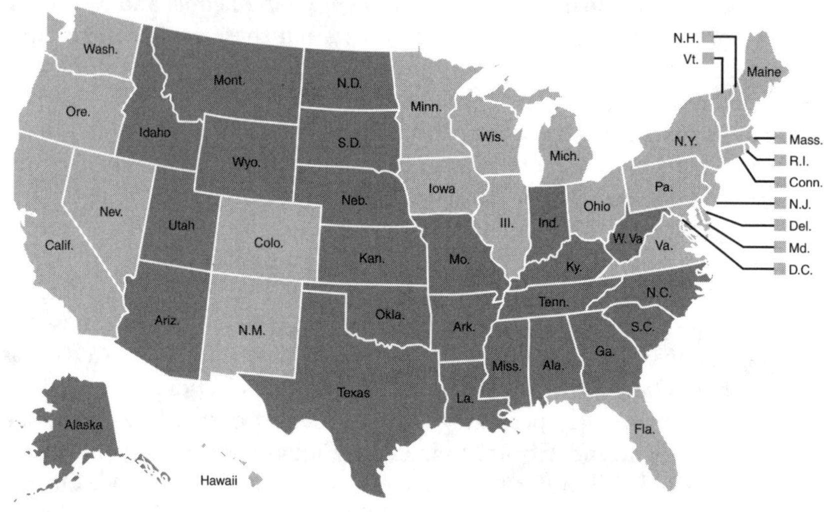

Source: Compiled by the author.

Table 3.1 State by State Results of the 2012 Election

State	Winner	Percentage	
		Obama	Romney
Alabama	Romney	38.4	60.7
Alaska	Romney	41.3	55.3
Arizona	Romney	44.1	54.2
Arkansas	Romney	36.9	60.5
California	Obama	59.3	38.3
Colorado	Obama	51.2	46.5
Connecticut	Obama	58.4	40.4
Delaware	Obama	58.4	40.0
District of Columbia	Obama	91.4	7.1
Florida	Obama	50.0	49.1
Georgia	Romney	45.4	53.4
Hawaii	Obama	70.6	27.8
Idaho	Romney	32.6	64.5
Illinois	Obama	57.3	41.1
Indiana	Romney	43.8	54.3
Iowa	Obama	52.1	46.5

(Continued)

Table 3.1 Continued

State	Winner	Percentage	
		Obama	Romney
Kansas	Romney	37.8	60.0
Kentucky	Romney	37.8	60.5
Louisiana	Romney	40.6	57.8
Maine	Obama	56.0	40.9
Maryland	Obama	61.7	36.6
Massachusetts	Obama	60.8	37.6
Michigan	Obama	54.3	44.8
Minnesota	Obama	52.8	45.1
Mississippi	Romney	43.5	55.5
Missouri	Romney	44.3	53.9
Montana	Romney	41.8	55.3
Nebraska	Romney	37.8	60.5
Nevada	Obama	52.3	45.7
New Hampshire	Obama	52.2	46.4
New Jersey	Obama	58.0	40.9
New Mexico	Obama	52.9	43.0
New York	Obama	62.6	36.0
North Carolina	Romney	48.4	50.6
North Dakota	Romney	38.9	58.7
Ohio	Obama	50.1	48.2
Oklahoma	Romney	33.2	66.8
Oregon	Obama	54.5	42.7
Pennsylvania	Obama	52.0	46.8
Rhode Island	Obama	62.7	35.5
South Carolina	Romney	44.0	54.6
South Dakota	Romney	39.9	57.9
Tennessee	Romney	39.0	59.5
Texas	Romney	41.4	57.2
Utah	Romney	24.9	72.8
Vermont	Obama	67.0	31.2
Virginia	Obama	50.8	47.8
Washington	Obama	55.8	41.7
West Virginia	Romney	35.5	62.3
Wisconsin	Obama	52.8	46.1
Wyoming	Romney	28.0	69.3

West both went for Obama by more than 20 percentage points. Republican support unmistakably comes from the South, Great Plains, and the upper Rocky Mountain West. Romney's margins in these states were often very large, too. Idaho and Oklahoma, for example, went for Romney by more than 30 percentage points.

The states that featured the closest margins tended to come from the border South (e.g., Virginia and North Carolina), the desert Southwest/lower Rocky Mountains (e.g., Colorado and Nevada), and the upper Midwest (e.g., Ohio, Wisconsin, Iowa, and Minnesota). Of course, the story of the election's outcome was that Obama won almost all these competitive states, a point we will revisit. Although the margins were not large, that is immaterial. To win all but two states' electoral votes, one need only win by a single vote.

The Electoral College encourages us to examine presidential elections using the state as the unit of analysis. Doing so causes us to lose sight of the fact that it is really population density that divides Republicans and Democrats these days.[5] Republicans win states that are disproportionately rural, while Democrats prevail in disproportionately urban states. If one were to break down a state like Pennsylvania, for example, it would make the population density story clearer. Obama ran up a huge margin in the greater Philadelphia metropolitan area and healthy margins in and around Pittsburgh. The rest of the state is very rural, which was strong Romney country. Given the urban-rural divide there, it produced a relatively close outcome, with Obama winning by just over 5 points. The same is true of similar city-country mix states like Ohio.

Also consequential is the fact that Obama won his states by, on average, smaller margins than Romney won his. This fact had the potential to produce an electoral vote winner that was different from the popular vote winner. Specifically, Obama had fewer "wasted" votes—votes more than the minimum one vote margin needed to win a state's electoral votes—in the states where he did well. Indeed, *New York Times* blogger Nate Silver estimated that, for Romney to win the electoral vote, he probably would have needed to win the popular vote by at least 2 percentage points.[6] This could be an interesting feature of future elections that lean just slightly in a Republican direction.

Do Campaigns Even Matter?

Political campaigns matter. They are at least part of why this specific electoral map emerged. In their infinite "cleverness," political scientists often argue that campaigns do not matter, suggesting that the outcomes of presidential elections are driven by "the fundamentals." Most often, the fundamentals they have in mind are measures of the economy's strength in the months leading up to the election. Political science has spawned a cottage industry of election forecasting models that often use economic data gathered well before the campaign starts in earnest to make projections about the outcome.[7] These forecasting models usually pick the correct winner. The political scientists' argument goes that, if we can pick the winner without knowing anything that happened between when these data were gathered and election day, that means the effect of the campaign is minimal. Instead it is merely sound and fury.

This view is wrong headed. The campaigns may not always (or even often) *change* the outcome of a race, but that is not the same as not mattering. Instead, it is probably most often the case that both sides in a campaign field evenly matched teams that, until recently, had exactly the same amount of money to spend on the race. As a result, the campaigns themselves have a tendency to cancel each other out. If one side gains an advantage for a time, the other has the skill to counter that advantage. The reasoning here is analogous to product advertising. Coke and Pepsi spend billions on marketing, with each spending roughly the same as the other. Despite a slew of memorable ads on both sides, Coke maintains a slight sales advantage. Presumably both employ the Don Drapers of the advertising world to make their case, making it difficult for one side to move ahead without the other making a major mistake (remember New Coke?). Is this, then, money wasted by Coke and Pepsi? Surely not. If one side spent more resources or if one side spent them much more effectively than the other, the outcome would be different. In that sense, marketing campaigns matter, even if all they do is reinforce people's existing preferences.

The same is true of political campaigns, specifically. To illustrate the point, it might be useful to explore examples occurring when the fundamentals were not the whole story. In 1988, the fundamentals suggested a narrow victory for George H. W. Bush. Instead, he won comfortably with 53 percent of the vote and 426 electoral votes. Why? His campaign was better than Michael Dukakis's campaign. Whereas the Dukakis campaign was slow and ineffective in responding to attacks, the Bush campaign produced a remarkable number of memorable advertisements, from Willie Horton to Boston Harbor to one that featured Dukakis himself, looking ridiculous, riding in a tank with a helmet that appeared four sizes too big. Not only were these short-term tactics important, but the Bush campaign was strategically successful in painting Dukakis as an out-of-touch liberal. In this case, the campaigns were not equally skillful, and the difference between the two manifested in an easier than expected Bush victory.

The effect of the campaign was similarly obvious in 2008. In this case, the campaigns were probably more similar in their skill level than they were in 1988, but Barack Obama outspent John McCain by better than a hundred million dollars. Such spending asymmetries had not been possible since the adoption of the Federal Election Campaign Act of 1974. In return for tens of millions of federal dollars, candidates agreed not to raise and spend cash in the general election beyond what the government gave them. In 2008, however, Obama became the first candidate to eschew federal campaign money for the general election while McCain accepted it. This allowed Obama to raise and spend an unlimited amount of money while McCain's spending was capped at $84.1 million.

As a result, Obama's team had resources to commit to a sophisticated ground game designed to mobilize voters who are usually difficult to reach. Making voter mobilization a centerpiece of the campaign has been rare in recent decades. The reason is that, because racial and ethnic minorities and young people are not frequent political participants, campaigns worry that they will not respond to their appeals. Concerned about wasting finite resources on these groups, campaigns often ignore them. Taking advantage of their resource advantage, however, the Obama campaign got these hard-to-reach voters to the polls in record numbers, which padded what the fundamentals predicted would be a reasonably comfortable win. Just how important these efforts were in 2008 is obscured because of the several percentage points of voters that political scientists estimate Obama lost because of the color of his skin.[8]

These examples suggest that the campaign mattered in 2012 even though the preconvention polls taken several months before the election had Obama up narrowly and he won relatively narrowly. In making this case, it is first important to note that Obama won, in the end, by about 3.5 percentage points, which is a couple points more than the roughly 1 point lead he enjoyed according to poll averages generated on the eve of the Republican National Convention in late August. Although 2.5 percentage points might not seem like much, it amounts to about 3 million people moving toward Obama during the general election campaign, given that 129 million people voted. A number that large seems significant. Although the campaign may not have altered the predicted winner, it almost certainly changed the margin.

Even if one does not believe that a 2.5 percentage point shift is much of anything, it is still important to note that there was nothing inevitable about the race ending in roughly the same way as it started. Only the skillful work of the campaign teams and the candidates themselves brought the twists and turns of the race back to where it roughly began.

Let's consider some of the reasons for the movements that we saw during the campaign season. In early September and again in mid-September we saw marked turns toward Obama. The first turn coincides with the end of the convention period, suggesting the Democratic convention was more successful than the Republican convention. Most credit Bill Clinton's nomination speech, which has been described as the best convention speech of the modern era, for the Democratic bounce. Perhaps even more significant was the second turn toward Obama. It coincided with what came to be known as the "47 percent" gaffe. A recording of a private Romney fundraiser was released to the press that showed Romney giving a speech to big donors. In it, he said, "There are 47 percent of the people who will vote for the president no matter what. All right, there are 47 percent who are with him, who are dependent upon government, who believe that they are victims, who believe that government has a responsibility to care for them, who believe that they are entitled to health care, to food, to housing to you name it... And so my job is not to worry about those people—I'll never convince them that they should take personal responsibility and care for their lives."[9] The implication was that 47 percent of the electorate, including veterans, senior citizens, active duty service members, and the like, were moochers being supported by a harder working 53 percent.

The 47 percent controversy raged for weeks. Had the election been held during this period, the polls suggest Obama would have won an even more comfortable victory than he did nearly two months later. But the election was not held then, and Obama suffered from the next major campaign event. Specifically, he gave a lackluster performance in the first presidential debate, which was held in Denver on October 3. At times, the president seemed disinterested and sleepy. His delivery was halting and weak, contrasting sharply with Romney's crisp performance. Indeed Romney's performance was probably the best by a Republican presidential candidate since Ronald Reagan in 1980. Although sitting presidents dating back to Jimmy Carter have tended to perform poorly in their first debate, the public provides them little quarter. The electorate in 2012 was no different. Just two days after the first debate, Romney seized his first lead in the poll averages, a lead he would enjoy for nearly three weeks. In fact, some individual polls had him up by more than 5 points at times. Had the election been held after the first debate, then Romney would likely have been the popular vote winner.

Although liberal Democrats appeared ready to hang themselves after the first debate, the race again moved back in their direction. As usual, the vice presidential debate made little difference in the polls, but Obama showed voters that he really did want to be reelected president by performing much better in the second debate than the first. He had more success parrying Romney's attacks on taxes, health care, and the economy. And Romney performed much worse than he had. Two gaffes stood out, both occurring in areas where the former Massachusetts governor was vulnerable. The first had to do with gender pay equality, an issue on which Republicans find themselves on the wrong side of public opinion. Most Americans think government should enact pay equity statutes, which the Obama administration successfully championed with the passage of the Lily Ledbetter Fair Pay Act in 2009. This law removes previous requirements that any lawsuits challenging pay determinations had to be filed within 180 days of the initial discriminatory pay decision. Under the new law, the 180-day window to file suit begins again with each paycheck that reflects the discriminatory wages, thereby facilitating easier legal challenges to pay discrimination.[10] The GOP tends to see such efforts as unnecessary intrusions on business.

In the debate, Romney attempted to counter charges that he was unsympathetic to women in the workplace by noting how invested he was in ensuring women equal opportunities when he was governor, especially as he assembled his cabinet. In doing so, however, he chose his words inartfully. Specifically he said that he had asked for assistance from women's groups in identifying qualified female candidates for cabinet posts, and the women's groups delivered "whole binders full of women."[11] His unfortunate phrasing became a social media sensation, causing some people, especially women, to focus on an area that was not a strong point for the Republican ticket.

The second gaffe occurred in another area in which Governor Romney had less experience and hence less credibility than his opponent—foreign policy. In the second half of the town hall debate, a member of the audience asked about the situation in Libya whereby the U.S. ambassador and three other Americans had been killed near the consulate in Benghazi. The deaths suggested a serious security lapse. In addition, Republicans were arguing that the Obama administration's evolving story about what had precipitated the attacks suggested a potential cover-up. The administration's original interpretation suggested the attack was part of a spontaneous protest that erupted after an anti-Islamic film showed up on YouTube. Later the administration allowed that it was probably a more coordinated terrorist attack. In pressing this line of argument, Romney ignored the fact that the president had, in his original comments the day after the tragedy, left open the possibility that it was a terrorist attack. When the governor refused to believe the president, the debate moderator, Candy Crowley, corrected him. This turned what seemed to be a positive for Republicans—a colossal security failure that led to the death of an ambassador—into a negative.

The third debate, which was held on October 22, contained no similarly memorable miscues. But Obama provided a commanding performance, which, according to snap polls of debate watchers, was on par with Romney's dominating performance in the first debate.[12] Two days later, the president took a slight lead in the national poll averages, a lead he did not relinquish over the last two weeks of the campaign. Although his margin was small, it was persistent. In short, the polls on election eve suggested a narrow Obama victory, but narrow enough so that even slight changes in the expected composition of the electorate could support a belief that Romney would emerge victorious.

Although the race ended where it started, that didn't mean the events of the campaign were meaningless. Had the election been held right after the 47 percent gaffe, Obama would have won easily. Had it been held after the first debate, Romney would have been elected. There was nothing inevitable about the return of the race to its late August starting line. The candidates and their campaigns needed to perform.

How the Campaigns Mattered in 2012

In assessing campaign effects, most pundits automatically frame the conversation in terms of one side changing voters' minds, turning Romney voters into Obama voters or vice versa. If changing minds is the main criterion when measuring whether campaigns matter, then they matter little. This is especially true now that the parties have polarized along ideological lines. Over the last forty years, Americans (1) have grown more partisan, (2) care more about who wins elections, (3) vote a straight party ticket more often, and (4) perceive larger differences between the parties.[13] As a result, most see the world as they want to see it and are not particularly open to persuasion.

Democrats and Republicans even tend to interpret objective facts differently. For example, less than a week before the election, the government released its October jobs report. Employers added 170,000 new jobs in October and the unemployment rate was 7.9 percent, a slight increase from September's rate of 7.8 percent. Democrats hailed it as great news—all those new jobs and an unemployment rate below 8 percent meant the economy was on the mend. Republicans noted that most of the decrease in the unemployment rate in recent months could be explained by people abandoning job searches—the economy was still broken. Social scientists call this tendency to see the world as people want *motivated reasoning*,[14] a tendency that has grown stronger as the political world has become more polarized.

Instead of persuasion, effective campaigns are more likely to measure success by their ability to change the shape of the electorate in ways advantageous to their side. Mobilizing voters who might otherwise have decided not to vote is central to this strategy. Recent research in political science, in particular, and behavioral social science more generally has uncovered a range of techniques to encourage people to participate, even as researchers remain largely in the dark about how to change minds. Political campaigns have started to use these tools. For example, we know that Americans respond to social pressure. When you tell people that voting records are public and that friends and neighbors can view them, people are more likely to vote.[15] People are also more likely to vote if they see on Facebook that members of their friend community have voted and believe that their friends can see that they have not.[16] These field experiments also provide campaigns ideas about the best ways to encourage participation. They find that people do not participate more in response to taped phone messages, and also that the effect of direct mail solicitations on voting is relatively weak. But people do respond strongly to canvassers visiting homes.[17] Hence, if you live in a battleground state, chances are you have had at least one person from at least one of the campaigns pay you a visit.

Old style political parties in the "boss era" relied on such tactics for decades, but they fell into disuse as television advertising rose in importance.

Campaign operatives from the 1970s to the 1990s believed they could reach more people more effectively through electronic media. Lately, though, politics has witnessed a resurgence of door-to-door canvassing, sometimes with decisive effects. In 2004, for example, George W. Bush's campaign succeeded in increasing the number of regular churchgoers in the electorate, a group that is overwhelmingly supportive of Republicans. Mobilizing people who belong to organizations like churches can be particularly effective because those in the organization can work to mobilize others in that social network.[18] Moreover, many think the mobilization that occurred around churches in Ohio was decisive in explaining Bush's narrow Electoral College victory. A swing of just 60,000 votes in Ohio would have thrown the election to John Kerry.

In 2012, voter mobilization was central to understanding the efficacy of the campaigns as well. Understanding the importance of mobilization also helps explain the foundation for one of the big controversies that raged through the campaign—whether the news media's preelection polls were accurate. Throughout the campaign, Republicans argued that the polls were skewed in favor of the Democrats. In fact, a website maintained by a conservative activist that was devoted to "unskewing" the media polls received significant attention. The crux of the controversy boiled down to two related questions. What percentage of Republicans and Democrats would make up the electorate on election day? And, what percentage of voters would be white? These two questions are related because of the immense racial polarization in voting that has emerged over the last generation. Since racial and ethnic minorities of almost all types identify and vote disproportionately Democratic, properly estimating how much of the electorate they will make up has a profound effect on the poll forecasts.

According to exit poll data, which appear in Table 3.2, whites supported Mitt Romney over Barack Obama by a 59 to 39 percent margin. Had the demographics of the country remained the same as they were in 1984, Romney, like Ronald Reagan, would have won handily. Back then, 86 percent of the electorate was white.[19] The racial makeup of the electorate has changed significantly since then, however. Although minorities made up only 13 percent of voters in 1992, that percentage had doubled to 26 percent by 2008. In contrast to whites, minority groups all provided overwhelming support to Obama. African American support was nearly unanimous, 93 to 6 percent. Latinos and Asian Americans were among the few groups whose support for Obama increased between 2008 and 2012. For Latinos the increase was from 67 to 71 percent, and for Asian Americans, it was from 62 to 73 percent. These gains are particularly impressive because Obama's overall margin decreased by 4 percentage points. Because Latinos are the fastest growing minority group in the United States, this gap became a particular concern to GOP political operatives after the election. Taken together, minority voters supported Obama over Romney by more than a 2-1 vote.

Table 3.2 Race, Ethnicity, and the Presidential Vote in 2012

Group	Obama	Romney
White (72% of electorate)	39	59
African American (13%)	93	6
Hispanic-Latino (10%)	71	27
Asian American (3%)	73	26
Other (2%)	58	38

Source: National Exit Poll, 2012.

In advance of the election, the question pollsters had to answer was just how large a percentage would nonwhites make up. As always, it would have to be an educated guess. Would the percentage continue to increase after 2008? Or was 2008 an anomaly, driven by the first major party presidential nominee of color? Republican pollsters tended to think the electorate would look more like it did in 2004. That year 24 percent of the electorate was nonwhite. Democratic pollsters thought the percentage would continue to grow, reflecting overall increases in the minority population in the United States, particularly Latinos and Asian Americans. Media polls tended to take the middle position—that the racial composition would be about the same as it was in 2008. The Democratic pollsters turned out to be right. The exit polls suggest that 28 percent of the electorate was nonwhite. That is why the Democratic polls tended to be closer to the mark than the Republican polls. Obama's pollster missed the popular vote total by about 0.1 percentage points. The Romney campaign polls apparently showed Romney winning.

The minority vote is more than a story about poll accuracy. It is also a marker of the success of the Obama campaign's mobilization efforts. Realizing that they would change few minds in the weeks leading up to the election, the campaign worked hard to get out as many of their potential voters as possible. The literature on political participation tells us that minorities are less likely to vote than whites. This gap can be explained by differences in socioeconomic status; minorities tend to be less well educated and less well off financially. The need for campaigns to mobilize such irregular voters is very important because, absent get-out-the-vote efforts, they are likely to stay home.[20]

Groups and Voting Behavior

The racial polarization in voting was not the only storyline in the 2012 election. Many different groups contributed to the result. Table 3.3 presents a systematic breakdown of groups and their voting behavior as reported in the 2012 exit polls.

Table 3.3 Coalitional Support of the Presidential Candidates, 2012

Group	Obama	Romney
Party Identification		
Democrats (38%)	92	7
Independents (29%)	45	50
Republicans (32%)	6	93
Ideology		
Liberals (25%)	86	11
Moderates (41%)	56	41
Conservatives (35%)	17	82
Gender		
Men (47%)	45	52
Women (53%)	55	44
Religion		
Protestant (29%)	37	62
White Evangelical	21	78
Catholic (25%)	50	48
White Catholic	40	59
Jewish (2%)	69	30
No Religion (12%)	70	26
Income		
Less than $50,000 (41%)	60	38
$50,000-$100,000 (31%)	46	52
Greater than $100,000 (28%)	44	54

Source: National Exit Poll, 2012.

The first thing to note is that party identifiers were more loyal to their party's standard bearer than any time in the history of polling. Twenty or thirty years ago, it was not uncommon for 90 percent of partisans in the winning candidate's party to support him or her but for only about 80 percent of the partisans in the losing candidate's party to vote for him or her. In 2012, 92 percent of Democrats voted for Obama and 93 percent of Republicans voted for Romney. This continues a trend toward more party-orienting voting that political scientist Larry Bartels first identified in the 1990s.[21] Increased party voting is a function of the clearer choices that Republicans and Democrats now provide voters. Back in the 1970s and 1980s, for example, the parties were ideological hodgepodges. Although the Democrats were the more liberal party, they had plenty of conservative leaders, especially from the South. Similarly, the Republican Party featured a more liberal wing, mostly from the Northeast, to go along with its conservative base. That heterogeneity has all but disappeared among office holders today, with Republicans homogenously conservative and Democrats homogenously liberal.

Not only do voters have a clear ideological choice, partisans have developed a real dislike of the other party over time. Consider how partisans say they feel about the other side. Since the 1970s, the American National Election Study (ANES) has been asking voters to rate people and groups on what it calls a feeling thermometer. If someone loves a group, they can rate it as high as 100 degrees. If they really despise a group, they can rate it as low as 0 degrees. And, if their feelings are neutral, they are instructed to rate the group at 50 degrees. They can choose any temperature between 0 and 100 degrees.

As Figure 3.2 shows, Republicans did not exactly love Democrats and vice versa back when Jimmy Carter and Ronald Reagan served as president, but they did not hate the other side either. The average scores they tended to provide were in the high 40s—chilly but not cold. Partisans have grown far more negative about the party they do not belong to. In 2010, for example, Democrats rated the Republican Party at about 17 degrees, while Republicans rated the Democratic Party around 18 degrees. To put those scores in some perspective, only groups like "student radicals" and "black militants" have ever received scores similarly low since the ANES started to ask these types of questions forty years ago. Polarization has not caused partisans to like their own party more, but has caused them to like the other party much less. It seems reasonable to conclude such negative affect is critical to understanding the big increase in party-based voting in 2012. The other party is simply not a viable option in the eyes of most partisans any longer.

Figure 3.2 Partisan Feelings About the Other Party

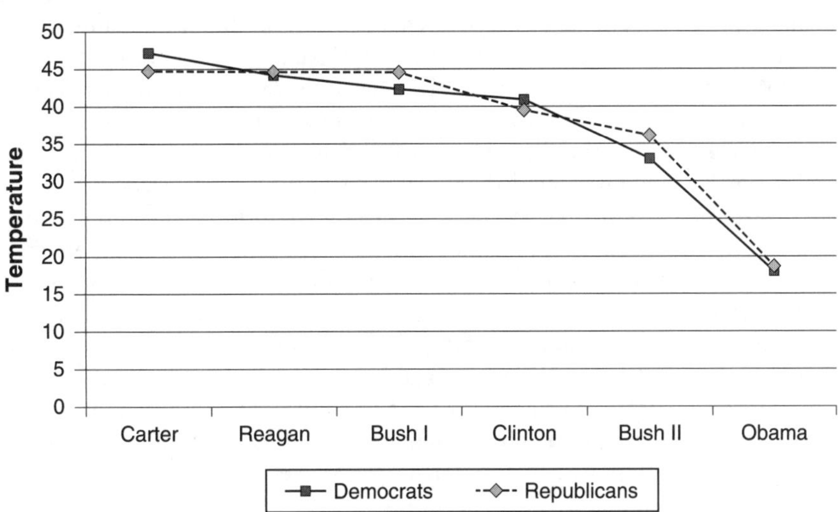

Source: Compiled by the author.

Not surprisingly, ideology affected vote choice as well. More than 80 percent of self-identified conservatives favored Romney while more than 85 percent of self-identified liberals favored Obama. Perhaps more significant, the percentage of self-identified liberals has been creeping upward over time. Although conservatives still outnumber liberals by a 35 to 25 percent margin, not long ago the difference was much larger. In 1988, when a Democratic presidential candidate was castigated for being "a card carrying member of the American Civil Liberties Union," only 17 percent of Americans said they were liberals.[22] Indeed from the mid-1960s until recently, the word *liberal* was often used as an insult. That appears to be changing.

Even more significant in the exit poll data on ideology is Obama's success with self-identified moderates. This group, which made up fully 41 percent of the electorate, preferred Obama to Romney, 56 percent 41 percent, a very large 15 percentage point gap. When pundits talk about swing voters, they often mistakenly pitch their analysis in terms of political independents, those who say they do not identify with a political party. Research suggests, however, that most people who say they do not identify with a party actually do.[23] Instead the percentage of pure independents voting in a presidential election is probably under 10 percent, much less than the 40 percent who identify themselves as moderates.

The fact that people who like to think of themselves as moderate provided Obama with such an advantage is surely indicative of the strongly conservative positions Romney felt compelled to saddle himself with in the Republican primaries. Although the exit polls asked few questions about specific policies, most that they did ask suggest the electorate as a whole was not on the far right. For example, when asked about their opinions on abortion, 59 percent said they believed it ought to be legal in all or most cases. Only 36 percent said it ought to be illegal in most or all cases. Similarly, exit polls asked respondents whether most illegal immigrants who are working in the United States should be "offered a chance to apply for legal status" or be "deported to the country they came from." When given this choice, 65 percent of voters favored a path to legal status while only 28 percent favored deportation. On most issues, Americans prefer something in the broad middle ground. All this suggests that Romney's efforts to woo the Republican primary constituency may have fatally wounded his candidacy in the general election.

Another group that received significant attention from pundits both before and after the election was women. Women comprised 53 percent of the electorate, significantly more than men did. Moreover, the presence of more women was bad news for Mitt Romney. Women favored Obama over Romney by 11 percentage points (55 to 44 percent), while men favored Romney over Obama by 7 percentage points (52 to 45 percent). Although pundits often ascribe this gender gap in voting to social issues like abortion rights and contraception, such issues have little to do with why men and women vote differently. In fact, men and women have basically the same opinions on them.

Instead, the gender gap is driven by women and men's differing opinions on the role of government and their differing preferences about foreign policy.[24] Specifically, women favor more government services and spending on social safety net programs than men do. Women also tend to favor a less hawkish foreign policy than men. It is also worth noting that the constant focus on women in understanding gender and voting is probably misguided. In fact, women have cast the majority of their ballots for Democrats in every election since 1988. It is men who tend to shift back and forth from election to election.[25] Although men have voted more Republican than women for decades, they have cast a majority of their ballots for Democratic candidates several times during that period, including 2008.

It is also a mistake to consider the genders as particularly descriptive. Let's face it; we all know people of the same gender who are very different from one another. Categorizing any 50 percent of the public into a single group is bound to be a pretty course treatment. Different types of women and men vote differently. For example, Romney actually won 53 percent of married women's votes, compared with 46 percent for Obama. Similarly, unmarried men favored Obama over Romney by 16 percentage points (56 to 40 percent). The largest voting gap between the candidates involved unmarried women, which is the fastest growing of the four groups. Unmarried women favored Obama by 67 to 31 percent, a remarkable 36 percentage point difference.

Religion has received significant attention from political observers in recent decades and it continues to have a significant effect on voting behavior. As usual, Protestants favored the Republican candidate, this time by a 15-point margin (57 to 42 percent). But Protestantism is a problematically lumpy category, insofar as it includes a wide array of different types of people—mainliners, evangelicals, whites, blacks. Breaking the data down further reveals clearer divisions. White evangelicals favored Romney over Obama by a whopping 51 points.

Interesting differences emerged among other religious groups as well. Catholics overall split their vote evenly between the candidates, but, as with Protestants, there is more to it than meets the eye. White and Latino Catholics behaved quite differently. Anglos actually favored Romney by 19 points (59 to 40 percent), while Latinos favored Obama by even more. In decades past, even white Catholics were a strongly Democratic constituency. This was because many were working class and hence beneficiaries of government programs. In addition, the Catholic Church's emphasis on social justice meshed well with the Democrats' use of government to lessen economic inequalities. As the group became more affluent and as the Church embraced conservative positions against abortion and gay rights, white Catholics have become a solidly Republican constituency. The evolution of white Catholics from ardent Democrats to Republicans provides conservatives hope in attracting Latino Catholics in the future. As the thinking goes, although Latinos are, on average, not well-off financially now, they will be in the future, allowing them to make political decisions on moral rather than material grounds. This thinking hinges on the belief that Latinos eventually will identify more strongly with their religious group than their ethnic group.

Finally, income returned to its customary role in structuring vote choice, unlike in 2008, when its effect was not particularly strong. In 2012, those making under $50,000 a year voted for Obama by a 60 to 38 percent margin, almost identical to the numbers in 2008. But those making more than $50,000 moved toward the GOP. Although Obama managed to tie John McCain among those making between $50,000 and $100,000 and those making more than $100,000 in 2008, Romney enjoyed an advantage among those with higher income in 2012. Those making between $50,000 and $100,000 favored Romney by 52 to 46 percent, while those making over $100,000 favored Romney by a 54 to 44 percent margin.

The Economy: An 800 Pound Gorilla?

The issue environment seemed advantageous to any Republican candidate in 2012. Although some issues wax and wane in importance from election to election, the state of the economy is almost always influential. Voters can act, in V. O. Key's famous words, as gods of vengeance or reward.[26] When the economy is bad, voters can send the incumbent president home. When the economy is good, voters can keep the president around. Usually the effect of the economy is asymmetric. Because people expect the government to succeed, they often give the president less credit for a good economy than they give blame for a bad one. The economic voting literature would seem to have portended a bad end for Barack Obama.

In 2012, the economy was anything but strong. Indeed the economy had been in the doldrums for Obama's entire presidency. Toward the end of George W. Bush's second term, a near collapse of the world financial sector brought the U.S. economy to the brink of collapse. Even though policymakers avoided the worst possible outcome, the aftermath became known as the "Great Recession," the worst economic downturn since the Great Depression of the 1930s. Flagging economies usually take time to recover, but the situation was particularly difficult to manage in the late Bush and early Obama years. Many of the usual levers used to stimulate the economy were not available. For example, policymakers often use interest rate cuts to stimulate growth. But interest rates were already at their minimum when the crisis hit. Making matters worse, although banks lending money at low interest rates can provide stimulus, the crux of the economic problems lay in the world credit markets, which led financial institutions to hoard money rather than lend it. Further exacerbating problems, disasters at home like the BP oil spill in the Gulf of Mexico and unrest abroad like the euro-zone crisis persistently pushed down any green shoots in the economy.

As a result, the depressed economy that Obama inherited never began to roar. Unemployment, which peaked just below 10 percent in 2009, remained relatively high. At election time, it stood at 7.9 percent, higher than it had been for any successful incumbent presidential candidate. Economic growth was similarly sluggish. Gross domestic product (GDP) grew at a paltry 1.97 percent in the year leading up to the election. Household incomes remained relatively flat and the housing market remained deeply depressed. As far as the economy was concerned, Obama had little good news to report except that inflation remained low and growth, while slow, was at least positive. His main argument was that he had kept the economy from getting much worse, always a politically tough sell.

Mitt Romney appeared on paper to be the ideal candidate to take advantage of the country's economic distress. He grew up around successful businesses; his father, George, was president of American Motors during its boom years. And Mitt Romney built his own professional reputation as a businessman, leading a very successful venture capital firm called Bain Capital. These skills also allowed him to solve problems in more public arenas. When the management of the 2002 Winter Olympics in Salt Lake City fell severely short of expectations, Romney was called in to save the Games. He was successful. Conventional wisdom held that he was better suited than most any other Republican to argue credibly that he could fix the economy.

But the effect of a bad economy did not play out as expected. On the one hand, it is clear that people realized the economy was not particularly strong. When asked about the condition of the nation's economy in the exit poll, 77 percent described it as being either "not so good" or "poor." Such perceptions would seem to predict an electorate ready to be the gods of vengeance. A deeper look at the data, however, suggests something more complicated. When asked whether President Obama or President Bush was more responsible for the negative economic circumstances, 53 percent said Bush while only 38 percent said Obama. If people do not believe the incumbent is responsible for the state of the economy, then in their minds it would not make sense for them to punish him at the ballot box.

In addition, voters were close to evenly split on which candidate would be better at handling the economy: 49 percent said Romney, and 48 percent said Obama. Romney's impressive business credentials clearly did not translate into much of a political advantage. Although people did acknowledge that conditions were poor, they did not necessarily think the challenger was better equipped than the incumbent to solve the problem. Given how poor the economy was for all four years of the Obama presidency, this is a remarkable finding.

That the electorate would split evenly on the economy between Romney and Obama is perhaps the biggest surprise from the exit poll data. Obama's economic stewardship during his four years as president had not produced great results as measured by most any economic indicator. Furthermore the Republican candidate's leading credential was his experience and success with economic matters. Something must have been operating below the surface to produce such an even split in opinion on management of the economy.

Part of the problem for Mitt Romney appears to have been his background. He was the scion of a wealthy family, perceived by many to have been born with a silver spoon in his mouth. Although Americans have elected presidents who were very wealthy, these presidents, more often than not, were liberals whose policies often demanded more, not less, of the well-off. Examples include John F. Kennedy and Franklin D. Roosevelt. That Romney argued in favor of lower tax rates for high income earners surely did not help his cause. In addition, his successes in the business world were not of the storied brick and mortar type. He came from a world of leveraged buyouts and high-stakes venture capital, not building factories that employed people for life.

Both of these factors probably contributed to the perception that Romney's policies would not benefit ordinary people. As evidence, the exit polls asked voters what type of people the candidates' policies would generally favor: the rich, the middle class, or the poor. For Obama, only 10 percent said the rich, while the most common response was the middle class (44 percent). Although 34 percent of the electorate thought Romney's policies were designed to help the middle class, too, 53 percent thought they would help the rich the most. Romney's problems with "ordinary" Americans showed up in people's assessments of the two candidates' personal qualities. The exit polls asked respondents which of four qualities mattered most to them in guiding their vote choice: "shares my values," "is a strong leader," "cares about people like me," and "has a vision for the future." About a fifth of Americans said "cares about people like me," which made it only the third most popular response option. But Obama trounced Romney by 81 to 18 percent among people who chose that option. Finally, the exit polls asked which of the two candidates was "more in touch with people like you." Obama enjoyed a 10-point advantage on this question as well. As compelling as Romney's background may have been and regardless of how weak Obama's record on the economy was, Romney's inability to cause voters to believe that his policies would help people like them rather than people like himself robbed him of whatever advantage he might otherwise have enjoyed on the economy.

The Battleground

Obama's campaign successes manifested in a near sweep of what are called the battleground states. These are states that both sides agree could go either way and are thus critical to winning the election. In 2012, ten states received almost all the candidates' attention: Florida, North Carolina, Virginia, New Hampshire, Pennsylvania, Ohio, Iowa, Wisconsin, Nevada, and Colorado. Taken together these states have only 130 electoral votes, or less than a fourth of all 538. Indeed the number of electoral votes that are truly up for grabs in presidential elections has decreased markedly over the last fifty years.[27]

At least as interesting as the ten battleground states are the states that do not appear on the list. Electoral College gold mines like California (55 votes), New York (29 votes), and Texas (38 votes), which combined have 122 electoral votes, merit no attention at all from the campaigns, except when the candidates parachute in to raise money from wealthy donors in private events. Because one party's candidate is assured of winning each of them, neither campaign has an incentive to spend scarce resources appealing to their voters. It does not matter if, say, the Republicans lose California by 20 points or 10 points; the Democrats still win all 55 electoral votes. Moreover, these three states are not alone. In 2012, thirty-four states were decided by 10 percentage points or more and, of those, eighteen were decided by 20 points or more. Only five states were decided by 5 percentage points or less. An electoral map like this produces a range of perversities. For example, the states that contain the five most populous metropolitan areas in the country (New York, Los Angeles, Chicago, Dallas, and Houston) received no public attention from either campaign. In short, even though presidential elections are nationally competitive, with the last several elections producing some of the closest Electoral College votes in history, they are not at all competitive at the state level, with more blowout states containing far more electoral votes than any time before.

Examining the battleground states offers some clues about how well the Obama and Romney campaigns did their jobs. It is in these ten states that the campaigns spent upwards of 95 percent of their resources. As a first cut, consider the candidates' win-loss record. Obama took nine of the ten states. Only North Carolina broke for Romney on Election Day. Consider that these ten states were viewed as toss-ups at the beginning of the campaign, with about a fifty-fifty chance of going either way. That Obama won 90 percent of them is a remarkable achievement.

Another way of assessing the campaigns is to examine how the actual election result differed from the polls taken just before the election. Because polling in the battleground states was ubiquitous during the lead-up to the election, it is possible to calculate averages based on many polls. Such averages are more reliable than the result of any single poll. If a candidate did better than the polls predicted, it could indicate that the candidate's organization did a superior job turning out supporters. The data presented in Table 3.4 suggest that, by this metric, Obama consistently outperformed his preelection poll average. Only in Ohio did Romney's actual share of the vote exceed his average predicted share of the vote in the polls. In the other nine battleground states, Obama's vote share exceeded his average poll share, sometimes by quite a bit. In New Hampshire, Iowa, Nevada, and Colorado, Obama's vote share exceeded his preelection poll average by more than 3 percentage points. In four of the other battleground states, he ran more than 2 points better than expected. One might argue that the differences here

Table 3.4 Candidate Vote Advantage Relative to Poll Advantage in Battleground States, 2012

State	Poll Margin	Election Margin	Difference
Florida	Romney 1.5	Obama 0.8	+2.3 Obama
North Carolina	Romney 3.0	Romney 2.2	+0.8 Obama
Virginia	Obama 0.2	Obama 3.0	+2.8 Obama
New Hampshire	Obama 2.0	Obama 5.8	+3.8 Obama
Pennsylvania	Obama 3.0	Obama 5.2	+2.2 Obama
Ohio	Obama 2.3	Obama 1.9	+0.4 Romney
Iowa	Obama 2.0	Obama 5.6	+3.6 Obama
Wisconsin	Obama 3.9	Obama 6.7	+2.8 Obama
Nevada	Obama 2.7	Obama 6.6	+3.9 Obama
Colorado	Obama 1.5	Obama 4.7	+3.2 Obama

Source: Compiled by the author.

could be driven by pollsters' inability to gauge minority turnout. Although this explanation might be true in racially and ethnically diverse states like Florida and Nevada, it does not hold for states like New Hampshire and Iowa, which are not at all diverse.

Instead these differences between Obama's support in the polls and in the actual vote might be better read as mobilization effects. When pollsters calculate their results, they usually focus on "likely voters." Different polling organizations have different ways of deciding who a likely voter is, but, regardless of how they do it, it requires a certain amount of guesswork. Pollsters can't read people's minds. And, if pollsters just ask people whether they plan to vote, almost all say they will because it is the socially desirable thing to say. Whatever likely voter screens were employed by pollsters, they had the effect of skewing results toward Romney. Throughout the campaign, samples of registered voters (that is, both likely and unlikely voters combined) were consistently more pro-Obama than samples of likely voters. Obama's campaign apparently turned registered voters whom pollsters judged unlikely to vote into actual voters on Election Day. That is a tangible metric on which campaigns can be judged. The Obama campaign did a demonstrably superior job encouraging potential supporters, who were not particularly enthusiastic, into actual participants when it mattered.

Conclusion

Much of this chapter has painted a discouraging picture for conservatives and Republicans. They lost an election that was winnable. Just two years before, the GOP enjoyed sweeping victories in the 2010 midterm elections. But the Obama campaign's successful mobilization of key groups changed the playing field enough so that the electorate in 2012 did not look like the one in 2010. It was much younger and more diverse, like the one that elected Obama in 2008. The numbers that have come out of the 2012 election have caused Democrats to become giddy with excitement about the future. The country is getting more racially and ethnically diverse, and these minority voters are voting overwhelmingly Democratic. Women also make up a larger share of the electorate, especially those who are not married—another overwhelmingly Democratic constituency. And young people are starting to develop a habit of voting Democratic, too. Although the support of eighteen- to twenty-nine-year-olds for Obama dropped from two-thirds to three-fifths between 2008 and 2012, they still provided a sizable edge for Democrats. Moreover, strong support among the elderly for Republicans will not last forever. The Grim Reaper eventually gets us all.

It is probably best not to turn demographic trends into inevitable future outcomes, however. Although demography definitely favors the Democrats, these demographics might not play out the same way in subsequent elections. First, a coalition that relies so heavily on difficult-to-mobilize groups like young people and minority groups is bound to suffer from a fair amount of surge and decline. High stimulus presidential elections may bring out irregular voters, provided mobilization efforts continue to be successful. But Democrats will be much more vulnerable in midterm elections when interest is lower and mobilization efforts less complete. The GOP sweep in 2010 is evidence of the limits of purely demographic arguments. Democrats may find similar problems in 2014, particularly if the economy does not improve demonstrably by then.

It is also possible that Republicans will change tactics by attempting to win minority voters as the country grows more diverse. Democrats probably will not continue to win more than three-fourths of the minority vote if Republicans begin pursuing policies that are attractive to nonwhites. In the aftermath of the election, for example, some prominent Republicans, such as senator Lindsay Graham of South Carolina and conservative radio and television host Sean Hannity argued that the party needed to moderate its stance on immigration. In 2004, when George W. Bush championed a comprehensive immigration reform plan, about 40 percent of Latinos supported him. Taking what many see as extreme and hostile stances on such issues is not only alienating the GOP from Latinos but is making Asian Americans feel like Republicans regard them as foreigners in their homeland, too. Of course, a more moderate position on immigration may distress some of the party's base, but it is unlikely they will vote Democratic as a result. Moreover, Republicans might be well served by losing some votes in the staunchly conservative South and Great Plains by pursuing policies that help them win votes in increasingly diverse swing states such as Colorado, Virginia, and Nevada.

Making such changes on issues to attract new coalition partners usually does not come easily. The reason party leaders are the leaders of their parties often has to do with their positions on issues that matter to the existing party coalition.[28] Change often requires an electoral shellacking in which party leaders cannot possibly misinterpret the public's message. Such a shellacking has not yet happened to the GOP. Although they have lost the last two presidential elections, they still control the House of Representatives and a majority of state governments. Indeed just two years before Obama's reelection, Republicans made among the most sweeping gains the party has ever achieved in off-year elections, picking up sixty-three House seats in 2010. Moreover, conservatives in the party can still argue that they would have won the 2008 and 2012 presidential elections if the GOP had nominated "real conservatives." Although they did not run as moderates, both McCain and Romney were drawn from the moderate part of the party.

Absent an old-fashioned beat down, old habits die hard. We saw evidence of this in 2012. Since Richard Nixon's southern strategy, Republican candidates have used resentments toward African Americans to win whites' votes. Although saying directly disparaging things about African Americans is no longer socially acceptable, Republicans have found that talking about "states rights," "welfare," "street crime," and "food stamps" act as proxies.[29] Following the usual playbook, Republican campaign operatives described Obama as being somehow less than American and his supporters as not coming from "the real America." They expressed a desire "to take the country back."

The use of such implicitly racial appeals almost became overtly explicit after Obama's poor performance in the first presidential debate. John Sununu, the former Republican governor of New Hampshire and White House chief of staff under George H. W. Bush, invoked a common racial stereotype in calling Obama "lazy." Around the same time, Newt Gingrich, the former Republican Speaker of the House and 2012 presidential candidate took his racialized criticism a step further. He said, "You have to wonder what he's doing. I'm assuming that there's some rhythm to Barack Obama that the rest of us don't understand. Whether he needs large amounts of rest, whether he needs to go play basketball for a while or watch ESPN, I mean, I don't quite know what his rhythm is, but this is a guy that is a brilliant performer as an orator, who may very well get reelected at the present date, and who, frankly, he happens to be a partial, part-time president."[30] The racial stereotypes in remarks like these are not hard to identify.

After their defeat in 2012, Republicans began some serious soul searching. Much of it was directed toward attracting votes from a more diverse group of Americans. Doing so would almost certainly serve the best interests of the party. Although they may lose a few votes in the South and Great Plains, they can afford such losses if it helps them arrest their slide among young people and people of color. To do so, however, will require grappling with established ways of doing things within the party. Convincing existing Republican leaders to change course will be made harder by the fact that 2012 was a close election. Parties find it hard to change without collapsing first.

Notes

1. As evidence, see www.realclearpolitics.com/articles/2012/02/06/a_demographic_divide_could_evangelicals__block_romney_113031.html.
2. 2012 Exit Poll Data, www.foxnews.com/politics/elections/2012-exit-poll.
3. Data taken from David Liep's Election Atlas, http://uselectionatlas.org/RESULTS/national.php.
4. Ibid.
5. John B. Judis and Ruy Teixeira, *The Emerging Democratic Majority.* (New York: Scribner, 2004).
6. See Nate Silver, "What State Polls Suggest about the National Popular Vote," http://fivethirtyeight.blogs.nytimes.com/2012/10/31/oct-30-what-state-polls-suggest-about-the-national-popular-vote/.
7. Ray Fair, Michael Lewis-Beck, Tom Rice, and Alan Abramowitz are all notable contributors to this genre.
8. Donald R. Kinder and Allison Dale-Riddle, *The End of Race: Obama, 2008, and Racial Politics in America.* (New Haven, Conn.: Yale University Press, 2012).
9. The transcript is from MotherJones, the original source for the secret video, www.motherjones.com/politics/2012/09/full-transcript-mitt-romney-secret-video#47percent.
10. The summary here is from a legislative summary by the bill's Senate sponsor, www.mikulski.senate.gov/_pdfs/Press/LedbetterSummary.pdf.
11. For context, see the debate transcript at Politico.com, www.politico.com/news/stories/1012/82484_Page4.html.
12. The CBS News postdebate snap polls found approximately the same gaps for the first and third debates, www.washingtonpost.com/blogs/post-politics/wp/2012/10/22/snap-polls-obama-won/.
13. Marc J. Hetherington, "Resurgent Mass Partisanship: The Role of Elite Polarization," *American Political Science Review* 95 (2001): 619–631.
14. See for example, Milton Lodge and Charles Taber, "Three Steps toward a Theory of Motivated Reasoning" in *Elements of Reason: Cognition, Choice, and the Bounds of Rationality,* eds. Arthur Lupia, Mathew D. McCubbins, and Samuel L. Popkin (New York: Cambridge University Press, 2000).
15. Donald Green, Alan Gerber, and Christopher Larimer, "Social Pressure and Voter Turnout: Evidence from a Large-Scale Field Experiment," *American Political Science Review* 102 (2008): 33–48.
16. James Fowler, Robert Bond, Christopher Fariss, Jason Jones, Adam Kramer, Cameron Marlow, and Jaime Settle, "A 61-million-person Experiment in Social Influence and Political Mobilization," *Nature* 489 (2012): 295–298.
17. Alan Gerber and Donald Green, "The Effects of Canvassing, Telephone Calls, and Direct Mail on Voter Turnout: A Field Experiment," *American Political Science Review 94* (2000): 653–663.
18. Steven Rosenstone and John Mark Hansen, *Mobilization, Participation, and Democracy in America* (New York: Macmillan, 1993).
19. See 1984 Exit Polls, www.ropercenter.uconn.edu/elections/how_groups_voted/voted_84.html.

20. Rosenstone and Hansen, *Mobilization, Participation, and Democracy in America.*
21. Larry M. Bartels, "Partisanship and Voting Behavior, 1952–1996," *American Journal of Political Science* 44 (2000): 35–40.
22. See the American National Election Studies' Guide to Public Opinion, www.electionstudies.org/nesguide/toptable/tab3_1.htm.
23. Bruce E. Keith, David B. Magleby, Candice J. Nelson, Elizabeth Orr, and Mark C. Westlye, *The Myth of the Independent Voter* (Berkeley: University of California Press, 1992).
24. Karen M. Kaufmann and John R. Petrocik, "The Changing Politics of American Men: Understanding the Sources of the Gender Gap," *American Journal of Political Science* 43 (1999): 864–887.
25. For this evidence and other observations about the gender gap, see Christina Wolbrecht, "Parties and the Gender Gap," http://mischiefsoffaction.blogspot.com/2012/10/parties-and-gender-gap.html.
26. V. O. Key Jr., *Politics, Parties and Pressure Groups,* 5th ed. (New York: T. Y. Crowell, 1964).
27. Alan I. Abramowitz, *The Disappearing Center: Engaged Citizens, Polarization, and American Democracy* (New Haven, Conn.: Yale University Press, 2011).
28. James Sundquist, *Dynamics of the Party System: Alignment and Realignment of Political Parties in the United States* (Washington, D.C.: Brookings, 1983).
29. See, for example, Martin Gilens, *Why Americans Hate Welfare* (Chicago: University of Chicago Press, 1999); Tali Mendelberg, *The Race Card* (Princeton, N.J.: Princeton University Press, 2001).
30. See http://thehill.com/video/campaign/258689-gingrich-obama-not-a-real-president.

4

Voting Behavior

How the Democrats Rejuvenated Their Coalition

Nicole Mellow

When Barack Obama was first elected to the presidency in 2008 it was by such a decisive margin that many wondered if a new Democratic political order was being inaugurated.[1] But by 2012, following a crushing midterm setback in 2010, Obama's reelection was in doubt. To some extent, this abrupt turnaround makes sense given the change in circumstances in four years. In 2008, Obama was the challenger, offering hope and change to a country dissatisfied with the previous leadership. In 2012, he *was* the status quo. In 2008, he promised to bring a new spirit of post-partisan leadership to Washington. In 2012, he had a record with little evidence of bipartisan support. In 2008, Obama critiqued the practices that had led to the emerging economic crisis. In 2012, he owned the still middling economy. In these new circumstances, Obama faced a tough reelection challenge.

In the final days of the campaign, the race between President Obama and his Republican challenger Mitt Romney was being heralded as the "closest in recent history."[2] This assessment followed weeks of punditry that described the race as "wildly unpredictable" given campaign events that seemed to shift the momentum back and forth between the candidates.[3] On election night, Americans settled in for what many anticipated would be a long night of tallying results.[4] Surprisingly, the race was over relatively early: with swing state returns in and the polls on the West Coast closed, the networks declared President Obama the winner shortly after 11:10 p.m. (EST). In the end, the president was reelected by a narrow popular vote margin of 51 percent to Romney's 47 percent but with a wide Electoral College margin, 332 to 206.

What accounts for the comfortable reelection of Obama despite circumstances that were dramatically different, and much less promising, than in 2008? Romney himself was reportedly "shell-shocked" by the outcome of the election.[5] This chapter argues that Obama's victory was built on ground that the Democratic Party prepared in the 1930s and 1960s. Few Democratic presidential candidates since the 1960s have been able to succeed in part because of tensions within the party's coalition. As the following sections illustrate, Obama succeeded for three reasons: (1) the current state of partisanship and the geography of the parties means that very few voters are truly "up for grabs" in an electorally consequential way; (2) the sustained economic class division in party support that has roots in the 1930s was underscored in 2012 because New Deal government activism was clearly on trial; and (3) the commitment to social justice and equality the Democratic Party made in the 1960s is yielding increasing electoral benefits in part because of demographic trends in the country. The combination of these three elements provided President Obama with the Democratic support he needed to win. And he did so in 2012 with much the same coalition, although slightly smaller, as he had in 2008. The question that remains is whether Obama's success is unique to him or evidence of a more lasting Democratic advantage.

A Partisan Affair

The depth of the ideological division between the two presidential candidates was abundantly clear in the 2012 election season. In their campaigns, through their surrogates, and in debates, President Obama and Governor Romney offered starkly different visions of the scope and responsibilities of the national government, primarily with regard to the economy but also on social issues.[6] These differences reflect an ideological divide between the Democrats and Republicans that has been increasingly evident in Washington, and especially in Congress, since the 1980s and that has continued largely unchecked despite presidential promises to overcome these divisions. For example, before taking office, George W. Bush pledged to be a "uniter, not a divider." Similarly, Barack Obama was elected in 2008 partly because of his promise to usher in a new era of "post-partisanship" that would emphasize practical ideas over ideology.[7] Despite efforts by both presidents early in their tenures to work with the opposition party, neither was ultimately successful in changing partisan dynamics, and indeed both have been accused of further inflaming partisan politics.

Many lament party polarization, claiming that the extreme views of party elites do not represent the views of the American electorate.[8] Although there may be truth to this claim, scholars find that clear party differences nonetheless engage voters and help them to make sense of their electoral choices.[9] Clarified choices, and stakes that are made more evident by the close electoral division of the parties, have increased voter participation in recent elections.[10] After decades of declining turnout, voters since 1996 have participated in increasing numbers. In 2008, 61.6 percent of the eligible electorate voted for president, the highest level of participation since the 1960s. This proportion dropped slightly in 2012, to 58.2 percent.[11]

With engagement comes loyalty. In recent years, voters have become increasingly loyal to the party with which they identify, and the overwhelming majority of voters in 2012 chose to endorse their own party's candidate. According to national exit polls, 92 percent of Democrats voted for Obama

Figure 4.1 Party Loyalty in Presidential Elections, 1976–2012

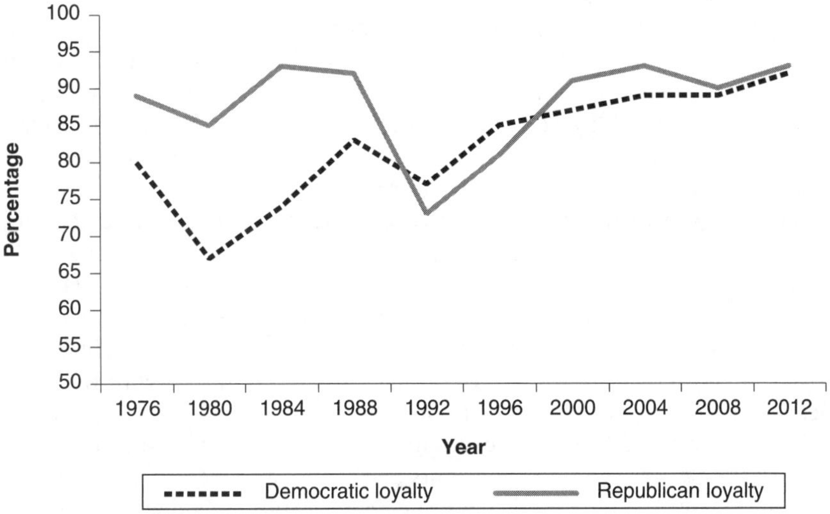

Source: 1976–2004, Roper Center NEP data; 2008–2012 NYT NEP data.

and 93 percent of Republicans voted for Romney. As Figure 4.1 makes clear, this degree of party loyalty is higher than at any point since the 1970s.

With the exception of 1992, Republican voters have been consistently loyal supporters of their party's candidate in recent decades.[12] More interesting is the steady increase, since 1980, in Democratic loyalty. In large part, this reflects the ideological realignment of voters in the two-party system in response to the clearer cues being sent by party elites. Conservative Democratic voters, who often voted for the Republican presidential candidate in the 1970s and 1980s, have migrated out of the Democratic Party over the years. To a lesser extent, liberal Republicans have shifted to the Democratic Party. The result is a more thoroughly liberal Democratic voter base and conservative Republican base. Thus even though party elites and the most politically engaged voters are more polarized than the electorate as a whole, within the parties there is an ideological consistency across all levels of the party system that is relatively new.[13]

This clear partisan division represents a departure from the middle part of the twentieth century when the similarities between Democrats and Republicans led observers to lament the tweedle-dee and tweedle-dum nature of the parties.[14] America at that time was characterized as having a politics of consensus, with nonideological parties and frequent demonstrations of bipartisanship among lawmakers. This was the height of the New Deal era, when the ideas of the Democratic Party about government activism defined normal politics. The party system dynamics of the era provide a useful baseline for understanding contemporary party divisions and the stakes in the 2012 election.

From the 1930s to the 1960s, the dominant ideas and interests in American politics were those of the New Deal Democratic Party. National institutions reflected the Democrats' commitments. Keynesian fiscal policy, the bureaucratic welfare state, a social contract between labor and capital, and containment of Soviet communism were regularly reauthorized by a broad majority of Americans from all regions of the country. Simply put, Democrats prevailed by using government activism to promote security at home and abroad, and Republicans were hard-pressed to compete. As political analyst E. J. Dionne has written, "To many in the late 1940s, it appeared that conservatives were doomed . . . to crankiness, incoherence, and irrelevance."[15] The one Republican president of the era, Dwight Eisenhower, was a moderate whose governance was more in step with the New Deal than with the conservatives in his own party.

By the 1970s, Democratic dominance was gone. The social disruptions of the 1960s from the civil rights and feminist movements, dissension over the war in Vietnam, and economic deterioration upended the political order. To many, Democratic solutions appeared obsolete or wrong-headed. Richard Nixon was the first Republican to capitalize on this weakness, and by 1980, with Ronald Reagan's election, the country seemed poised to embrace a new governing philosophy. Reagan summed up this new philosophy in his 1981 inaugural address to the nation, saying "government is not the solution to our problem; government is the problem."

Although skepticism of national government power has existed since the founding, Reagan's victory in 1980 restored the idea to public prominence in American politics. Republican philosophy combined military strength with limited government, stressing the benefits that would accrue with unfettering capital from excessive governmental control and intervention into the economy. When the effects of this approach appeared volatile, conservative social values became the Republicans' new ballast. Churning economic and social change, they argued, was best answered with the stability and security of traditional values.[16] In the new Republican agenda, tax cuts, deregulation of industry, monetary policy, and devolution of power to the states were joined with an emphasis on race-neutral individual rights, a resurrection of traditional "family" values, and support for law and order. When Reagan's election was followed by a resounding reelection in 1984 and then the election, in 1988, of his Vice President George H. W. Bush, the string of Republican presidential victories seemed, at last, to be a repudiation of the New Deal. Indeed, recent works of political history tend to characterize the late twentieth century as a conservative, Republican era that began with Reagan, or possibly Nixon.[17]

But unlike the New Deal and earlier party eras, voters have reacted with ambivalence to the new Republican regime. With the exception of the Senate from 1981 to 1987, Congress stayed under Democratic control throughout the 1970s and 1980s. When Republicans finally won control of both the House and Senate in 1994, Democrat Bill Clinton remained in the White House, and was reelected two years later. Indeed, divided party control has become the norm in Washington, with the same party ruling both houses of Congress and the presidency for just twelve of the last forty-four years. This is not merely an artifact of the difficulty of dislodging congressional incumbents. No recent president has been able to secure a "big win," or a significant electoral mandate. Pluralities prevailed in three of the four elections won by Clinton and George W. Bush (1992, 1996, and 2000), and Bush's reelection, in 2004, was earned with a very slim popular vote majority (51.0 percent).

President Obama has fared only a little better. Although his victory with 53 percent in 2008 was decisive, Obama won a smaller majority in 2012, making his reelection not unlike George W. Bush's reelection. And after Democrats gained unified control of government in 2008, the party lost its majority in the House in the midterm elections of 2010. This partisan balance was unchanged by the 2012 results. In short, with pluralities and small popular vote majorities deciding most presidential contests and with divided government the norm, the evidence suggests that while the New Deal faltered in the 1970s, the Republican order that replaced it has not achieved the same kind of electoral validation. As the two parties war with each other over their distinct visions for governance, the electorate as a whole has yet to unequivocally embrace either.

The Democrats' New Deal vision of government activism and longstanding Republican calls to roll back the welfare state framed the 2012 election, especially in the aftermath of President Obama's first term economic recovery efforts. Although Obama campaigned in 2008 on a theme of post-partisanship, the major legislative victories of his first term—economic stimulus and health care reform—were largely traditional New Deal Democratic initiatives. Reflecting the conservative shift of the last thirty years and Obama's bipartisan aspirations, both of his signature bills had elements conservatives favored: the economic stimulus bill paired government spending with tax cuts, and health care reform did not include the government option liberals desired. Nonetheless, neither garnered Republican support, and both were passed along party lines. Indeed, Obama's activist agenda spurred Tea Party anger and the victory of conservative Republicans in the 2010 midterm elections. Because of the internal cohesion, base loyalty, and rough parity of the two parties, the clarity of their opposing visions of government set the election up to be a showdown over the merits and commitments of the New Deal.

Not a Red Nation, Not a Blue Nation, But a Red and Blue Nation

The outcome of the election was a cautious nod to President Obama to continue on the New Deal–style path to economic recovery that he began in 2009. As is clear from the previous discussion, he did not receive an overwhelming show of support. Part of the reason that neither party has been able to claim a mandate of the sort that scholars have observed in past eras is that neither party has been able to secure a majority that is truly national in strength. Rather, the closely divided parties represent different regions of the country. The difference in their geographic strengths explains why, no matter how big the win in recent elections, a substantial partisan opposition has remained in government.

The geographic division of the parties first became apparent to the media in the 2000 election and was quickly labeled the "red state/blue state" divide. Red, or Republican, states captured in 2000 by Bush were largely in the South and interior West, while the blue, or Democratic, states captured by Al Gore were concentrated in the Northeast, Midwest, and Pacific Coast. This basic division of red and blue states has been sustained in every election since then, including the 2012 election. In fact, as the map in Figure 4.2 suggests, over the course of the last five presidential elections, the vast majority of states in the country have consistently voted for one party or the other.[18]

When the number of Democratic victories in the five elections from 1996 to 2012 is added up for each state, the Northeast, Midwest, and Pacific Coast emerge as the most consistently Democratic regions. States in these regions chose the Democratic presidential nominee at least four times in the last five elections. Conversely, states in the South and interior West have chosen the Democratic nominee either once or not at all in the last five elections.

Figure 4.2 Geography of Presidential Elections Results, 1996–2012

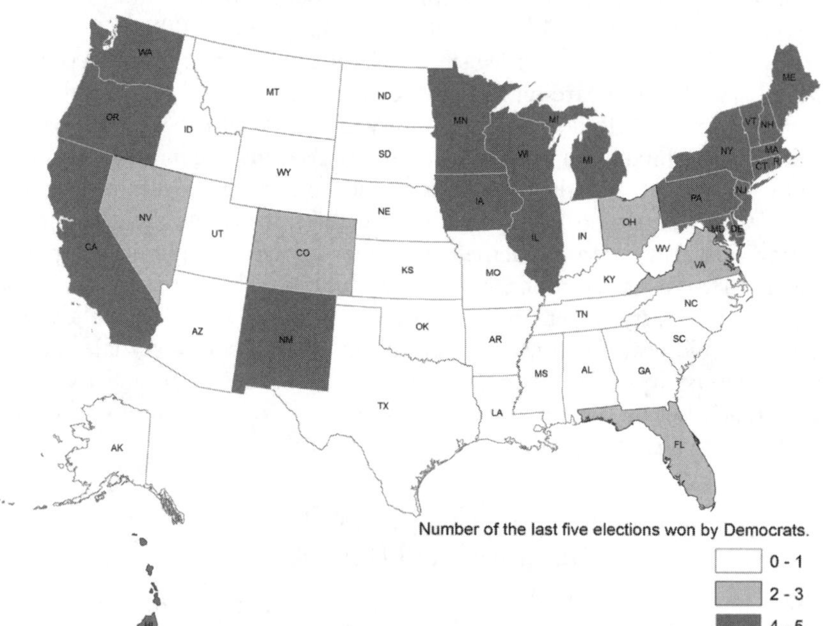

Source: Compiled by the author.

Underscoring the magnitude of this durable pattern is the number of states at each end of the spectrum of party loyalty. Fully twenty-one states—largely in the Northeast, Midwest, and the Pacific Coast regions—have voted for the Democratic candidate four or five times in the last five elections. Another twenty-four states—largely in the South and interior West—have voted for the Republican candidate at a similar rate. This stability accounts for the voting outcomes of the vast majority of the country: forty-five of the country's fifty states. Only five states—Florida, Ohio, Nevada, Virginia, and Colorado—have a mixed record, voting Democratic two or three times in the last five elections. All five of these swing states went to Obama in 2008 and again in 2012.

Part of the stark division of the red and blue map derives from institutional contrivances; simple majorities dictate how nearly all states cast their electoral votes. The fact that majorities in one set of states have voted in a consistently different fashion from majorities in the other set of states is by itself compelling. Yet further evidence of these longstanding geographical trends can be seen in Figure 4.3, which shows the percentage of major party voters in each region who supported the Democratic presidential candidate from 1960 to 2012.[19]

In every election since 1960, major-party voters in the North (including the Northeast and the Midwest) and Pacific Coast regions have supported

Figure 4.3 Percentage of Major Party Voters Selecting Democratic Presidential Candidate, 1960–2012, by Region

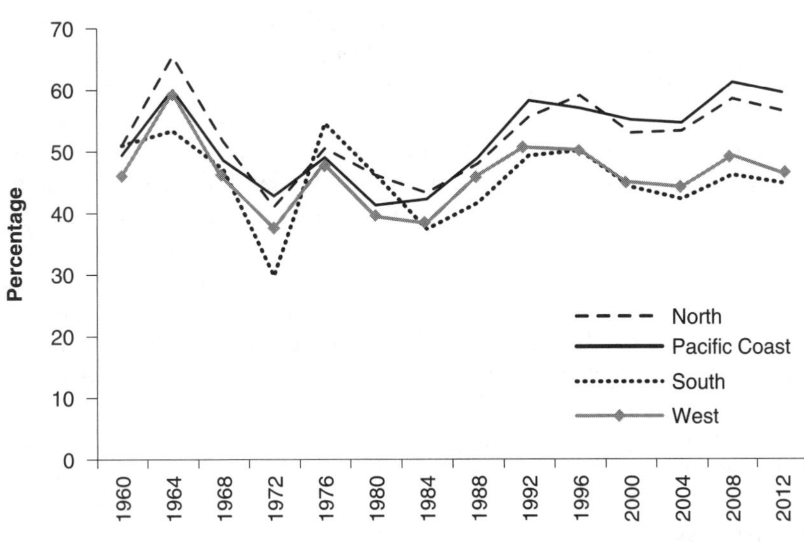

Source: Presidential Elections, 1789–2000 (Washington D.C.: CQ Press, 2002); CNN.com (2004 data); and David Leip, *Atlas of U.S. Presidential Elections* (2008 and 2012 data), available at http://uselectionatlas.org.

the Democratic presidential candidate to a greater degree than voters in the South and West. The exception is 1976, when Georgia's Jimmy Carter headed the Democratic ticket and did better in the South than elsewhere. Although the general trend since 1984 has been toward greater Democratic support, the partisan gap between voters in the North and Pacific Coast and voters in the South and West has become increasingly wide in that time.

This regional split stayed essentially the same in 2012. Although Obama's total support declined by between 2 and 3 percentage points from the levels of 2008 in each of the four regions, the gap in the support he received between the regions remained roughly the same. In 2012 as in 2008, Obama had reasonably strong majority support from voters in the North and Pacific Coast, stronger than that of his party predecessors, John Kerry (2004) and Al Gore (2000). Although he also had a higher proportion of southern and western support than either of those candidates, it was not enough to gain him a majority in either region.

The current regional organization of the party system has its origins in the 1960s, when the New Deal Democratic Party still dominated national elections. The party's electoral strength since the 1930s had derived from an accord brokered between its regional halves in the North and South. The basis of this accord was that national policy would be tailored to accommodate the dominant interests in each region: organized labor and manufacturers in the North, and agriculture and labor-intensive industry in the South. Issues that defied regional tailoring, such as civil rights for African Americans, were suppressed by the party. By the late 1960s and early 1970s, this accord was in jeopardy. Republican leaders were quick to exploit the emerging fissures in the New Deal coalition—most obviously, but not entirely, in the area of civil rights. The Republicans gained an advantage at this time by appealing to white southern Democrats, not just on racial issues but on other social issues and economic and foreign policy matters as well.

The regional discord that marked the late New Deal era led to a dramatic reorganization of the geographic basis of the party system. The most transparent outcome of Republican efforts to destabilize the Democrats' geographical base was an acceleration of the GOP's capture of the South. But Republican leaders concentrated their attention on the West as well, a region that, like the South, contained states with fast growing economies and populations. Also as in the South, the farming, ranching, and mining states of the West had a political history of antagonism toward a perceived domination by northern financial and political elites. These economic, social, and symbolic similarities were fodder for a growing Republican Party.[20]

With the regional crackup of the Democratic Party, the New Deal coalition was revealed to be an ultimately unstable sectional fusion. Two new versions of the Republican and Democratic Parties replaced the New Deal party system in the 1970s. One was an "emerging Republican majority" that was centered in the fast-growing suburbs and small towns of the South and West.[21] The other was a refashioned Democratic Party, with enhanced electoral muscle in the historically urbanized, densely populated, and commercially developed states of the North and the Pacific Coast. Just as Republicans displaced Democrats in some regions, such as the South, Democrats, in turn, displaced Republicans in other regions, such as New England, where the GOP had historically reigned.

As the demands made by the South and West on the national government began to clash with those of the North and Pacific Coast, the parties responded. For example, in the 1970s, as Northern lawmakers came to dominate the Democratic Party, they abandoned that party's long-held commitment to free trade in the face of the deindustrialization of their region. As Republicans simultaneously shifted south and westward into the trade-dependent regions of the rising Sunbelt, the two parties came into increasing conflict with one and another over trade policy.[22] On trade as on a range of foreign and domestic policy measures, "red versus blue" partisan conflict intensified as the parties' geographic bases shifted. Less than a national realignment, the current party system has been one of partisan stalemate between two regionally centered parties.

The consistency of the geographic pattern in recent decades means that few states are truly competitive—much of the vote in 2012 was already set. Simply by winning the Democratic-leaning states of the Pacific Coast and the North (as it is broadly defined earlier), Obama assured his victory in 2008, even as he won a number of additional "red" and swing states in that election as well. In 2012, he did the same.[23] He gained a wider electoral vote than popular vote margin because he again captured several states that had recently been red, including Virginia, Colorado, and Florida.

Debating the New Deal

> *There are 47 percent of the people who will vote for the president no matter what. All right, there are 47 percent who are with him, who are dependent upon government, who believe that they are victims, who believe the government has a responsibility to care for them, who believe that they are entitled to health care, to food, to housing, to you-name-it—that that's an entitlement. And the government should give it to them.*
>
> —Mitt Romney, May 2012

One of the most memorable gaffes of the 2012 campaign was revealed when the liberal magazine *Mother Jones* released a secretly recorded video that it had obtained of Mitt Romney speaking at a private fundraiser in Florida in May. In his remarks, Romney appeared to conflate a reasonably accurate number about non-income taxpayers with a mildly inaccurate number about party loyalty and a wholly inaccurate characterization of Democratic voters as government dependents with a particular set of ideas and identities.[24] The comment haunted Romney, whom Democrats had already portrayed as elitist and out of touch, throughout the remainder of the campaign. The comment resonated in part because the election turned, in no small way, on the debate about the role of government in economic recovery when that recovery was still sluggish. Underneath this, the chord Romney struck reverberated with a more enduring divide in partisan attitudes about New Deal government activism. As discussed previously, party loyalty and the geography of party strength tell us much about voter behavior and the 2012 outcome. But the story is more complex in that voters were asked, perhaps more directly than in any election since the 1980s, to endorse or repudiate the New Deal.

Low-income and working-class voters have played a foundational role in Democratic victories since Franklin D. Roosevelt put the New Deal coalition together. This is unsurprising given the programmatic commitments of the party, especially initiatives, like Social Security and the G.I. Bill, that helped working-class voters move into the middle class in the middle decades of the twentieth century. The correlation between economic class and party affiliation, with affluent voters more likely to vote for the Republican Party, remains strong.[25] The election of 2012 provided further evidence of this continued relationship and especially of the support of lower-income voters for the Democratic Party. Individuals with family incomes of less than $50,000 a year made up 41 percent of all voters, and 60 percent of them supported Obama. By comparison, 28 percent of all voters had family incomes above $100,000, and 54 percent of them supported Romney. To the extent that Romney's "47 percent" comment invoked a basic economic class division animating party support, there was still some truth to it.

Yet several developments since the 1970s have made it difficult for the Democratic Party to invoke its record of economic management as a way of retaining majority status or consistently winning presidential elections. Stagflation in the 1970s called into question traditional New Deal Keynesian solutions. Unions, a key coalition partner that helped mobilize northern working-class voters to the Democratic Party, declined in size and strength. And even though low-income and working-class voters continue to support the party, many white middle-class voters have drifted away.[26] This is especially evident in the South. Once solidly Democratic, southern whites of all economic classes, but especially middle- and upper-income whites, began to abandon the Democratic Party after it endorsed African American civil rights in the 1960s.[27]

The effects of these developments can be seen in the mixed support for the Democratic Party of the very middle class that the party helped to build. Although "middle class" is a fungible category that has as much to do with identity as it does with economics, 2012 exit polls showed that 52 percent of solidly middle- and upper-middle-class voters, those with family incomes between $50,000 and $100,000, supported Mitt Romney. Obama commanded the support of only 46 percent of these voters. Thus although

Obama repeatedly drew attention during the campaign to Democratic programs that benefit the middle class, the message did not take hold as it did for lower-income voters.

Another, less tangible, development that has hurt the Democratic Party is the inability of its leaders to convince working- and middle-class voters that the party is still committed to addressing their economic needs. Some of this has to do with changes in the global economy that have constrained policymakers' abilities to solve problems with new programs. Regardless, despite the significant growth in income inequality in the last forty years (which would seem to politically benefit the Democratic Party), national public policy outcomes reflect the preferences of affluent voters far more than they do low- and middle-income voters. Even when Democratic Party initiatives benefit low- and middle-income voters, this fact is often obscured by partisan rhetoric and by the timing of economic growth relative to the election cycle.[28]

In 2012, President Obama appears to have bucked these trends. The incumbent in a bad economy typically fails to be reelected, and yet Obama won. Recent work by political scientist Lynn Vavreck suggests that how candidates frame their message can make a difference.[29] In 2012, faced with middling economic indicators, the Obama campaign told a story of an economy on the mend, and exit poll data suggest that this frame worked or at least was consistent with the experiences of a large majority of voters. Forty-one percent of voters indicated that their personal financial situation was "about the same" as it was four years ago (up from 34 percent who said that in 2008), and another 25 percent said that they were "better off" than four years ago (up from 24 percent). These two groups, representing 66 percent of all voters, voted strongly in favor of Obama's reelection: 58 percent of voters who were "about the same" and 84 percent of "better off" voters chose Obama. Among the 33 percent of voters who indicated that they were "worse today," only 18 percent supported Obama—down from 71 percent in 2008.

In the 2012 election, voters were given a choice about whether to continue on the path of government activism laid out by Obama or to change direction. To make his case, Obama was able to call on a long Democratic Party history of promoting the interests of low- and middle-income Americans and point to the New Deal–like accomplishments of his first term. If the economy had not been as important to voters as it was in 2012, this legacy and record may not have been helpful. The stakes were also clearer than they've been in decades. Media coverage of the Tea Party, congressional Republicans' strong resistance to Obama's first-term agenda, and Romney's selection of the GOP's leading fiscal conservative, Rep. Paul Ryan of Wisconsin, as his running mate, signaled a Republican Party with a renewed zeal for rolling back the New Deal. Even if voters have had doubts about the efficacy and commitment of the Democratic Party, it was nonetheless clear in this election which party would sustain programs that the public still broadly supports.[30] With sufficient numbers of voters feeling that they were not worse off than they were four years ago, Obama's Democratic message prevailed.

The Emerging Democratic Majority?

Obama's victory can be interpreted in part as the country's confirmation of its commitment to New Deal–like economic management. But his success also signals shifts in the voter universe that may have important implications for both parties in the future. In 2002, at a high point of Republican popularity, Democratic strategists John Judis and Ruy Teixeira published *The Emerging Democratic Majority* in which they outlined the demographic changes that they predicted would result in a boon for the Democratic Party.[31] The prospects they saw for a new national majority were rooted in social and political changes of the 1960s, which combined Democrats' traditional appeals to working-class voters with appeals to ethnic and racial minorities and to young professionals working and living in "ideopolises." Fast growing and information-focused metropolitan areas like Seattle, Denver, and Austin were likely to be especially receptive to the Democratic Party's social tolerance and environmental policies, argued Judis and Teixeira. The young professionals these authors described are similar in some respects to what Richard Florida has dubbed "the creative class"—highly educated, high income–earning individuals attracted to cities known for the diversity of their populations as well as their recreational and cultural offerings.[32] The demographic factors Judis and Teixeira identified appear to have played a critical role in Obama's victory, in ways that at times intersect with his party's traditional economic appeals and at other times cut against it.

As the previous section of this chapter noted, affluent voters tend to support Republicans and Romney benefitted from this in 2012. Nonetheless, Obama received 44 percent of the votes of those with family incomes over $100,000. In 2008, he received 49 percent of their vote. Economic anxiety, given the severity of the recent financial crisis, may explain this Democratic support, but it may have another source as well. Attracting affluent supporters to the Democratic cause did not begin with Obama. The party began gaining support from some higher income earners in the 1960s, when the party embraced a set of "post-material" goals, such as equality for historically marginalized groups, environmentalism, and opposition to war.[33] Researchers have demonstrated that there is a red state–blue state dimension to the departure from traditional economic class loyalties. Although affluent voters still support Republicans at much higher rates than low-income voters in poor states, most of which are Republican, the correlation is virtually nonexistent in rich (mostly Democratic) states, where both low- and high-income voters support the Democrats.[34] This is one reason why Democratic presidential candidates have consistently done well in recent elections (see Figure 4.2) in the relatively wealthy, traditionally blue states of the North and Pacific Coast.

Judis and Teixeira saw the Democratic Party's post-1960s emphasis on post-material concerns as a key element in building a national majority. In particular, they argued that this emphasis would attract highly educated, often high-income earning, professionals who were unlikely to be swayed by the Democrats' traditional economic message. In 2012, while those with a high school diploma or less gave majority support to Obama, the only other group to do so was at the other end of the educational spectrum: the 18 percent of voters with postgraduate education supported Obama over Romney by a margin of 55 to 42 percent. This helps to account for Obama's success in the more educated, generally blue regions of the country, and it may help to explain why Obama captured the states that he did outside of these traditional Democratic strongholds.

Figure 4.4 shows where advanced degree holders are concentrated.

With the single exception of Kansas, every state with a higher than average percentage of advanced degree holders voted for Obama. Generally, these are among the consistently blue states of the Pacific Coast and the North. But important battleground states in the 2012 election—Pennsylvania, Colorado, and Virginia—also have a higher than average

Figure 4.4 Percentage of Population With an Advanced Degree

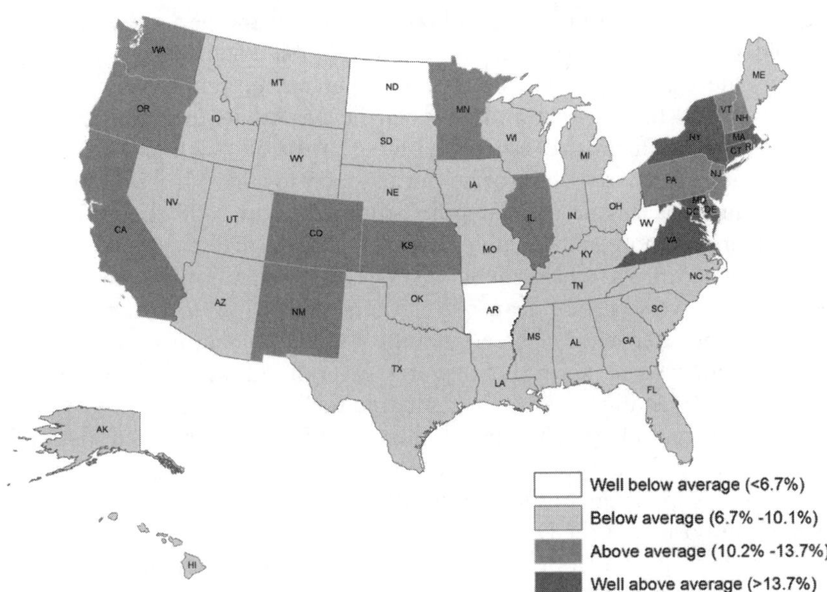

Note: Category breaks based on mean +/- 1 Std. Dev. 2009 data.

Source: U.S. Census Bureau, 2009 American Community Survey.

percentage of advanced degree holders. These states are home to many of the high-tech industries central to today's economy, and they have the type of metropolitan ideopolises that Judis and Teixeira identified as crucial to Democratic growth, places like Philadelphia, Boulder/Denver, the northern Virginia suburbs, Albuquerque, and Minneapolis-St. Paul. Highly educated voters in these states helped to tip their states to Obama in 2008 and again in 2012.

Another feature of ideopolises is the relative youthfulness of their residents, and these areas are often home to one or more institutions of higher education. Here, too, Obama found some of his strongest support. While Romney won among voters aged forty-five and over, Obama won 52 percent of the vote of thirty- to forty-four-year-olds and a full 60 percent of the vote of those under thirty. Together, these younger age cohorts made up nearly half—46 percent—of all voters. Although Obama's appeal to young voters owes partly to his personal style, his celebrity supporters, and his campaign's use of social media, it is also possible that his well-publicized commitment to making higher education more affordable and accessible along with his health care reform bill (which extended insurance coverage for young people on their parents' plans through age twenty-six) solidified his support among young people. Regardless, young ideopolis voters helped Obama in states in the South and West where Democrats recently have struggled.[35]

Obama's success in 2008 and 2012 with young voters is significant for multiple reasons. First, the youth turnout rate has historically been relatively low, and past presidential candidates have rarely spent significant time courting young voters. In recent elections, however, young people have begun to turn out in greater numbers, narrowing the gap between them and older voters.[36] In 2012, turnout among eligible voters aged eighteen to twenty-nine was 49 percent, down just 2 percentage points from 2008.[37] This was good for Obama, and may benefit Democrats in the long run as well. A person's first vote, especially in turbulent or "high stakes" times, can be a good indicator of his or her future party loyalty.[38] If this holds true, then Obama's success in attracting first-time voters in 2008 and 2012 may translate into a more enduring Democratic success.

Obama's inroad with young voters is also significant because they are a more diverse group than older voters. According to exit poll data, 18 percent of voters aged eighteen to twenty-nine self-identified as Hispanic/Latino, compared to 8 percent of voters overall. Similarly, 17 percent in this age group identified as black, compared to 12 percent of voters overall. Finally, 9 percent identified as gay, lesbian, or bisexual, compared to 4 or 5 percent among the electorate as a whole.[39] Latinos and African Americans were strong supporters of Obama in 2012, and they have historically been reliable supporters of the Democratic Party.

Although a small portion of the electorate overall (4 or 5 percent), voters who identified as gay, lesbian, or bisexual gave 76 percent of their votes to Obama. This no doubt reflects this group's general preference for the socially tolerant values that the Democratic Party has expressed since the 1960s. Also important, President Obama was the first president to endorse same-sex marriage and his administration advanced gay rights issues in a number of arenas.

The only other demographic group that surpassed this level of support for Obama is black voters. In 2012, Obama received 93 percent of their vote, down 2 percentage points from 2008. African American support for the Democratic Party is nothing new. When the New Deal Democratic Party foundered in the 1960s, one of the deepest regional fissures that emerged was over the issue of civil rights for African Americans. Northern Democratic support for civil rights, while alienating the white South, helped secure the lasting support of African American voters for the Democratic Party. Since 1972, Democrats have regularly earned more than 80 percent of the black vote while never surpassing 45 percent of the support of white voters, as Figure 4.5 makes clear.

Since the 1960 election, African American support has been important for Democrats in the large urban states of the North. But more recently, black voters have helped the Democrats and President Obama break into the Republican stronghold of the South. African Americans currently represent between 20 and 30 percent of the total population in many southern states. The strong support of these voters has not been enough for the Democratic Party to make large gains in the South, but it was critical in helping Obama capture states like Virginia and Florida, and it made him competitive in North Carolina, which he won in 2008 and lost by a slim margin in 2012. In these states, blacks represented 20 percent, 13 percent, and 23 percent of voters respectively.

Figure 4.5 Support for Democratic Candidate among Black and White Voters, 1972–2012

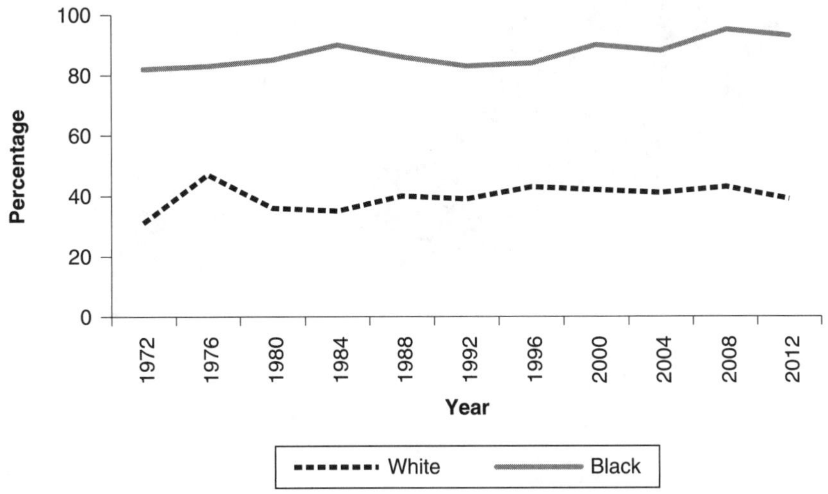

Source: NYT exit poll data.

Hispanic voters were also crucial to Obama's victory in 2012, as in 2008. He increased his support by 4 percentage points among Hispanic voters, to 71 percent in 2012. Although President Obama oversaw the deportation of more immigrants than any of his recent predecessors, in the summer of 2012, after failing to get congressional approval for the pro-immigrant Dream Act, he used executive action to enable young migrants to stay and work in the United States. A survey from December 2011 found that 91 percent of Latinos supported the Dream Act, and Obama's action was widely heralded by Latino activists.[40] It, along with the Democratic Party's economic agenda, may account for the increase in his support among Hispanics.

As with African American voters, strong support from the Latino community helped Obama in states in traditional blue strongholds, like California and New York, but more crucially in states outside of these regions. Nevada, Colorado, and Florida supported George W. Bush, the Republican candidate, in 2000 and 2004. But Obama won all three of these states in 2008 and again in 2012, and Hispanic support was critical.

Figure 4.6 shows the percentage of each state's population that is of Hispanic origin. Florida, Nevada, and Colorado are well above average in the size of their Hispanic populations.[41] In each of these three states, the

Figure 4.6 Percentage of Population of Hispanic Origin

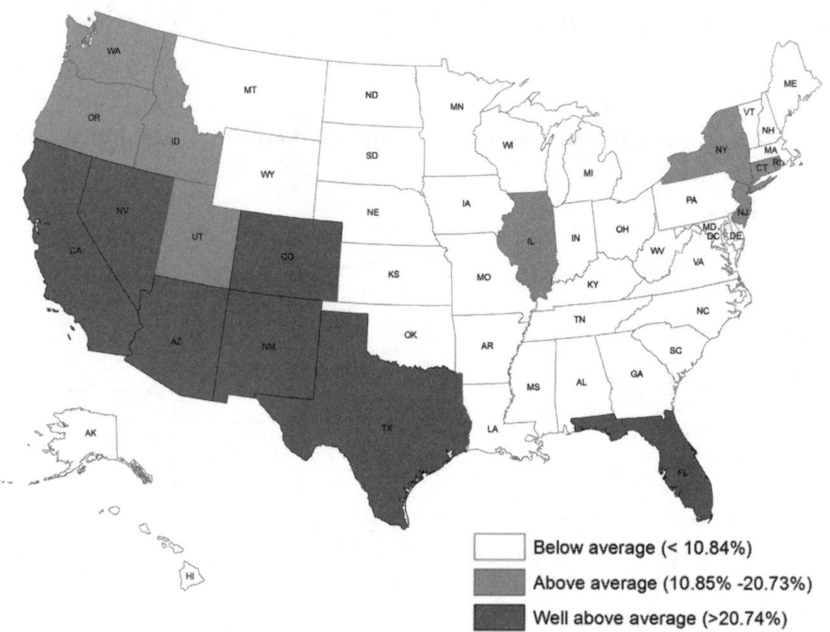

Note: Category breaks based on mean +/- 1 Std. Dev. 2010 data.

Source: U.S. Census Bureau, Population Division.

size of the Hispanic share of the vote grew from 2008 to 2012 by between 1 percentage point (Colorado) and 4 points (Nevada). Obama captured the majority of the Hispanic vote in each of these states. In Nevada and Colorado, Obama won 71 and 75 percent of the Hispanic vote respectively. In Florida, which has a substantial and generally conservative Cuban American population, Obama nevertheless captured 60 percent of the total Hispanic vote.

Hispanic and black voters were vital to Obama's success in 2012, as they were in 2008. And the electoral significance of these groups is growing: racial and ethnic minorities are now one-third of the population, and are expected to become the majority by 2042. This is largely due to the forecasted growth in the Hispanic population, which is expected to triple by 2050. At that point, Hispanics will make up 30 percent of the total population. Additionally, although Asians are currently only 5 percent of the population, by 2050, their number is expected to grow to nearly 10 percent.[42] The growth in Democratic support among this group in recent years (Asian voters represented 3 percent of all voters in 2012 and 73 percent of them chose Obama) is also potentially promising for the Democratic Party.

In securing and increasing support from racial, ethnic, and sexual identity minority voters, Obama has built on long-standing relationships between the Democratic Party and these constituencies. The party's economic message as well as its commitment to using national government to promote social equality has made it a generally more hospitable home for minority voters since the 1960s. Another demographic group that scholars have long seen as friendly to Democrats for these reasons is women. As Figure 4.7 indicates, the gap between women's and men's support for the Democratic presidential candidate has generally grown since the 1970s.

Figure 4.7 Gender Gap in the Support for the Democratic Presidential Candidate, 1976–2012

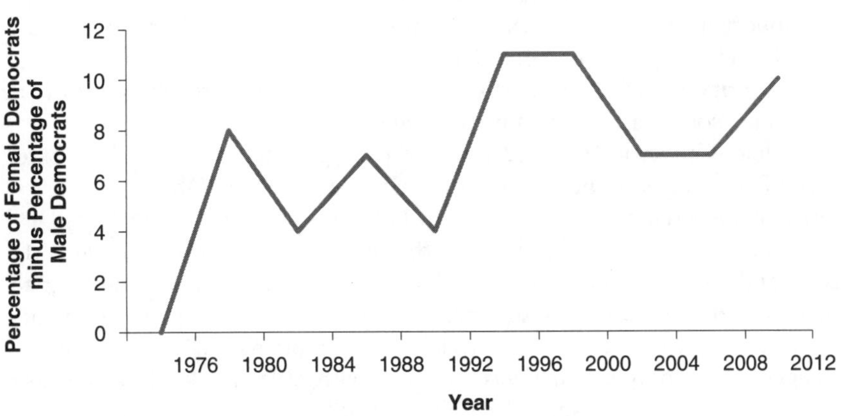

Source: 1976–2004, Roper Center NEP data; 2008–2012 NYT NEP data.

The story here is complex however. Part of the reason for the gender gap is that men, especially white men, have increasingly left the Democratic Party.[43] In 2012, Obama won 45 percent of the male vote but 55 percent of the female vote. Even more telling, Obama won 67 percent of the vote of unmarried women but only 38 percent of married men's vote. How to interpret these results is not clear. On the one hand, the number of single adults has been on the rise and if single women continue to vote cohesively, Democrats stand to gain.[44] On the other hand, the differences between Obama and Romney, and between Democrats and Republicans generally, on policies and attitudes about women were highly visible in the 2012 election, due in part to a number of high-profile incidents and remarks in the preceding year. For example, Republican resistance to health insurance coverage of contraception, a Republican Senate candidate's reference to "legitimate rape," and a controversial abortion bill in Virginia received extensive coverage in the media as well as attention from late-night comedians. These may have elevated the gender gap temporarily, in ways that will not endure beyond the structural divide that exists because of the departure of white men from the Democratic Party.

The Same, but Different, Ground of the Blue Coalition

In the 1930s, Franklin D. Roosevelt established Democratic Party dominance under the principle that the national government should intervene actively in the economy to protect the welfare of its citizens. Beginning in the 1960s, the Democratic Party combined economic with social justice appeals in an attempt to build a broader, multiracial and multiethnic base. This helped the party gain the support of minority voters and women, both of which are themselves disproportionately represented among the poor, and it attracted new support from educated, often more affluent, voters, especially in the states of the North and Pacific Coast. The cost was a loss of support in the white South, and among white middle-class voters more broadly. The Republican gains that resulted have led to several decades of rough parity between the parties and an increasing partisan standoff on economic, social, and foreign policy issues.

Obama's victory in 2012 builds on the ground paved by the Democratic Party. Responding to the economic crisis of 2008, Obama in his first term pursued relief and recovery efforts largely consistent with New Deal philosophy, and this record became the main point of debate between the two candidates. Obama also promoted the social justice and equality goals of a number of groups, including women, Hispanics, and gays and lesbian.[45] This appears to have yielded an electoral pay-off as well. Despite a still struggling economy, Obama was rewarded with reelection by the same basic coalition of voters that supported him in 2008.

Notably, in both 2008 and 2012, Obama succeeded where other recent Democrats, such as Gore in 2000 and Kerry in 2004, had failed. He did so by securing swing states in the blue regions, like Ohio and Pennsylvania, and capturing red states in the South and interior West, like Virginia and Colorado. To the extent that his victories came through his appeal to young professionals in ideopolises and to Hispanic and Black voters more generally, President Obama's coalition has extended and perhaps shifted the proportions of the Democratic Party base.

With the 2012 election in their column, Democrats have now won the popular vote in five of the last six presidential elections. Since 1988, Republicans have won the popular vote for the presidency only once, in 2004. Because of the demographic shifts forecasted for the country, this trend could continue if the Democratic candidates who follow Obama can sustain his party building. This would result in the Democratic majority prophesied by Judis and Teixeira a decade ago.

But in the world of politics, demographics are not destiny. The two major parties have histories of shifting, even flip-flopping, positions on issues and of winning—and losing—constituents as a result. The Republican Party is already retooling on issues ranging from immigration to gay marriage. Further, identities that are politically salient in one moment can become less relevant over time, especially after key aims are achieved. The erosion of white middle-class support for Democrats is some evidence of this. In a party system as closely divided as the current one, small shifts among voters can spell victory or defeat. Democrats appear to have the advantage, for now.

Notes

1. This reasoning made more sense given the significant Democratic gains in Congress in 2006, when the party reclaimed control of both houses of Congress and made large gains at the state level as well.
2. Scott Bomboy, "Why the 2012 Election is the Closest in Recent History," *Yahoo News,* November 5, 2012, http://news.yahoo.com/why-2012-election-closest-recent-history-175835847.html.
3. This was the characterization of the conventional wisdom made by Nate Silver in his blog post for October 28, 2012. In the post, Silver used state polls to dispute the conventional wisdom about unpredictability, concluding instead that the race was extremely tight yet slightly favoring Obama. See Nate Silver, "In Swing States, a Predictable Election?" *New York Times,* October 29, 2012, http://fivethirtyeight.blogs.nytimes.com/2012/10/29/oct-28-in-swing-states-a-predictable-election/?hp. There is a larger, interesting story about the rise, ubiquity, and public consumption of polling in this election season. Variability in poll outcomes is in part what drove the media narratives of the close and unpredictable race. Several blogging analysts, including Nate Silver at the *New York Times,* Sam Wang at Princeton University, and Drew Linzer at Emory University, saw a more consistent story of a tight race favoring Obama.
4. Michael Calderone, "2012 Election Night: TV Networks, Associated Press Prepare to Call Winners," *Huffington Post,* November 5, 2012, www.huffingtonpost.com/2012/11/05/2012-election-night_n_2078385.html.
5. Daniel Lippman, "Mitt Romney 'Shellshocked' after Lost Election, Advisor Says," *The Huffington Post,* November 8, 2012, www.huffingtonpost.com/2012/11/08/mitt-romney-lost-election_n_2095013.html.

6. There was less evidence on display of the differences over foreign policy, especially noted during the presidential debate devoted to foreign policy.
7. On the mix of post-partisanship and partisanship in the Obama presidency, see Sidney Milkis, Jesse Rhodes, and Emily Charnock, "What Happened to Post-partisanship? Barack Obama and the New American Party System," *Perspectives on Politics* 10:1 (2012): 57–76; for a characterization of Obama's post-partisanship and broader ambitions with regard to the presidency and constitutional governance, see Jeffrey Tulis, "Plausible Futures," in Charles Dunn (ed.) *The Presidency in the Twenty-first Century* (Lexington: University Press of Kentucky, 2011).
8. Morris Fiorina (with Samuel J. Abrams and Jeremy Pope), *Culture War? The Myth of a Polarized America* (New York: Pearson Longman, 2005).
9. For an example of the argument that polarization characterizes the "engaged" American electorate and is increasing engagement generally, see Alan Abramowitz, *The Disappearing Center: Engaged Citizens, Polarization, and American Democracy* (New Haven, Conn.: Yale University Press, 2010).
10. From the mid-1980s until 2006, roughly a third of the electorate identified as Republicans and a third as Democrats (though Democrats held a consistent edge in party identification). Roughly a third identified as Independents. Since 2006, the difference between Republican and Democratic identification has grown (largely due to a drop in Republican identification) and Independent identification has grown as well. PEW Research Center, "Partisan Polarization Surges in Bush, Obama Years: Trends in American Values, 1987–2012," June 4, 2012, www.people-press.org/2012/06/01/trend-in-party-identification-1939–2012/. It is important to note that scholars have found that most "Independents" are actually "leaners" who tend to vote consistently for one of the two parties. See Bruce Keith, David Magleby, Candice Nelson, Elizabeth Orr, and Mark Westlye, *The Myth of the Independent Voter* (Berkeley: University of California Press, 1992).
11. Turnout figures are available at George Mason University's United States Election Project website, http://elections.gmu.edu/voter_turnout.htm.
12. The exceptional nature of the 1992 election for Republicans is likely the result of Ross Perot's strong showing in that election; he captured 19 percent of the overall vote.
13. See Matthew Levendusky, *The Partisan Sort: How Liberals Became Democrats and Conservatives Became Republicans* (Chicago: University of Chicago Press, 2009).
14. The American Political Science Association's Committee on Political Parties, "Toward a More Responsible Two-party System," *The American Political Science Review* XLIV:3:2 (September 1950).
15. E. J. Dionne, *Why Americans Hate Politics* (New York: Simon & Schuster, 1991), p. 152.
16. This is not new. Similar impulses have been observed in reactions against industrial modernization at the turn of the twentieth century. See Richard Hofstadter, *The Age of Reform: From Bryan to F.D.R.* (New York: Knopf, 1955).
17. There are numerous examples of such works, but for a few, see: Donald Critchlow, *The Conservative Ascendancy: How the Republican Right Rose to Power in Modern America* (Lawrence: University Press of Kansas, 2011); Matthew Lassiter, *The Silent Majority: Suburban Politics in the Sunbelt South* (Princeton, N.J.: Princeton University Press, 2006); Bruce J. Schulman, *The Seventies: The Great Shift in American Culture, Society, and Politics* (New York: The Free Press, 2001); Lisa McGirr, *Suburban Warriors: The Origins of the New American Right* (Princeton, N.J.: Princeton University Press, 2001); Sean Wilentz,

The Age of Reagan: A History, 1974–2008 (New York: Harper, 2008); Stephen Skowronek, *The Politics Presidents Make: Leadership from John Adams to George Bush* (Cambridge, Mass.: Harvard University Press, 1993); Rick Perlstein, *Nixonland: The Rise of a President and the Fracturing of America* (New York: Scribner, 2008).

18. The author would like to thank Sharron Macklin for her assistance in producing the maps in this chapter.
19. Calculations based on all major-party voters in each of the four regions. The South includes: Alabama, Arkansas, Florida, Georgia, Louisiana, Mississippi, North Carolina, South Carolina, Texas, Virginia, Kentucky, Oklahoma, Tennessee, and West Virginia. West includes: Iowa, Kansas, Minnesota, Missouri, Nebraska, North Dakota, South Dakota, Arizona, Colorado, Idaho, Montana, Nevada, New Mexico, Utah, and Wyoming. Pacific Coast includes: California, Oregon, and Washington. North includes Connecticut, Delaware, Illinois, Indiana, Maine, Maryland, Massachusetts, Michigan, New Hampshire, New Jersey, New York, Ohio, Pennsylvania, Rhode Island, Vermont, and Wisconsin. Alaska and Hawaii, which were added to the Union after World War II and which regularly vote Republican and Democratic respectively, are not included in the analysis.
20. See Nicole Mellow, *The State of Disunion: Regional Sources of Modern American Partisanship* (Baltimore: Johns Hopkins University Press, 2008). Also, Lassiter, *The Silent Majority*; Schulman, *The Seventies*; and McGirr, *Suburban Warriors*.
21. The phrase “emerging Republican majority” was coined by Republican strategist Kevin Phillips in his book, *The Emerging Republican Majority* (New Rochelle, N.Y.: Arlington House, 1969).
22. Mellow, *The State of Disunion*, ch. 3.
23. Though in 2012 he lost Indiana.
24. This comment was extensively analyzed and fact-checked in the press. See Lucy Madison, “Fact-checking Romney’s ‘47 percent’ comment,” *CBS News*, September 18, 2012, www.cbsnews.com/8301-503544_162-57515033-503544/fact-checking-romneys-47-percent-comment/. Also see Philip Rucker, “Romney’s ‘47 percent’ Comments Aren’t Going Away, and They’re Taking a Toll,” *Washington Post*, October 1, 2012, www.washingtonpost.com/politics/decision2012/romneys-47-percent-comments-arent-going-away/2012/10/01/17604654-0be5-11e2-a310-2363842b7057_story.html.
25. Although, scholars have found that the relationship between income and party is mediated by geography. On the persistence of class divisions in party identification, see Jeffrey Stonecash, *Class and Party in American Politics* (Boulder, Colo.: Westview Press, 2000). For an account that stresses the geographic variation in the income–party relationship, see Andrew Gelman, Boris Shor, Joseph Bafumi, and David Park, *Red State, Blue State, Rich State, Poor State: Why Americans Vote the Way They Do* (Princeton, N.J.: Princeton University Press, 2009).
26. For a review of some of the reasons for middle-class drift, see Thomas Byrne Edsall and Mary D. Edsall, *Chain Reaction: The Impact of Race, Rights, and Taxes on American Politics* (New York: W.W. Norton, 1992); also Lassiter, *The Silent Majority*; McGirr, *Suburban Warriors*; Kevin Kruse, *White Flight: Atlanta and the Making of Modern Conservatism* (Princeton, N.J.: Princeton University Press, 2005).
27. See Kruse, *White Flight*; Lassiter, *The Silent Majority*; for a breakdown of white abandonment of the Democratic Party by class, see Larry Bartels, *Unequal Democracy: The Political Economy of the New Gilded Age* (Princeton, N.J.: Princeton University Press, 2008).

28. See Bartels, *Unequal Democracy*; Martin Gilens, *Affluence and Influence: Economic Inequality and Political Power in America* (Princeton, N.J.: Princeton University Press, 2012).
29. Lynn Vavreck, *The Message Matters: The Economy and Presidential Campaigns* (Princeton, N.J.: Princeton University Press, 2009).
30. For a breakdown of the policy preferences of lower-, middle-, and upper-income Americans, see Gilens, *Affluence and Influence.*
31. John B. Judis and Ruy Teixeira, *The Emerging Democratic Majority* (New York: Scribner, 2002).
32. Richard Florida, *The Rise of the Creative Class: And How It's Transforming Work, Leisure, Community, and Everyday Life* (New York: Basic Books, 2002).
33. Everett Carll Ladd Jr., "Liberalism Upside Down: The Inversion of the New Deal Order," *Political Science Quarterly* 91 (1976–77) : 577–600.
34. Andrew Gelman, Boris Shor, Joseph Bafumi, and David Park, "Rich State, Poor State, Red State, Blue State: What's the Matter with Connecticut?" *Quarterly Journal of Political Science* 2 (2007) : 345–367; also see Gelman, et al. *Red State, Blue State.*
35. The importance of young voters in key swing states such as Florida, Ohio, Pennsylvania, and Virginia was also the finding of The Center for Information and Research on Civic Learning and Engagement. See their November 13, 2012, fact sheet, "Young Voters in the 2012 Presidential Election," www.civicyouth.org.
36. "Why Youth Voting Matters," *The Center for Information and Research on Civic Learning and Engagement,* November 10, 2012, www.civicyouth.org/quick-facts/youth-voting/.
37. Ibid.
38. Angus Campbell, Phillip Converse, Warren Miller, and Donald Stokes, *The American Voter* (Chicago: University of Chicago Press, 1976 [orig. 1960]); note, in particular, their description of Democratic growth after the 1932 election: "When we ask from what levels of society the Democratic Party drew this new strength, we find from our survey data and from the aggregative election figures that the impact of the events of that period appears to have been felt most strongly by the youth, the economically underprivileged, and the minority groups" (p. 153).
39. "Young Voters in the 2012 Presidential Election," *The Center for Information and Research on Civic Learning and Engagement,* November 13, 2012, www.civicyouth.org; note that the *New York Times* exit poll data has gay, lesbian, or bisexual voters as representing 5 percent of the electorate as a whole (not 4 percent).
40. Julia Preston and John Cushman Jr., "Obama to Permit Young Migrants to Remain in U.S.," *New York Times*, June 15, 2012, www.nytimes.com/2012/06/16/us/us-to-stop-deporting-some-illegal-immigrants.html?smid=pl-share.
41. Well above average is defined as more than one standard deviation above the national mean.
42. U.S. Census Bureau, "An Older and More Diverse Nation by Midcentury," *U.S. Census Bureau Press Release*. August 4, 2008.
43. Janet Box-Steffensmeier, Suzanna De Boef, and Tse-Min Lin, "The Dynamics of the Partisan Gender Gap," *American Political Science Review* 98 (2004): 515–525; Karen Kaufmann, "The Gender Gap," *PS: Political Science and Politics* (July 2006): 447–453.

44. According to U.S. Census Bureau data, 44.1 percent of all U.S. residents age eighteen or over are unmarried. Available at www.census.gov/newsroom/releases/archives/facts_for_features_special_editions/cb12-ff18.html; also see, Rachel Swarns, "More Americans Rejecting Marriage in 50s and Beyond," *New York Times,* March 1, 2012, www.nytimes.com/2012/03/02/us/more-americans-rejecting-marriage-in-50s-and-beyond.html?pagewanted=all.
45. Obama has been criticized for not being responsive to African Americans. On these criticisms and the challenges Obama has faced as the country's first black president, see Ta-Nehisi Coates, "Fear of a Black President," *The Atlantic,* September 2012, www.theatlantic.com/magazine/archive/2012/09/fear-of-a-black-president/309064/.

5

The Media

Different Audiences Saw Different Campaigns

Marjorie Randon Hershey

Are the media liberal, as many charge? Or are they conservative, portraying negative stereotypes of blacks and other minorities? Generalizations about the media are almost as inescapable as the media themselves. Yet we might ask whether we can continue to generalize about media coverage at all, given that the term *media* now encompasses a huge and ever-expanding collection of diverse outlets ranging from NBC News to Facebook, from *The Daily Show with Jon Stewart* to the Drudge Report, from the *New York Times* to *The Maury Povich Show*. What generalization about the coverage of the 2012 presidential race would apply to both the *Wall Street Journal* and *Ellen*?

Because media outlets have become so diverse, Americans can be selective about where they get their political information. A recent study by the Pew Research Center's Project for Excellence in Journalism found that in the run-up to the 2012 elections, no single media platform dominated as the source for Americans' political learning. Although the largest numbers of people turned regularly to cable TV news (41 percent) and local news (38 percent) for information about campaigns, almost as many (36 percent) relied on the Internet—greater than the percentage who said they used network news—and as many as one in six (17 percent) mentioned at least one social medium (Facebook, Twitter, or YouTube) as their regular source for campaign news. More than one in ten said that they regularly get their news fix from programs such as *The Daily Show, Saturday Night Live,* and the *Tonight Show with Jay Leno*. And significantly, only about one in twenty Americans (6 percent) reported turning regularly to just one platform for campaign news.[1]

This chapter asks how the great increase in the diversity of media outlets affected the 2012 presidential race. Did these varied outlets carry similar types of political information? Or were they as different in their content and political slant as in their appearance and location? What were the dominant themes or frames various types of media used to portray the race between President Barack Obama and former governor Mitt Romney? Is it possible that Americans were not all seeing the same presidential campaign in 2012?

In fact, there is a lot of evidence that consumers of different media outlets saw different campaigns.

A Media Revolution

While current college students and their older siblings were growing up, the media world was experiencing a technological revolution. Just thirty years ago, three-quarters of all households watching television at about 6 p.m. on a week night were tuned in to the evening network news,[2] because that was almost the only programming available on TV at that time of day. Then came the rise of cable TV, followed by satellite TV and widespread use of the Internet to access political information. Internet sources varied from CNN.com to the online platforms of traditional print newspapers and network TV news to the explosion of all sorts of blogs: partisan, nonpartisan, and just plain wacko. Even on network TV, politically relevant information now reaches viewers from such "soft news" sources as *Dr. Phil* and the *Late Show with David Letterman*, as well as from *NBC, ABC,* and *CBS News*.[3]

These changes have had profound consequences for media coverage of political campaigns. Different types of outlets lend themselves to different types of presentations. Someone who watches a candidate's appearance on an entertainment-oriented outlet, such as *The View,* is more likely to learn about the candidate's personality, family, and religious faith than is someone who watches the candidate on *CBS Evening News*—and is less likely to see the candidate exposed to tough questioning by the interviewer.[4] Cable and satellite political programming and especially Internet blogs carry much more opinionated content, with a more partisan slant, than do network and local news.[5] Moreover, when individuals have much more choice in the programming they get from their screens, they can not only be more selective in their media consumption but can avoid political content altogether if they choose—and large proportions do. This can increase the gap in political knowledge between those who choose to watch or read political news and those who choose not to, which can lead in turn to a greater gap in political participation.[6]

It would be easy to assume that in this profusion of presumably biased sources, politically involved Americans tend to choose media outlets that favor their own preexisting points of view. In fact, we don't have much proof of this selective exposure. One recent study finds that to the contrary, most people consume relatively nonpartisan local newscasts rather than more partisan media, and even those who use partisan sources consume news programming from different parts of the political spectrum: a politically balanced diet.[7] But there is ample support for the idea of selective perception (or confirmation bias), in which individuals are more likely to attend to and retain messages that reflect their existing attitudes, regardless of the medium they get them from.[8] If different media outlets carry different messages about the presidential election, then this may be contributing to the ideological and partisan polarization that characterizes American political life.

Coverage during the Invisible Primary

A lot of evidence shows that Americans did see different campaigns in 2012, depending on the types of media they consumed. For example, the Pew Research Center compared the coverage of presidential candidates on Twitter with that of a collection of hundreds of thousands of blogs and more than 10,000 mainstream online news sites beginning with the 2011 invisible primary (the months that precede the first primary election).[9] Researchers classified the tone of each candidate's coverage as positive, neutral, or negative, *based not on any perceived bias in the reportage* but on the positive or negative content of the activities, events, polling data, and interpretations being reported. For example, stories containing criticisms of a candidate by his or her opponents present negative statements about that candidate to viewers or readers, whereas stories showing a candidate rising in the polls provide positive statements about that candidate.[10]

The most striking finding is that on all of these media platforms, when we compare positive to negative content, the tone of both candidates' coverage was disproportionately negative (see Table 5.1). During the months prior to the 2012 primaries and caucuses, the traditional online media carried the least negative coverage, but even here, negative outweighed positive coverage of Obama, in particular, by a ratio of four to one. In fact, in all of these platforms, the impression conveyed of the president was more negative and less positive than that of his opponent. Finally, coverage in the traditional online media was more likely to be neutral about both candidates than in either Twitter or blogs.

Why would a sitting president face such a disadvantage, especially a Democratic president portrayed by the supposedly liberal mainstream media? A major reason was that the disappointing state of the American economy was the most-covered issue in the campaign, and the candidates jockeying to win the Republican nomination were even more critical of Obama's handling of the Great Recession than they were of one another. As a result, all three media platforms conveyed a substantial amount of criticism of Obama.

Table 5.1 Tone of Media Coverage of Obama and Romney in Twitter, Traditional Online Media, and Blogs, 2011

	Obama			Romney		
	Positive	Neutral	Negative	Positive	Neutral	Negative
Twitter	17	33	51	19	41	40
Traditional Online Media	9	56	35	25	47	28
Blogs	14	48	38	33	32	35

Note: Coverage was coded from May 2, 2011, through November 27, 2011.

Source: Pew Research Center's Project for Excellence in Journalism, www.journalism.org/analysis_report/candidates_twitter.

The negative tone of candidates' media coverage reflects the media's need for an audience. Candidates make news when they give speeches or take actions. In reporting these events, journalists are especially likely to focus on the attacks or charges made, because attacks fit the media's definition of what is news. Attacks and countercharges are more dramatic, more conflict-filled, and therefore more likely to draw an audience than is milder content, and the for-profit media need to attract audiences in order to sell commercial time at favorable rates. A presidential speech, for instance, often has greater news value when it elicits a harsh response from a critic. When these attacks or charges dominate the coverage, it takes on a negative tone. In addition, journalists have been censured so often for biased reporting—often from both liberals and conservatives at once[11]—that they may find it safer to report criticism of both sides, which probably gives their coverage a more analytical and investigative air than if they were to transmit praise of both sides.

Yet these media platforms weren't equally negative, as Table 5.1 shows. Twitter's coverage was consistently harsher toward both candidates than were blogs and traditional online media. In Romney's case, only 19 percent of the assertions about him on Twitter were positive, compared with 25 percent in the mainstream media and 33 percent on blogs. Similarly, only 17 percent of Obama's Twitter coverage was positive, and a full 51 percent was negative. The negative slant of Obama's tweets abated only during the week when Navy SEALs killed Osama bin Laden in a daring raid.

Negative tweets about Romney in 2011 often referred to him as a "RINO," a "Republican in Name Only," suggesting that the former Massachusetts governor was more of a moderate than a conservative—an interesting charge in light of Romney's effort during the primaries to appeal to the very conservative Republican base. Romney was also blamed for having changed his positions on a number of important issues. A frequent re-tweet in November 2011 originated with humorist Andy Borowitz: "Romney Admits He Is Flip-flopper, Then Denies It." Tweets about most of the other candidates for the Republican nomination were predominantly negative as well, including those about former Pennsylvania senator Rick Santorum, representative Michele Bachmann of Minnesota, businessman Herman Cain, Texas governor Rick Perry, and (in almost all of these weeks) former House Speaker Newt Gingrich. The only Republican candidates whose tweets tended to be more positive than negative were those with no real chance of winning the party's nomination: Texas representative Ron Paul and Utah's former governor, Jon Huntsman.

Why was Twitter's coverage of both candidates more negative than that of other platforms? Twitter was the new kid on the block in 2012. Although this microblogging site began in 2006 and was used to some degree in the 2008 campaign, political professionals had still been trying to figure out how best to apply it. By 2011, however, Twitter had found its way into the set of tools with which major campaigns injected material into the body politic. One reason is its ease of use. Tweets are limited to 140 characters, so they can be posted quickly, read quickly, and passed on to others with the tap of a key. Facebook, another social medium, shares this ease of distribution.

For example, in April 2012, a Democratic activist complained on CNN that Romney's wife, Ann, had never worked a day in her life. A few minutes after the activist's comment, tweets mentioning her or Ann Romney were being issued at a rate of 150 a minute. Within two hours, Mrs. Romney had taken to Twitter to say, "I made a choice to stay home and raise five boys. Believe me, it was hard work." By noon the next day, 2,800 people had re-tweeted Ann Romney's response to tens of thousands of other Romney activists—and a Democratic campaign that had considered women's issues to be one of its strongest talking points found itself on the defensive and distinctly off message. The Democrat's comment and Romney's response were spread by traditional media as well, but more slowly, lacking the urgency and the individual involvement that social media offer.

In addition to their speed, tweets differ in several other ways from the style and content of blog posts and stories in the mainstream media. Because tweets must be very brief, writers are less able to explain themselves or to qualify their claims than is a blogger or writer of a newspaper story or column. Thus, a typical tweet about a presidential candidate is likely to be provocative, ironic, and highly opinionated—for instance, "ROMNEY WAS PROBABLY THAT KID IN CLASS THAT REMINDED THE TEACHER ABOUT LAST NIGHT'S HOMEWORK" or "WHAT'S THE DIFFERENCE BETWEEN GOD AND **OBAMA**? GOD DOESN'T THINK HE'S **OBAMA**. #VoteWhite." Provocation and humor will also gain the tweeter more attention, via re-tweets, than will a statement such as, "Obama talked about unemployment levels in Ohio today." Candidates and activists can post shocking charges more comfortably on Twitter than in the more professional setting of interviews with network or newspaper reporters. A Twitter feed relates to political discussion as a sound bite relates to a news story: it accommodates short attention spans and the need for novelty.

Most important, Twitter and other digital media permitted campaigns to talk directly with supporters without having their messages interpreted or ignored by the traditional media outlets. Campaigns used Twitter as a means of testing citizen response to events and ads. When Obama or Romney gave a campaign speech, the Twitter feed served up instant reaction. The campaigns could later turn to Facebook to see how the story lines played out in that broader arena, and could use Google the next day to find out where the story had gone in the larger media universe. The "instant response" teams of earlier presidential campaigns "or even Obama's own technology-savvy 2008 effort—seem almost glacial by comparison."[12] Although Facebook far outpaced Twitter in number of users (141 million for Facebook, 29 million for Twitter in 2012),[13] politicians, political activists, and campaign professionals constituted a larger proportion of the Twitterverse than of Facebook's more undifferentiated clientele. The politicized nature of Twitter's audience compensated for its smaller size. The Obama campaign even began incorporating Twitter hashtags into presidential speeches, Facebook posts, and almost everything else the campaign sent out.

The "conversations" between campaigns and their followers on Twitter were largely one-sided in most cases. Neither campaign did much to incorporate citizen responses into its use of social media. Even so, the arrival of Twitter and other new media in 2012 changed the campaign environment and carried different coverage than the mainstream media in both content and tone.

The Nomination Race

Even before the primaries began, journalists had been reporting for months on the "horse race"—candidates' strategy, movement in the polls, fund-raising, and other indicators of their likely success or failure.[14] In an analysis of a sample of key news outlets on- and offline, researchers found that almost two-thirds of Obama's coverage between November 2011 and mid-April 2012 referred to campaign strategy and momentum, and only about one-fifth dealt with policy issues.[15] In short, Obama was being reported throughout this time as a candidate more than as a president. Coverage of the Republican primary race devoted a similar amount of attention to horse race coverage and even less (11 percent) to the candidates' stands on issues.

The biggest failure of the coverage was the very limited information it provided about the candidates' often-lengthy records of political experience, which certainly should be relevant to their future performance. During this period, only 6 percent of the coverage referred to the candidates' public records. Various aspects of their personal lives received an unusual amount of attention only during the month of November (39 percent of that month's total coverage), particularly the religious faith of Mitt Romney and Rick Santorum and the interesting marital history of Newt Gingrich. As the campaign proceeded, these personal characteristics never occupied more than 10 percent of the coverage. And on such questions as Romney's performance as governor of Massachusetts and Obama's leadership of the executive branch since 2009, viewers and readers found little to enlighten them.

Although the content of both candidates' coverage emphasized strategy and momentum, its tone differed. Analyzing more than 11,000 news outlets, Pew researchers found that Romney's coverage was mixed or negative in the early primaries, emphasizing his personal wealth, his experience with the venture capital firm Bain Capital, and his challenges in attracting conservative support. The turning point came in late February, after the Michigan primary. Even though Romney won only narrowly in his home state, journalists reported that his nomination had become inevitable. The tone of his coverage then became more favorable, and the space given to his Republican rivals shrank. According to the Pew analysis, positive coverage of Romney jumped from 33 percent during January and February to 47 percent between the Michigan primary and April 15 (see Figure 5.1).[16]

Obama's coverage remained predominantly negative in tone, however (see Figure 5.2), due mainly to the steady barrage of criticisms leveled against him

Figure 5.1 Tone of Romney's Media Coverage, November 2011–May 2012

70
60
50
40
30
20
10
0
Percentage
10/31–11/6
11/14–11/20
11/28–12/4
12/12–12/18
12/26–1/1
1/9–1/15
1/23–1/29
2/6–2/12
2/20–2/26
3/5–3/11
3/19–3/25
4/2–4/8
4/16–4/22
4/30–5/6
Negative tone
Positive tone

Note: The data are derived from coding of 11,000 news websites around the United States and the full public feed of tweets on Twitter. Coverage judged to be neutral is not shown. Positive, negative, and neutral coverage add up to 100 percent.

Source: Data made available by Pew Research Center's Project for Excellence in Journalism, using Crimson Hexagon Technology, http://features.journalism.org/campaign-2012-in-the-media/tone-of-news-coverage/.

Figure 5.2 Tone of Obama's Media Coverage, November 2011–May 2012

60
50
40
30
20
10
0
Percentage
10/31–11/6
11/14–11/20
11/28–12/4
12/12–12/18
12/26–1/1
1/9–1/15
1/23–1/29
2/6–2/12
2/20–2/26
3/5–3/11
3/19–3/25
4/2–4/8
4/16–4/22
4/30–5/6
Negative tone
Positive tone

Note: The data are derived from coding of 11,000 news websites around the United States and the full public feed of tweets on Twitter. Coverage judged to be neutral is not shown. Positive, negative, and neutral coverage add up to 100 percent.

Source: Data made available by Pew Research Center's Project for Excellence in Journalism, using Crimson Hexagon Technology, http://features.journalism.org/campaign-2012-in-the-media/tone-of-news-coverage/.

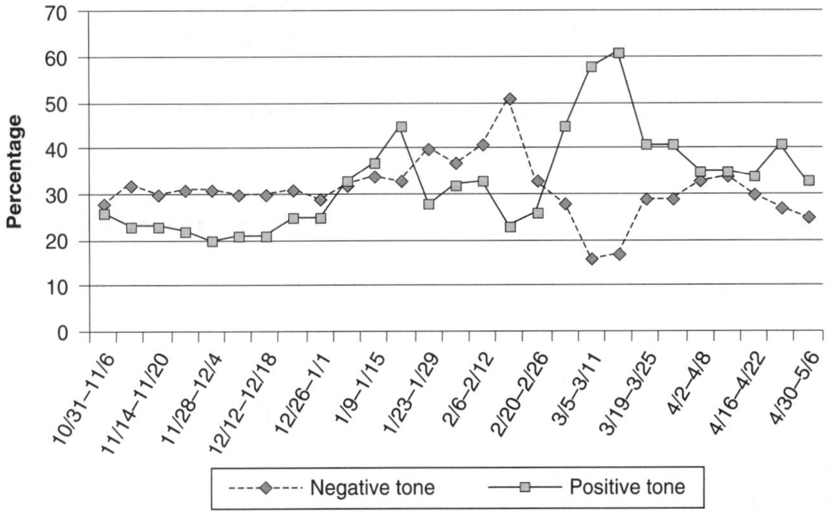

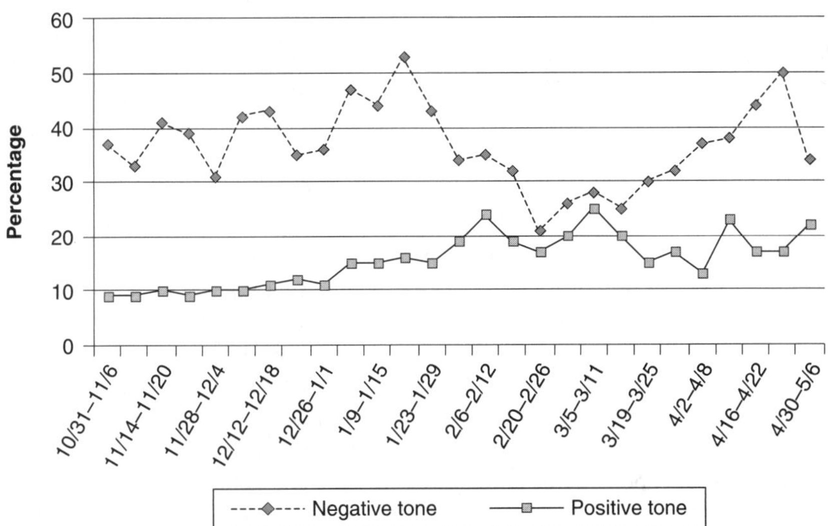

during this time by candidates for the Republican nomination. These criticisms dealt especially with the 2010 health care reform law, rising gas prices, continuing high rates of unemployment, and Obama's handling of the economy.

Through the Parties' National Conventions

The news for both campaigns got worse in the summer. During the ten weeks preceding the national conventions in August, coverage of the two presidential candidates on network TV, cable, radio, newspaper, and online major news outlets was "as negative as any campaign in recent times, and neither candidate has enjoyed an advantage over the other."[17] Of the stories and posts classified as negative or positive in tone, almost three-quarters of both candidates' coverage was negative at this time.

The Romney campaign was facing a growing drumbeat of criticism from within his own party. Some of this "friendly fire" contended that Romney was failing to drive home his charges against the administration. Conversely, others blamed Romney for criticizing Obama without making Romney's own agenda clear. Many liberal voices agreed that Romney's issue stands were difficult to pin down. As a *New York Times* writer had earlier jibed, "Frustrating as it may be, the rules of quantum campaigning dictate that no human being can ever simultaneously know both *what* Mitt Romney's current position is and *where* that position will be at some future date. This is known as the 'principle uncertainty principle.'"[18]

As these varied claims indicate, the characterization of Romney in the overall media coverage was negative but diffuse. The most frequent narratives were that he was a "vulture" (rather than venture) capitalist who didn't empathize with workers (14 percent), too rich and elite to understand the average American (13 percent), and an awkward campaigner (11 percent) whose policies would hurt the economy (10 percent).[19] Interestingly, although Romney was the first Mormon to become his party's candidate for president, media coverage rarely took note of that fact. In contrast, coverage in 2008 dwelled on the fact that Barack Obama was the first serious black presidential candidate.[20] Perhaps journalists felt that the controversy over Romney's religion had already been dealt with when he had run for the Republican nomination in 2008. More likely, breaking the racial barrier in a presidential contest seemed more historic than again departing from the once-powerful norm that only Protestants could be elected president.

The narrative about Obama during the summer was much more focused, centering on his handling of the nation's economic performance. The most frequent theme was that his policies had not improved the economy (about 36 percent of references) but on the other hand (and about half as frequently—16 percent), that most Americans would be even worse off without these policies. Next most frequent was the curious question as to whether Obama really believed in American values, such as individualism and capitalism (11 percent). (This theme often cited a partial quote from an Obama speech about the importance of government in stimulating business growth: "If you've got a business, you didn't build that.") These three themes comprised about two-thirds of all the mentions of Obama during this time. Thus, viewers and readers were exposed to a more uniform portrayal of the president than they were of Romney.

Again we find that different media outlets portrayed the two candidates differently. Fox carried about six times more negative (86 percent) than positive (14 percent) assessments of Obama's character and accomplishments, though its coverage of Romney was mixed rather than predominantly positive. MSNBC tilted in the opposite direction (88 percent negative to 12 percent positive) on Romney, with mixed coverage of Obama.[21] However, the tone of the coverage remained predominantly negative in all types of media platforms.

One way for a candidate to combat this negative coverage is to address citizens directly. Social media and websites make this possible. As in 2008, the Obama campaign started the race with a more sophisticated online and electronic presence than any of his rivals. In June 2012, for instance, Obama's campaign posted almost four times more digital content than Romney's campaign did, issuing an average of twenty-nine tweets a day, compared with one for Romney.[22] The Romney campaign moved to generate an online campaign soon after the close of the primaries. But Obama's head start was difficult to overcome; by mid-July, the president's campaign had 27 million supporters on Facebook, while Romney had 2 million.[23]

Both campaigns relied extensively on microtargeting to use these and other contact tools effectively. To microtarget, an organization gathers hundreds of pieces of information about individual voters—what they buy, what issues concern them, even what websites they visit—not only from public opinion polls but also from supermarkets' and other stores' loyalty and frequent shopper cards, the party's own canvassers, and the tracking of individuals' Internet surfing that is done routinely by websites. By analyzing these individuals' characteristics and preferences, campaigns can send specific types of appeals to the types of individuals most likely to respond to those appeals. For instance, the Obama campaign's data mining showed that if the campaign were to offer prospective donors a chance to have dinner with a Hollywood star, West Coast females between the ages of and forty-nine were most likely to respond positively if the star in question were George Clooney. These techniques permit a campaign to personalize a message in a way that network television advertising cannot, and often at less expense.

One simple application of microtargeting uses online searches. When you enter a candidate's name into your browser, or a search term identified with that candidate, the campaign's media buyers can then place an ad next to your search. The ad can be targeted more narrowly by using additional information they have obtained about you, such as whether you are young or older, or drive a Prius or a pickup, to present an appeal likely to induce you to donate money or support the candidate. And the campaign has to pay for the ad only if you actually click on it, which makes it cost-effective.[24] Or a campaign can use your browsing history to identify your interest in a candidate and then attach the candidate's pop-up ad to any video you request on YouTube. Because Internet users are increasingly watching TV programs online, this has become fertile ground for campaign strategists to till.

Republicans had been the pioneers in microtargeting, adapting it from businesses' market research in the early 2000s, but the Obama campaign developed much more sophisticated forms of the technique than the Romney campaign did.[25] Obama's website also permitted visitors to access content tailored to their own state and invited them to join one or more constituency groups, such as young Americans, women, Latinos, or veterans and military families. Those who clicked on a group would then receive continuing information aimed at that constituency. The Romney website followed suit in August, but targeted only half as many groups and directed users to a specific web page rather than sending ongoing messages to those users.

The volume of these messages foreshadowed the avalanche of political ads that was about to descend on viewers and readers in battleground states. During July alone, for instance, even before the parties had officially nominated their candidates, citizens of the small industrial town of Mansfield, Ohio, were the targets of more than 12,000 presidential campaign ads: nearly 400 per day, or 16 each hour.[26] It was an unprecedented ad assault, driven in part by the flotilla of independent spenders unleashed by the *Citizens United* and *SpeechNOW* court decisions permitting corporations, unions, and other groups to raise and spend unlimited funds on ads that were ostensibly independent of the campaigns themselves (see Chapter 6).

The General Election Campaign Begins

In this first phase of the general election campaign, media coverage of both candidates remained negative—especially Romney's. This was true even during each candidate's nominating convention, when he would star in a carefully staged presentation of his greatest strengths. Only the mainstream media offered a very brief respite—the traditional "convention bounce"—from the negativity. In social media, it was more like a convention bust. The tone of Obama's coverage on Facebook was three-to-one negative during the Democratic convention. Romney's coverage was negative to a similar degree on both Facebook and Twitter during the week he was named the Republican presidential candidate.[27]

Media coverage of Romney was at its lowest ebb in the month between the Republican convention and the first presidential debate. So was his campaign. The list of the candidate's stumbles kept growing. In the summer, Romney insulted Great Britain while visiting the London Olympics by raising questions about its security preparations. During the Republican convention, rising GOP star Chris Christie gave the keynote speech mainly about Chris Christie, and Clint Eastwood had a quirky conversation with an empty chair that overshadowed Romney's acceptance speech. After the U.S. ambassador to Libya was killed weeks later in an attack on the American embassy, Romney was widely criticized for speaking out immediately to blame Obama even though only scanty details of the story had yet been told. The most devastating blow was the release of a tape, secretly recorded, in which Romney told campaign donors that 47 percent of voters would never support him because they felt entitled to government subsidy, so his job was "not to worry about those people." On blogs, the tone of Romney's coverage deteriorated, from two-to-one negative during the last week in August to four to one in late September. Even the mainstream media's coverage of Romney, which had long been more positive than in blogs or social media, became mixed. Obama's negative coverage also substantially outstripped the positive during this time.[28]

From the Debates until Election Day

Romney's decline was halted abruptly by the first presidential debate on October 3. That was probably inevitable. During his disastrous month of September, Romney had reached the danger point for a candidate: he had become the frequent butt of jokes on late-night talk shows. When Jay Leno and David Letterman find a candidate to be a good source of comedy material, popular culture has deemed the candidate all but hopeless. For example, readers of the website Politico saw this damning evaluation of the Republican candidate: "It isn't the chair or the ho-hum convention. Or the leaked video. Or Stuart Stevens. Or the improving economy. Or media bias. Or distorted polls. Or the message. Or Mormonism. It's Mitt. . . . Slowly and reluctantly, Republicans who love and work for Romney are concluding that for all his gifts as a leader, businessman and role model, he's just not a good political candidate in this era."[29]

Given the growing narrative that Romney was a bad candidate, even a laughingstock, it is difficult to imagine how he could have failed to perform much "better than expected" in his next opportunity to address the public directly. Nobody could have been as bad a candidate as the comedians were portraying. And Romney had debated other contenders for the Republican nomination regularly for almost a year. His candidacy had been honed and vetted since before the 2008 presidential race. To seal the verdict, Obama appeared to be listless and uninspired in the first debate.

At least in the traditional media, the debate shook up the narrative and introduced the second of three distinct phases in coverage of the general election campaign. A spate of headlines in the mainstream media and on blogs quickly claimed that the tide of the race had turned. As even the left-leaning Huffington Post website put it, "Romney was able to unambiguously win the first debate because Obama so clearly lost. . . . The impact of the first debate on the polls was almost instantaneous. A host of national polls showed Romney enjoying a significant bounce, closing Obama's lead and even gaining a slight advantage in some surveys."[30]

Romney's coverage in the mainstream media, which had been grim until the first debate, now took on new life. From late August until the first debate, only 11 percent of his coverage was positive in tone, compared with 44 percent negative (the rest was mixed). In the days right after the debate, his positive coverage rose to 32 percent, settling then at 20 percent overall between October 4 and 21 (compared with 30 percent negative and the remainder neutral). In response to this new narrative, Obama's stock sank after the first debate. His positive-to-negative ratio in coverage, which had been only slightly negative in September, turned very substantially negative in this second phase.[31]

The story changed again in the closing weeks of the campaign—the third phase of the coverage. As polls showed that Obama was continuing to hold a slight but persistent lead, reporting about Obama, led by the horse-race stories, became much more positive in tone. The president's lead in swing states, whose Electoral College votes would decide the election, was an important component of these stories.[32]

These three phases looked different on other media platforms than they did in the mainstream media, however. Immediately after the first debate, when the mainstream coverage was becoming more favorable to Romney, reaction in the Twitterverse still trended against him, and posts on Facebook were more closely divided.[33] Overall, coverage of both candidates on Twitter, Facebook, and blogs was considerably more negative from late August to late October than was coverage in the traditional media[34] (see Table 5.2). And during the final two weeks of the campaign, the Twitter feed again moved contrary to the mainstream media. Coverage on Twitter became less negative toward Romney, while Obama's coverage on blogs finally moved from negative to mixed.

All these data support the conclusion that what we see depends on what we watch. Individuals who watch or read one media platform are exposed to different coverage, in terms of the tone of the reporting or interpretation, than are those who use another media platform. Beginning in the summer of 2012, those whose information about the campaign came from social media saw a more negatively-toned picture of the presidential candidates than did those who were reading mainstream media.

The picture becomes even more varied when we examine the various outlets within a particular media platform. For instance, viewers of some ideologically oriented cable news channels were exposed to markedly different portrayals of the candidates than were viewers of other cable channels. On MSNBC during September and the first three weeks of October, there were

Table 5.2 Tone of Media Coverage of Obama and Romney, August 27–October 21, 2012

	Ratio of Negative to Positive Tone in Coverage of			
Media Platform	Obama	% Negative	Romney	% Negative
Mainstream Media	1.6	30	2.5	38
Blogs	2.3	44	2.6	46
Twitter	1.8	45	3.6	58
Facebook	2.2	53	2.7	62

Source: Calculated from Pew Research Center Project for Excellence in Journalism, "Winning the Media Campaign 2012," November 2, 2012, www.journalism.org/analysis_report/winning_media_campaign_2012.

almost twenty-four negative references to Mitt Romney for every positive reference; 71 percent of Romney's coverage on MSNBC was negative in tone. In contrast, on Fox News, Obama's coverage included almost eight negative references for every positive reference, with 46 percent of Fox's coverage negative in tone. And then it got more polarized. In the campaign's final week, none of MSNBC's stories on Romney carried a positive tone, and none of the network's Obama stories were negative. Fox's record was not as starkly biased, but it came close.

These findings are congruent with the fact that the viewership of Fox, MSNBC, CNN, and PBS (on *NewsHour*) became more differentiated by partisanship between 2000 and 2010. Fox's audience trended substantially more Republican during the decade, and the other three outlets trended more Democratic. The difference was even more marked among those who tell pollsters that they see a lot of political bias in news coverage. The gap between Democrats and Republicans in viewership of MSNBC increased from 4 percentage points among those who do not see a lot of media bias to 24 points among those who perceive a lot of bias, and the partisan gap among Fox viewers grew from 19 to 42 points.[35] In short, those who suspect that there is a lot of media bias are much more likely to enclose themselves inside a network that reflects their political views.

In fact, we can even identify differences in the tone of coverage within a given media outlet based on the time of day that an individual chooses to watch. Among those who are partial to network news programming, for instance, Pew found that those who watched the morning network news were exposed to a different perspective than were those who watched the evening network news. On the three networks' morning newscasts, the tone of Romney's coverage was somewhat more positive than Obama's. On the evening news programs, Obama's coverage was mixed, and Romney's leaned negative.[36]

The differences among media platforms extended to the content they carried. Although horse-race stories were a much less substantial portion of the 2012 general election media coverage (38 percent) than had been the case in 2008 (53 percent),[37] the mainstream media cut down on its diet of horse-race reporting more than did social media and blogs (see discussion in the following section).

Huffington Post and the Drudge Report versus the Associated Press

To uncover more of these differences among media outlets, we may compare a sample of campaign coverage in the Associated Press (AP) news wire—a pillar of the mainstream media—and the two most widely read websites containing news stories and blogs on politics: the left-leaning Huffington Post and the Drudge Report, which tilts to the right. In addition to the frames of each article or post, two measures of slant in the coverage are examined. The first involves the long-standing concern as to whether the language used by the reporter or poster was "colored" or biased in favor of or against Obama or Romney. The second analyzes, as Pew did, whether the overall tone of the article presented positive or negative news for either candidate's campaign.[38]

With regard to frame, as Figure 5.3 shows, the AP devoted substantially more of its coverage to public policy—stories in which domestic or foreign policy was the primary frame or theme—than did either of the blogs. Both the Drudge Report and the Huffington Post focused to a greater extent than did the AP on strategic or horse-race stories. For the AP, policy issues outweighed strategic stories by about two to one, whereas almost 45 percent of the coverage in both blogs was primarily about strategy. Note that little or none of the coverage in any of these outlets focused on the candidates' personal characteristics or their record in office, as important as these qualities are in the selection of a president. Thus, despite all the criticism of the mainstream media for its focus on horse-race stories, those who were exposed to the AP's coverage had the chance to learn more about policy issues than did those who read either of the two blogs.

As would be expected, journalists used much more colored language in blog posts than in the AP's coverage (see Figures 5.4a and 5.4b). Although neutral language was used in a majority of the articles or posts in all three media, nearly all of the AP's stories used neutral language, whereas between 25 percent and 40 percent of the blogs' posts contained biased terms. Most of the bias in the blog posts was directed at the opposing candidate. Negative terms for the opposition far outnumbered positive terms used to describe the blog's favored candidate. In the Drudge Report, articles containing negative language in the reporter's writing about Obama outnumbered those containing positive terms by a factor of seven to one. In the Huffington Post,

Figure 5.3 Frames in Campaign Coverage, July-November 2012

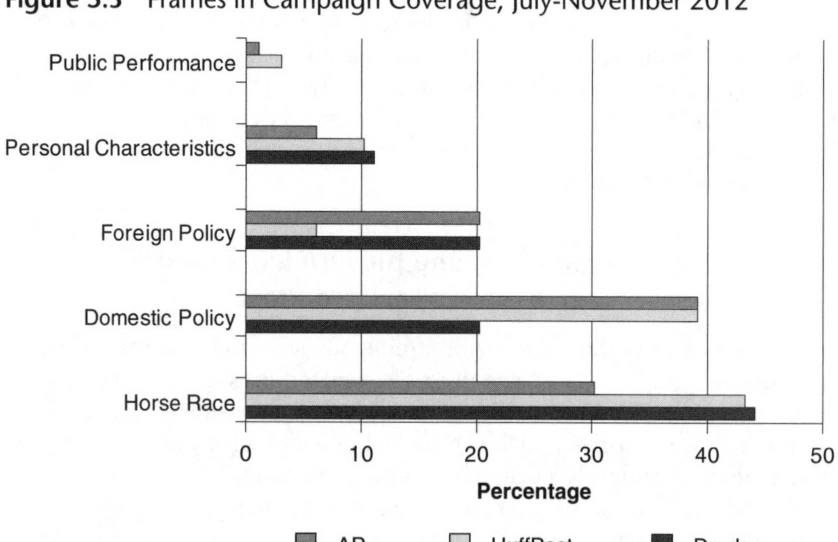

Source: Compiled by the author.

Figure 5.4a Language in Obama's Coverage, July–November 2012

AP
Huffington Post
Drudge
0
20
40
60
80
100
Percentage
Negative
Positive
Neutral

Source: Compiled by the author.

Figure 5.4b Language in Romney's Coverage, July–November 2012

AP
Huffington Post
Drudge
0
20
40
60
80
100
Percentage
Negative
Positive
Neutral

Source: Compiled by the author.

stories containing negative language in the reporter's writing about Romney swamped those containing positive terms by thirteen to one.

The three media outlets differed much more in the overall tone of their articles or posts (see Figures 5.5a and 5.5b).[39] Again, the greatest differences appeared in stories about the opposing candidate. In the Drudge Report,

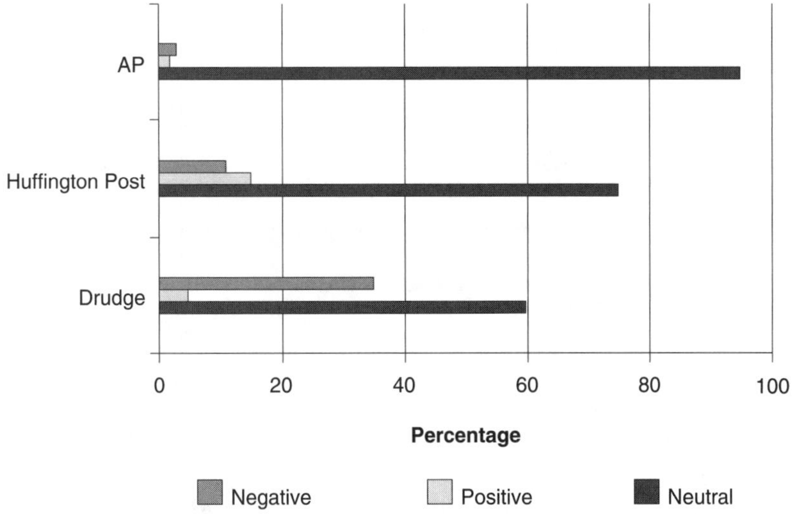

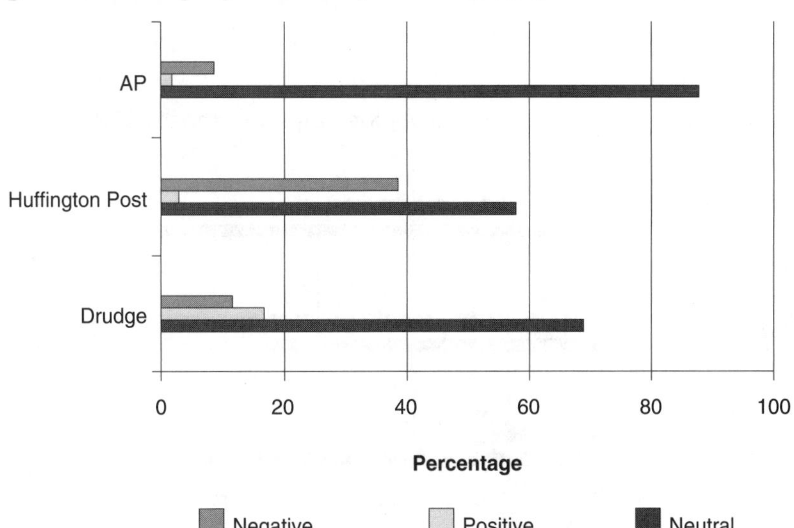

Figure 5.5a Tone of Obama's Coverage July–November 2012

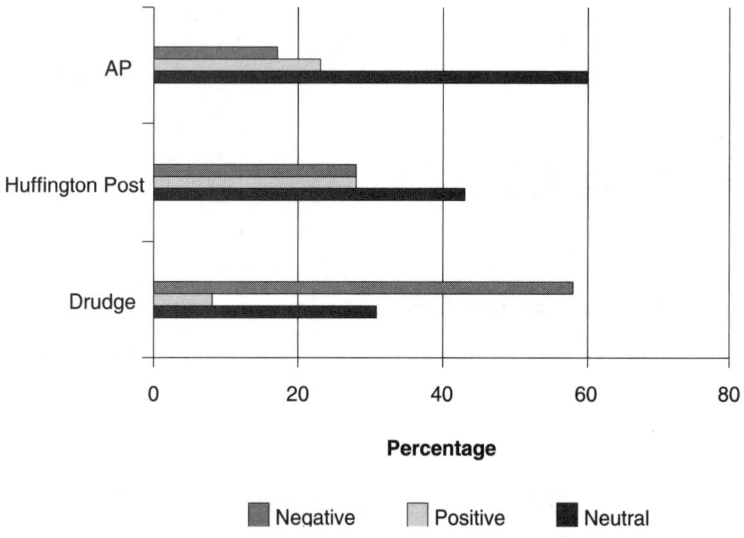

Source: Compiled by the author.

Figure 5.5b Tone of Romney's Coverage, July–November 2012

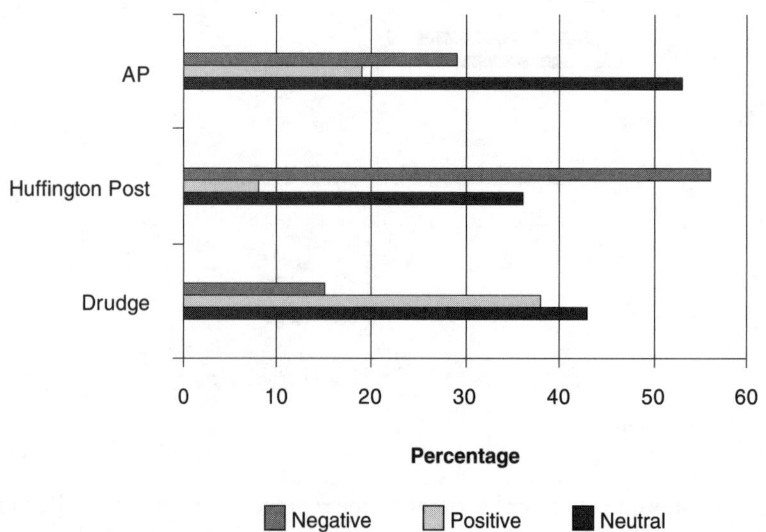

Source: Compiled by the author.

posts showing the Romney campaign in a favorable light outnumbered those showing him in a negative light by more than two to one. In Drudge stories mentioning Obama, negative news outweighed positive news by 58 percent to 8 percent, or seven to one. In contrast, the percentage of Huffington Post stories with good news about Obama exactly equaled the percentage with bad news, and 56 percent of the posts had bad news about Romney compared with only 8 percent that were favorable. Again, a larger proportion of the AP stories were neutral in tone. The AP's positive stories about Obama outdistanced negative stories by a small proportion. In stories about Romney, 19 percent of the AP stories were positive and 29 percent negative, often reflecting bad poll news for the Republican candidate.

In short, we see again that the audiences of different media outlets were exposed to different types of accounts of the campaign. Regular readers of the Huffington Post were presented with stories and columns that differed substantially, in both content and tone, from those presented to the audiences of the Drudge Report and the Associated Press. Although the language used by the journalists themselves was generally neutral in tone, the audience for the Drudge Report saw a series of stories whose overall tone was largely unfavorable toward Obama. Readers of the Huffington Post saw stories carrying primarily negative information about Romney, and those who saw AP's coverage were exposed to a much more even-handed perspective.

What Did the Election Mean?

As these differences in media interpretation indicate, campaign events and election results don't explain themselves. Campaigns, partisans, and media commentators promote their preferred explanations of any election result in order to build support for their agenda, and media outlets pick up on some of these explanations more than others.[40] Immediately after the votes were counted, journalists and activists constructed a series of explanations for Obama's victory.

The most conservative elements of the Republican Party—the Tea Party and its sympathizers—offered two explanations for Romney's loss. First, they suggested that he wasn't a very good candidate. Second, they argued, he shifted his positions on so many issues that conservatives did not trust him. In their view his moderate record as governor of Massachusetts was set aside during the Republican primaries in favor of very conservative positions on economic and social issues, only to return during the concluding month of the campaign, when he moderated his stands on immigration, cuts to social services, and other issues. In other words, Romney validated his adviser Eric Fehrnstrom's widely quoted statement about the campaign's intention to recast its stands after winning the nomination: "It's almost like an Etch A Sketch. You can kind of shake it up, and we start all over again."[41]

Other Republicans disagreed. Some argued that Romney lost because, as a son of privilege and a buyout specialist, he wasn't seen as being "on people's side." Romney's own post-election remarks encouraged this view; he charged that young people, women, blacks, and Latinos had voted for Obama in exchange for the "gifts" they had received from the president. Many analysts pointed to the demographics of the presidential vote and especially to the growing proportion of Hispanics and Latinos as well as blacks in the electorate. As Al Cardenas, a longtime Republican activist, summed up this view: "Our party needs to realize that it's too old and too white and too male and it needs to figure out how to catch up with the demographics of the country before it's too late."[42] Closely related was the explanation that several prominent Republican candidates for the Senate and other offices had made statements about abortion and rape that offended many people, particularly including women and younger voters.

Left-leaning outlets were often drawn to explanations of Obama's victory that featured his campaign's innovations in technology and voter targeting. Post-election interviews with campaign insiders touted the campaign's tactical wizardry as "elite talent," "world-class technologists," and "the most sophisticated email fundraising program ever."[43] The president's narrow margin of victory made it difficult for his supporters to claim overwhelming public enthusiasm for his policies. But the fact that Obama won reelection at all—in a long-term economic downturn, with a marginal public approval rating, a narrative ("Tea Party success!") that had moved against him, and a small but persistent proportion of voters who would not vote for him because of his race—led many to explanations based on strategy and tactics and to the missteps of his opposition, rather than to policy-based interpretations.

Conclusion

Does it make a difference that the overall tone of candidates' media coverage was negative, reflecting bad news about their campaigns rather than coverage of more favorable developments? It may make less difference than we assume. Keep in mind that during the period when Romney's coverage was the most dismal—his stumble-rich month of September—polls showed that Obama was able to open up a lead of only 3 or 4 percentage points, up from a single percentage point lead just prior to that time. So the negative tone of Romney's coverage may not have made much difference in his public approval—and in fact may have reflected a slight decline in his public approval rather than causing one.

Yet even if the tone of coverage doesn't change an election result, it could still have a major effect. The slant of the findings in some media outlets may have deprived their audiences of accurate information about the campaign. Commentators on many conservative blogs, Fox News, and other dominantly conservative outlets were predicting a sizable Romney victory in the weeks leading up to election day, contrary to the models of most other analysts. Even on the election night broadcast, Fox commentator and conservative strategist Karl Rove insisted that the network retract its projection of an Obama victory, citing a confidential tip from a Romney adviser that the network's projections were wrong. As one observer wrote,

> Barack Obama just trounced a Republican opponent for the second time. But unlike four years ago, when most conservatives saw it coming, Tuesday's result was, for them, an unpleasant surprise. So many on the right had predicted a Mitt Romney victory, or even a blowout . . . [or] scoffed at the notion that the election was anything other than a toss-up. . . . . Even Karl Rove, supposed political genius, missed the bulls-eye. These voices drove the coverage on Fox News, talk radio, the *Drudge Report,* and conservative blogs. Those audiences were misinformed.

That, the observer argued, produced a "self-imposed information disadvantage."[44] Partisans may enjoy hearing their beliefs validated, but inaccurate information did not help Republican supporters adapt their tactics to have a better chance of electing Mitt Romney.

The predominantly negative tone of the media coverage could also influence its audiences. Although the tone of coverage can vary a great deal from election to election, several recent campaigns (2004, for instance) have had similarly negative coverage, and in 2000, Al Gore's press was even more negative in tone than that of the 2012 campaigns.[45] Some portion of the negativity, of course, reflects the campaigners' own choices. Journalists regularly report about campaign ads, and the presidential candidates' TV ads in 2012 were more consistently negative (86 percent of Obama's ads and 79 percent of Romney's) than has been true of other recent presidential campaigns.[46]

During this same time, public approval ratings of Congress and other parts of government have dropped to a stunning degree. Congress's approval rating hit an all-time low of 10 percent on two occasions in 2012.[47] Virtually no one would argue that government has done nothing to deserve this public disgrace. But highly negative media coverage does little to encourage citizens to become more active in dealing with the problems that have been made so apparent to them. It does not excite people to learn more about government and politics or to support those who brave the shark-infested waters of American campaigns.

Finally, these findings that media outlets differ markedly in their campaign content and tone make it all the more important to determine the extent to which people selectively expose themselves only to media outlets that bolster their preexisting preferences. Research has shown that media interpretation can change people's views of events.[48] If viewers and readers choose to sample Fox News as well as the Huffington Post, then they may enrich the information that they receive from the more neutral mainstream media. But if most people embed themselves in "media silos" or "echo chambers" in which they hear nothing but reflections of their own preconceptions, then the polarization of American political life is likely to become even more entrenched. It would certainly be ironic if the explosion of information now available at a touch of a finger were to be matched by a large-scale retreat of political activists and informed citizens into the emotional comfort of a few like-minded media sources.

Notes

1. Pew Research Center's Project for Excellence in Journalism, "Internet Gains Most as Campaign News Source but Cable TV Still Leads," October 25, 2012, www.journalism.org/commentary_backgrounder/social_media_doubles_remains_limited.
2. Markus Prior, *Post-broadcast Democracy* (Cambridge, U.K.: Cambridge University Press, 2007), 37.
3. On "soft news," see Matthew A. Baum and Angela S. Jamison, "The *Oprah* Effect: How Soft News Helps Inattentive Citizens Vote Consistently," *Journal of Politics* 68, no. 4 (2006): 946–959.
4. Matthew A. Baum, "Talking the Vote: Why Presidential Candidates Hit the Talk Show Circuit," *American Journal of Political Science* 44, no. 2 (2005): 213–234.
5. See James T. Hamilton, *All the News That's Fit to Sell* (Princeton, N.J.: Princeton University Press, 2006) for a well-reasoned argument that changes in technology affecting the costs of news production are a major reason for the shifts over time in news content.
6. Markus Prior, "News vs. Entertainment," *American Journal of Political Science* 49, no. 3 (2005): 577–592.
7. Michael J. LaCour, "A Balanced News Diet, Not Selective Exposure: Evidence from a Direct Measure of Media Exposure," Paper prepared for the 2012 American Political Science Association Annual Meetings, http://ssrn.com/abstract=2110621.
8. See, for example, Silvia Knobloch-Westerwick and Jingbo Meng, "Reinforcement of the Political Self through Selective Exposure to Political Messages," *Journal of Communication* 61, no. 2 (2011): 349–368.
9. Pew Research Center's Project for Excellence in Journalism, "Twitter and the Campaign: The Candidates on Twitter," December 8, 2011, www.journalism.org/analysis_report/candidates_twitter; Pew's sample is discussed at www.journalism.org/about_news_index/methodology.
10. For details of the classification process, see "An Example," www.journalism.org/analysis_report/methodology_17.
11. Russell J. Dalton, Paul Allen Beck, and Robert Huckfeldt, "Partisan Cues and the Media," *American Political Science Review* 92, no. 1 (1998): 111–126.
12. Karen Tumulty, "Twitter Becomes a Key Real-time Tool for Campaigns," *Washington Post,* April 26, 2012, www.washingtonpost.com/politics/twitter-becomes-a-key-real-time-tool-for-campaigns/2012/04/26/gIQARf1TjT_story.html.
13. "Facebook's US User Growth Slows but Twitter Sees Double-digit Gains," eMarketer, March 5, 2012, www.emarketer.com/Article.aspx?id=1008879&R=1008879.
14. For example, see Marjorie Randon Hershey, "The Campaign and the Media," in Gerald M. Pomper, ed., *The Election of 2000* (New York: Chatham House, 2001), 46–72.
15. Tom Rosenstiel, Mark Jurkowitz, and Tricia Sartor, "How the Media Covered the 2012 Primary Campaign," April 23, 2012, Pew Research Center's Project for Excellence in Journalism, www.journalism.org/analysis_report/romney_report.
16. Rosenstiel et al., "How the Media."

17. Project for Excellence in Journalism, "The Master Character Narratives in Campaign 2012," August 23, 2012, www.journalism.org/analysis_report/2012_campaign_character_narratives.
18. David Javerbaum, "A Quantum Theory of Mitt Romney," *New York Times,* March 31, 2012, www.nytimes.com/2012/04/01/opinion/sunday/a-quantum-theory-of-mitt-romney.html?hp.
19. Project for Excellence in Journalism, "The Master Character Narratives."
20. See Marjorie Randon Hershey, "The Media: Coloring the News," in Michael Nelson, ed., *The Elections of 2008* (Washington, D.C.: CQ Press, 2009), 130–133.
21. Project for Excellence in Journalism, "The Master Character Narratives."
22. Project for Excellence in Journalism, "How the Presidential Candidates Use the Web and Social Media," August 15, 2012, www.journalism.org/analysis_report/how_presidential_candidates_use_web_and_social_media.
23. Philip Rucker, "Romney Advisers, Aiming to Pop Obama's Digital Balloon, Pump Up Online Campaign," *Washington Post,* July 13, 2012, www.washingtonpost.com/politics/romney-advisers-aiming-to-pop-obamas-digital-balloon-pump-up-online-campaign/2012/07/13/gJQAsbc4hW_story.html.
24. Beth Fouhy, "Campaigns Mine Online Data to Target Voters," Associated Press, May 28, 2012, www.google.com/hostednews/ap/article/ALeqM5g5IqenDmEunDOxRKNfQv7rYCScxA?docId=4a2481d5f77f4b53b326b8e62ce045e4.
25. See, for instance, Alexis C. Madrigal, "When the Nerds Go Marching In," *The Atlantic,* November 16, 2012, www.theatlantic.com/technology/archive/2012/11/when-the-nerds-go-marching-in/265325/.
26. David Nakamura, "Obama Campaigns in Ohio, a State Drowning in Political Ads," *Washington Post,* August 1, 2012, www.washingtonpost.com/politics/obama-campaigns-in-ad-saturated-swing-state-of-ohio/2012/08/01/gJQAT3f50X_story.html?hpid=z10.
27. Project for Excellence in Journalism, "How Social and Traditional Media Differ in Treatment of the Conventions and Beyond," September 28, 2012, www.journalism.org/commentary_backgrounder/how_social_and_traditional_media_differ_their_treatment_conventions_and_beyond.
28. Project for Excellence in Journalism, "How Social and Traditional Media Differ."
29. Mike Allen, Jonathan Martin, and Jim Vandehei, "In the End, It's Mitt," *Politico,* Sept. 28, 2012, www.politico.com/news/stories/0912/81772.html?hp=t1.
30. Ryan Grim and Sabrina Siddiqui, "Obama-Romney Debate Won by President," *Huffington Post,* October 17, 2012, www.huffingtonpost.com/2012/10/17/obama-romney-debate_n_1970693.html.
31. Project for Excellence in Journalism, "Winning the Media Campaign 2012," November 2, 2012, www.journalism.org/node/31438. During the first phase, from late August until the first debate, 22 percent of Obama's coverage had a positive tone and 27 percent was negative. (The rest was rated as neutral or mixed in tone.) Between the first debate and October 21, his negative coverage outweighed positive by 36 to 13 (with 51 percent neutral).
32. Project for Excellence in Journalism, "The Final Days of the Media Campaign 2012," November 19, 2012, www.journalism.org/analysis_report/final_days_media_campaign_2012.
33. Project for Excellence in Journalism, "Social Media Debate Sentiment Less Critical of Obama than Polls and Press Are," October 5, 2012, www.journalism.org/commentary_backgrounder/social_media_debate_sentiment_less_critical_obama_polls_and_press_are.
34. Project for Excellence in Journalism, "Winning the Media Campaign 2012."
35. Jonathan Ladd, untitled post, April 27, 2012, on "The Monkey Cage," http://themonkeycage.org/blog/2012/04/27/distrust-in-the-media-and-confirmation-bias.

36. Project for Excellence in Journalism, "Winning the Media Campaign 2012."
37. Ibid.
38. For details on the coding and examples of the types of language coded as positive or negative, and stories or posts coded as favorable or unfavorable, see the online appendix for this chapter at http://polisci.indiana.edu/docs/Nelson_appendix.pdf.
39. See also Matthew A. Baum and Tim Groeling, "New Media and the Polarization of American Political Discourse," *Political Communication* 25, no. 4 (2008): 345–365.
40. See Marjorie Randon Hershey, "Do Constructed Explanations Persist? Reframing of the 1994 Republican Takeover of Congress," *Congress and the Presidency* 38, no. 2 (2011): 131–151.
41. Quoted in Jackie Kucinich and Paul Singer, "Several Factors Were behind Romney's Loss," *USA Today,* November 8, 2012, p. 5A.
42. Jonathan Martin, "Election Aftermath: GOP Soul-searching: 'Too Old, Too White, Too Male'?" *Politico,* November 7, 2012, www.politico.com/news/stories/1112/83472.html?hp=t2_3.
43. Madrigal, "When the Nerds Come Marching In."
44. Conor Friedersdorf, "How Conservative Media Lost to the MSM and Failed the Rank and File," *The Atlantic,* November 7, 2012, www.theatlantic.com/politics/archive/2012/11/how-conservative-media-lost-to-the-msm-and-failed-the-rank-and-file/264855/# .
45. Project for Excellence in Journalism, "The Master Character Narratives."
46. Donovan Slack, "RIP Positive Ads in 2012," *Politico,* November 4, 2012, www.politico.com/news/stories/1112/83262.html?hp=13.
47. See the trend data linked to Jeffrey M. Jones, "U.S. Congress' Approval Rating at 21% Ahead of Elections," Gallup.com, October 24, 2012, www.gallup.com/poll/158372/congress-approval-rating-ahead-elections.aspx.
48. Kim L. Fridkin, Patrick J. Kenney, Sarah Allen Gershon, Karen Shafer, and Gina Serignese Woodall, "Capturing the Power of a Campaign Event," *Journal of Politics* 69, no. 3 (2007): 770–785.

6

Campaign Finance

*Campaigning in a Post–*Citizens United *Era*

Marian Currinder

Recent changes in the way federal campaigns are financed can be explained through the actions of one man: Sheldon Adelson. Worth over $21 billion, Adelson committed to spending $100 million by election day to defeat President Barack Obama in 2012. To put this in perspective, he vowed to contribute more campaign money in one year than sixty-five average Americans will earn in their combined lifetimes. What makes Adelson's pledge even more surprising is his support earlier in the presidential campaign for Newt Gingrich, who competed for the Republican nomination against Mitt Romney. After contributing $15 million to Gingrich's failed bid, the casino magnate switched candidates and backed Romney, an antigambling Mormon. As of September 2012, Adelson had already spent $70 million on Republican candidates and conservative causes. He entertained Republican "royalty" at the party's national convention in Tampa, had dinner with House Speaker John Boehner, had private meetings with House Majority Leader Eric Cantor and Republican vice presidential nominee Paul Ryan, hosted a $50,000-a-couple fundraiser in Jerusalem for Romney, and was seated front-and-center at a $1 million Las Vegas fundraiser for Romney. "I do whatever it takes," says Adelson, "as long as it's moral, ethical, principled, and legal."[1]

Thanks to recent Supreme Court decisions, Adelson's vast campaign spending was perfectly legal. In addition to contributing directly to candidates and their political action committees (PACs), individuals can make unlimited independent expenditures on behalf of candidates and causes. Now corporations and unions can, too. As a result, there are more legal outlets for campaign cash than ever before. Adelson's estimated $100 million investment in the 2012 campaign almost makes the $24 million George Soros spent trying to defeat President George W. Bush in 2004 seem quaint by comparison.

Every four years, new fundraising records are set. Every presidential race earns—then four years later, retires—the title of "most expensive in history." The escalating amount of campaign money spent in presidential and congressional races is as surprising as it is predictable. Less predictable is the means by which candidates and outside groups raise and spend record-breaking amounts of money. Campaign finance law is continually tested in court by those seeking new opportunities to influence electoral outcomes. The laws that govern federal campaign finance are fluid: what was illegal in the last campaign may be legal in the next.

Such was the case in the 2012 elections. This chapter examines post-2008 changes in the campaign finance landscape, and spending in the 2012 presidential and congressional races. As was the case in 2008, massive deficits, high unemployment, and a sluggish economy did not deter campaign spending. While candidates for federal office fought over how to best address looming financial disaster, donors forked over $6 billion in campaign money. We begin with a look at how the Supreme Court laid the groundwork for record-breaking campaign spending in 2012, then examine how the sources and uses of campaign funds in this election differ from previous elections.

Citizens United and SpeechNow.org: Independent Expenditures Move Front and Center

In his 2010 State of the Union address, President Obama rebuked the Supreme Court for overturning a century of campaign finance law. As he listened to the president's remarks, Justice Samuel Alito shook his head and mouthed the words, "not true." The exchange was a rare event, as presidents typically avoid direct confrontation with members of the Court, and justices avoid any public display of emotion. At issue was the Court's 5-4 decision in *Citizens United v. Federal Elections Commission.* The case took aim at the "electioneering communications" provision in the Bipartisan Campaign Reform Act (BCRA) of 2002. In 2008, Citizens United, a conservative nonprofit group, funded and filmed an anti-Hillary Clinton video. *Hillary: The Movie* was advertised as an on-demand video, but the Federal Elections Commission (FEC) ruled that the group had violated the law by running the video within thirty days of a primary and paying for it with its general treasury funds, rather than tightly regulated PAC funds. The Federal Elections Campaign Act of 1974 prohibited corporations and unions from using their treasury funds for independent expenditures; BCRA extended this prohibition to electioneering communications. Independent expenditures explicitly call for the election or defeat of a candidate, may run at any time, and must not be coordinated with a candidate's campaign. Electioneering communications (also known as issue advocacy) may not explicitly call for the election or defeat of a candidate, and cannot air within thirty days of a primary election or sixty days of a general election.

Citizens United deliberately paid for *Hillary: The Movie* with general treasury funds and ran the video within thirty days of a primary so that the violation would serve as a test case. In arguments before the Supreme Court, the FEC held that the video was a form of electioneering communications while Citizens United claimed that it was a form of free speech. Justice Ginsburg, who sided with the FEC, memorably declared that a corporation, unlike an individual, "is not endowed by its creator with inalienable rights." The Supreme Court usually decides cases on the narrowest possible legal grounds, but in *Citizens United*, the majority wrote a more expansive decision that encompassed aspects of the law not argued before the Court. Writing for the minority, Justice Souter was highly critical of the Court's majority—particularly its willingness to rule on issues not presented in litigation. Chief Justice John Roberts responded by withdrawing the case and ordering it reargued to clarify which provisions of the law could be considered.

Unsurprisingly, the re-argument of *Citizens United* did not change the minds of the Court's nine justices. In a 5-4 decision, the Court struck down the electioneering communications provisions of BCRA, thereby allowing corporations and unions to use their treasury funds to pay for independent expenditures and issue advocacy. As a result, corporations and unions can legally spend unlimited amounts of money on behalf of federal candidates, as long as they do not coordinate their efforts with candidate campaigns.

President Obama made a fair point during his 2010 State of the Union address. By allowing corporations and unions to spend unlimited amounts of money in federal elections, *Citizens United* represents a dramatic change in campaign finance law. Previously, such groups had to finance their political advertising with voluntary contributions raised by their PACs. But Justice Alito also made a fair point. Since 1904, it has been illegal for corporations and unions to contribute treasury funds directly to candidate campaigns. The *Citizens United* decision did not change this provision of the law. The Court reasoned that Congress can limit direct contributions to candidate campaigns, but cannot limit what individuals, corporations, and unions can say on their own, independently of a campaign.

Shortly after *Citizens United*, the U.S. Court of Appeals for the District of Columbia issued a decision that legalized a new player in the campaign finance game: the super PAC. In *SpeechNow.org v. Federal Election Commission,* the court ruled that contributions to PACs that make only independent expenditures cannot be limited. Most PACs make direct contributions to candidates, party committees, and other PACs and can accept up to $5,000 per year from individuals, party committees, and other PACs. Super PACs can accept unlimited contributions from corporations, unions, and individuals, and then use that money to advocate on behalf of federal candidates. Like regular PACs, super PACs have to disclose their contributions and expenditures to the FEC. And because super PACs operate in the realm of independent expenditures, they cannot coordinate with candidate campaigns.

The lines that separate candidate campaigns from the super PACs that support them can be extremely fuzzy, however. Republican presidential nominee Mitt Romney's campaign committee and Restore Our Future, the super PAC that has spent $143 million supporting him, both used the same consultant, and had offices in the same building, on the same floor. Several former Romney staffers founded Restore Our Future, including Charles Spies, Romney's general counsel in 2008, and Carl Forti, the 2008 Romney campaign's political director. Bill Burton and Sean Sweeny, two former Obama White House staffers, ran Priorities USA 2012, a super PAC that supported President Obama. Alixandria Lapp, a former Democratic Congressional Campaign Committee (DCCC) official, ran House Majority PAC, a Democratic super PAC. Both committees focused on electing Democrats to the House. The DCCC conveniently made its congressional ad-buy list publicly available this election cycle, presumably so super PACs could see where the committee was investing its money and follow suit. The appearance of coordination, apparently, was not a concern.

Super PACs are an extremely efficient campaign vehicle because there are no limits on what they can raise and spend. Some donors, however, are reluctant to give to a committee that is required to disclose all contributions. Fortunately for these donors, there are 501(c)(4) groups. The Internal Revenue Service (IRS), rather than the FEC, regulates these "nonprofit social welfare" groups and they do not have to disclose donors. The IRS says these groups "must be operated exclusively to promote social welfare," but they are allowed to spend money on electioneering and lobbying activities, provided that is not their "primary activity."

Because 501(c)(4) groups can give unlimited amounts of money to super PACs, they in effect provide donors with a way to "launder" their contributions en route to super PACs. For this reason, contributions from these groups are often referred to as "shadow money" or "dark money" because the source of the money is not transparent. Republican operatives Karl Rove and Ed Gillespie, for example, founded American Crossroads, one of the wealthiest, most active super PACs in the 2012 election. They also founded Crossroads Grassroots Policy Strategies (GPS), a 501(c)(4) that could (and did) contribute millions to their American Crossroads super PAC. But where GPS's money comes from is a mystery.

As of election day, there were 1,063 registered super PACs, reporting total receipts of $661 million and total independent expenditures of $619 million in the 2012 election.[2] Even comedian Stephen Colbert formed a super PAC, which raised more than $1.2 million, essentially to mock the current "anything goes" nature of political fundraising. Colbert shut down his super PAC after the 2012 election and released the following statement: "During this time of mourning, we ask that you respect our privacy, and more importantly, the privacy of our money. It wishes to stay out of the public eye, so please don't go trying to find it. Rest assured, you won't. We have a really good lawyer."[3]

Campaign finance law has traditionally emphasized the need to prevent corruption, reduce the influence of wealthy individuals, and enhance transparency in the electoral process. Reconciling these goals with the current system is increasingly difficult.

Unless changes occur in the membership of the Supreme Court, there is little chance of meaningful campaign finance reform. In June 2012, the Court summarily overturned a Montana law banning corporate spending in campaigns for state office. *American Tradition Partnership v. Bullock* was the first direct challenge to *Citizens United*. The Supreme Court of Montana upheld the state's ban (which had been in place since 1912), but the Court reversed the lower court's ruling, citing *Citizens United*.[4] Twenty-two other states and the District of Columbia ban corporate spending in political campaigns, so more cases like this one will certainly wind up before the Court.

So far, congressional responses to the Court's actions have been unsuccessful. The DISCLOSE (Democracy Is Strengthened by Casting Light on Spending in Elections) Act was introduced in 2010 to ban foreign owned corporations from making contributions, require more disclosure, and enhance transparency mechanisms. After it was revealed that the bill's sponsors had carved out an exception for the National Rifle Association, unions demanded a similar carve-out. The controversy ultimately led to the bill's defeat in the Senate. DISCLOSE 2, a bill that would require independent groups to disclose the names of donors who give $10,000 or more, was introduced by Sen. Sheldon Whitehouse (D-RI) in the 112th Congress, but failed on a procedural vote. Even if the bill had passed the Senate, House Republicans would not have brought it to the floor for a vote.

Senator Dick Durbin (D-IL), Rep. John Larson (D-CT), Rep. Walter Jones (R-NC), and Rep. Chellie Pingree (D-ME) reintroduced the Fair Elections Now Act in the 112th Congress. The act would provide public funding for candidates who first attract a predetermined number of small donations ($100 or less) from citizens in their states. Despite attracting over 100 cosponsors, the act is unlikely to go anywhere. Asking taxpayers to fund federal elections when Congress's approval ratings are at all-time lows and deficits are at all-time highs is probably not a winning political strategy. Indeed, a majority of House members in 2012 voted in favor of a bill to repeal the presidential public financing program. The bill's Senate companion, however, went nowhere. Table 6.1 lists current contribution limits for federal elections.

The *Citizens United* and *SpeechNow.org* decisions opened the floodgates to previously prohibited forms of fundraising and expenditures, allowing wealthy individuals like Sheldon Adelson to legally spend unlimited amounts of money on federal campaigns. He contributed to candidate campaigns, PACs, super PACs, 501(c)(4) groups, and Republican party committees—all in the name of doing "whatever it takes" to defeat President Obama. Ironically, Adelson does not believe one person should influence an election; he contributes because he believes that "other single people influence elections," and he wants to beat them at their own game.[5] Ultimately, Adelson's $100 million gamble did not pay off, proving that electoral politics can be an expensive game of chance. Indeed, never before has so much money been spent to maintain the political status quo. As was the

Table 6.1 Federal Contribution Limits 2011–12

	To Each Candidate or Candidate Committee per Election	To National Party Committee per Calendar Year	To State, District, and Local Party Committee per Calendar Year	To Any Other Political Committee per Calendar Year[a]	Special Limits
Individual may give	$2,500*	$30,800*	$10,000 (combined limit)	$5,000	$117,000* overall biennial limit: • $46,200* to all candidates • $70,800* to all PACs and parties[b]
National party committee may give	$5,000	No limit	No limit	$5,000	$43,100* to Senate candidate per campaign[c]
State, district, and local party committee may give	$5,000 (combined limit)	No limit	No limit	$5,000	No limit
PAC (multicandidate)[d] may give	$5,000	$15,000	$5,000 (combined limit)	$5,000	No limit
PAC (not multicandidate) may give	$2,500*	$30,800*	$10,000 (combined limit)	$5,000	No limit
Authorized campaign committee may give	$2,000[e]	No limit	No limit	$5,000	No limit

Source: Federal Elections Commission.

*These contribution limits are indexed for inflation.

[a]A contribution earmarked for a candidate through a political committee counts against the original contributor's limit for that candidate. In certain circumstances, the contribution may also count against the contributor's limit to the PAC. 11 CFR 110.6. See also 11 CFR 110.1(h).

[b]No more than $46,200 of this amount may be contributed to state and local party committees and PACs.

[c]This limit is shared by the national committee and the national Senate campaign committee.

[d]A multicandidate committee is a political committee with more than fifty contributors which has been registered for at least six months and, with the exception of state party committees, has made contributions to five or more candidates for federal office. 11 CFR 100.5(e)(3).

[e]A federal candidate's authorized committee(s) may contribute no more than $2,000 per election to another federal candidate's authorized committee(s). 11 CFR 102.12(c)(2).

case before the election, the Democrats control the White House and Senate and the Republicans control the House.

The Race for the White House

The *Citizens United* and *SpeechNow.org* decisions loomed large, making the 2012 presidential election the first in which outside money dominated the financial landscape. Before winning his party's nomination, Romney had to beat back challenges from an unusual number of fellow Republicans vying to take on President Obama. Romney had hoped to lock up the Republican nomination in early 2012, but thanks to the help of some very wealthy outside contributors, candidates like Newt Gingrich and Rick Santorum were able to drag out the nomination process until April 24, when Romney won the New York, Pennsylvania, Rhode Island, Delaware, and Connecticut primaries and became the party's presumptive nominee. Romney had the resources to far outraise and outspend his competition, but the protracted race forced him to spend a lot of money during the primaries and "run to the right" to compete with his more conservative challengers—disadvantages heading into the general election.

The Money Chase Begins. The field of candidates seeking the Republican nomination was as varied as it was expansive. Ten Republicans, including four current or former governors, five current or former members of Congress, and one business executive threw their hats in the ring.[6] Table 6.2 provides overall campaign finance data for the Republican candidates who ran unsuccessfully.

From the moment Mitt Romney announced his candidacy on June 2, 2011, he was considered the Republican front-runner. During his 2008 presidential bid, he raised over $107 million, second only to senator John McCain, who ultimately won the Republican nomination. He entered the 2012 race with a well-oiled fundraising machine, having kept his Free and Strong America PAC up and running after the 2008 election. The PAC raised $9.1 million and spent $8.7 million during the 2010 election.

July 15, 2011, marked the first campaign finance filing deadline for candidates who entered the 2012 presidential race.[7] At that point, the pool of Republican candidates included Mitt Romney, Ron Paul, Michele Bachmann, Tim Pawlenty, Herman Cain, Newt Gingrich, and Rick Santorum; together, they raised less than President Obama, who was running unchallenged for the Democratic nomination. Obama raised $42 million for his prenomination campaign, while the Republican candidates raised a combined $36 million.

These early reports provided a snapshot of the candidates' fundraising operations. Small donors (those who gave $200 or less) were the main drivers of Obama's, Bachmann's, and Paul's numbers. Romney, by contrast, relied heavily on large donors. Of the $18.2 million that Romney reported receiving during the first half of 2011, 89 percent came from donors who

Table 6.2 Summary Data for Unsuccessful Republican Presidential Candidates

Candidate	Total Raised	Total Spent	Individual Contributions	PAC Contributions	Self-financing	Federal Funds	Other
Michele Bachmann	$9,244,228	$8,885,504	$7,236,396	$7,500	$0	$0	$2,000,332
Herman Cain	$16,227,060	$16,208,566	$15,892,455	$18,832	$275,000	$0	$40,772
Newt Gingrich	$23,616,988	$23,582,988	$23,185,680	$74,323	$0	$0	$356,985
John Huntsman	$8,814,088	$8,812,224	$3,646,875	$24,982	$5,139,481	$0	$2,750
Thad McCotter	$547,389	$540,315	$78,577	$250	$0	$0	$468,562
Tim Pawlenty	$5,151,118	$5,151,118	$4,911,448	$133,816	$0	$0	$105,854
Ron Paul	$40,627,094	$39,329,241	$39,618,285	$2,670	$0	$0	$1,006,139
Rick Perry	$19,707,936	$19,306,876	$19,438,435	$250,380	$0	$0	$19,121
Rick Santorum	$22,358,245	$22,228,998	$22,241,810	$67,340	$0	$0	$49,095

Based on data downloaded from the Federal Election Commission on October 25, 2012.

Source: The Center for Responsive Politics.

gave $1,000 or more. And three-quarters of the money Romney raised came from donors who maxed out—that is, gave the legal maximum an individual can donate to a candidate—with contributions of $2,500. Pawlenty raised 79 percent of his money from donors who gave $1,000 or more, and 62 percent of his overall funds came from donors who maxed out.[8] Small donors, as President Obama adeptly demonstrated in 2008, provide candidates with a resource they can continue to tap over the course of a campaign. Romney's early reliance on large donors meant that he would have to keep finding new donors as his campaign moved forward.

By October 2011, when the third campaign finance filing deadline of the year rolled around, Texas governor Rick Perry had entered the race and proved himself a worthy challenger to Mitt Romney on the fundraising front. Like Romney, Perry attracted large donors; in fact, 80 percent of the money he collected in his first quarter as a candidate came from donors who maxed out. Romney continued to attract support from large donors, collecting 74 percent of his third quarter haul from individuals who gave $1,000 or more. Both Perry and Romney reported about $15 million in cash on hand—considerably more than the rest of the Republican pack.

Ron Paul finished the third quarter of 2011 with $3.7 million in cash on hand and continued to find support among small donors. Michele Bachmann and Herman Cain each wrapped up the third quarter with about $1.3 million in cash on hand. The remaining Republican candidates reported having less than $500,000 in the bank. Like Paul, Bachmann, and Cain, President Obama continued to rely heavily on small contributions. Of the President's third quarter contributions, 60 percent came from donors who gave $200 or less.[9] Obama raised about $39 million in the third quarter, bringing his cash on hand total to $61 million.

Heading into the 2012 primary and caucus season, some clear fundraising patterns had emerged. Mitt Romney and Rick Perry were relying heavily on donors who were maxing out, while the other Republican candidates were collecting most of their money from small donors. In previous presidential elections, the Romney and Perry "large donor strategy" might have raised red flags, simply because both candidates were burning through money from contributors who could no longer give. But thanks to the Supreme Court, Romney and Perry could redirect maxed out contributors to super PACs. For this reason, candidate campaign finance reports presented an incomplete picture of what the financial landscape really looked like.

Most super PACs are required to disclose their fundraising and spending numbers to the FEC twice per year, on January 31 and June 30. This meant that the candidates entered the January races without knowing how much money the competition really had on hand. By late 2011, most of the presidential candidates were backed by super PACs, but just how much these committees intended to spend was a mystery. The January 31 filings revealed that the pro-Romney super PAC, Restore Our Future, raised $30.2 million in 2011. Most of Restore Our Future's money came from donors with ties to the financial and real estate industries, including a few million-dollar donors with ties to Bain Capital, the equity fund that Romney once ran.[10] Over one-quarter of the PAC's contributions came from corporations that would not have been able to give prior to the *Citizens United* decision.

Make Us Great Again, a pro-Perry super PAC, raised $5.5 million in 2011, 32 percent of which came from corporate contributors. The rest of Make Us Great Again's money came mostly from wealthy individuals, as did almost all of the money raised by super PACs supporting Newt Gingrich, Rick Santorum, and Ron Paul. Meanwhile, Priorities USA Action PAC, a pro-Obama super PAC, closed out 2011 with $4.4 million, $1 million of which came from the Service Employees International Union.[11] Republicans were ahead of the curve on super PACs; by the end of 2011, Democrats were racing to catch up.

Primary and Caucus Season Begins, and Outside Spending Commences. Mitt Romney cemented his front-runner status with victories in Iowa and New Hampshire. Having raised a total of $56.7 million in 2011, he also established himself as the financial leader of the shrinking GOP pack. Although impressive, Romney's 2011 totals came nowhere near the $118.8 million that President Obama raised, half from small donors. Just nine percent of Romney's 2011 contributions came from small donors.[12]

With Michele Bachmann, Rick Perry, Herman Cain, and John Huntsman out of the race by January 2012, Romney believed he was closing in on the nomination. His early success also came courtesy of the $7.8 million Restore Our Future spent in the first two weeks of 2012. The PAC spent millions in Iowa attacking Newt Gingrich. Even though Romney appeared at a fundraiser for Restore Our Future, he claimed he had nothing to do with the committee's ads and was powerless to stop them. Romney and the other Republican candidates continued to run their own ads (with the legally required "stand by your ad" cameos), but super PAC advertising far surpassed candidate ads in both number and negativity.[13]

Super PACs spent more than $15 million on behalf of Republican candidates in Iowa and New Hampshire. Heading into the South Carolina primary, these committees were outspending the candidates by a two-to-one margin, which gave Newt Gingrich and Rick Santorum a chance to break Romney's run. The largest contributor by far was Sheldon Adelson, who gave $5 million to Winning Our Future, a pro-Gingrich super PAC. Winning Our Future made headlines for attacking Romney in a series of ads that were riddled with inaccuracies. Gingrich distanced himself from the super PAC, but clearly benefited from the committee's anti-Romney advertising. On January 21, the second anniversary of the *Citizens United* decision, Newt Gingrich won the South Carolina primary, thereby delaying Romney's plans to quickly wrap up the nomination.

At the end of January, Mitt Romney continued to lead the GOP pack in fundraising. For the first time, however, Newt Gingrich, Rick Santorum, and Ron Paul reported one-month fundraising totals that came close to matching Romney's. While the other candidates attracted contributions from small donors, Romney continued to rely on big givers. Donors who gave $1,000 or more made up 81 percent of Romney's money, and 40 percent of his donors had maxed out by January 31, 2012. Obama's January 2012 numbers showed continued support from small donors; in fact, 88 percent of those who gave in January had already made one or more contributions to his reelection campaign.[14]

Fundraising reports for February 2012 continued the already established patterns: Mitt Romney raised more money—$12 million—and had more cash on hand than his Republican rivals. Large donors continued to supply most of Romney's campaign cash; in fact, his campaign managed to find 2,479 new donors to max out in February. Santorum's campaign was given a boost when he performed well in a few February primaries. Half of the $8.9 million he raised came from small donors. Santorum and Ron Paul each finished February with about $1.5 million in cash on hand, while Romney checked in with $7.3 million. And in what would become an indicator of the overall direction his campaign was headed, Newt Gingrich reported $500,000 more in debt than cash. President Obama reported $67.7 million in cash on hand, putting him way ahead of his Republican challengers.[15]

As the race for the Republican nomination dragged on, super PACs began to increasingly pick up the fundraising slack. Because many major Republican donors opted to sit on the sidelines until a nominee was chosen, the candidates had a hard time keeping their campaign coffers flush. Romney spent more than he raised in February, as did Newt Gingrich. As the flow of money to candidate committees slowed, the campaigns were forced to cut back on spending in states that had yet to vote. In states like Georgia, Idaho, and Ohio, super PACs stepped in to fill the void and outspent candidate committees. Romney spent about $1.1 million in Illinois, while Restore Our Future spent $2.5 million. The Red White and Blue Fund, a pro-Santorum super PAC, outspent Santorum's campaign by about $100,000 in Illinois. And leading up to the March 13 Mississippi primary, Gingrich's campaign spent about $20,000 in the state while Winning Our Future spent $250,000.[16] By mid-March, super PACs supporting individual presidential candidates reported spending just over $80 million in the prenomination campaign.[17] Table 6.3 lists presidential candidate super PAC receipts and expenditures through April 30, 2012.

After finishing behind Mitt Romney in the April 3 Wisconsin, Maryland, and D.C. primaries, Rick Santorum officially ended his campaign for the Republican presidential nomination. He had been Romney's most successful opponent, winning eleven states, but he failed to broaden his appeal beyond the South. Two weeks later, as more and more Republican leaders lined up behind Romney and urged an end to the difficult and expensive nomination contest, Newt Gingrich ended his troubled, debt-ridden

Table 6.3 Presidential Candidate Super PAC Receipts and Independent Expenditures, Through April 30, 2012

Super PAC	Candidate Supported	Total Receipts	Independent Expenditures
Priorities USA Action	Obama	10,578,305	2,221,371
Restore Our Future and Citizens for a Working America	Romney	56,968,493	42,965,013
Winning Our Future and Strong America Now	Gingrich	24,157,390	17,214,733
Red White and Blue Fund and Leaders for Families	Santorum	8,635,733	7,650,152
Endorse Liberty, Santa Rita, and Revolution	Paul	5,320,143	3,951,694
Make Us Great Again	Perry	5,585,945	3,959,824
Our Destiny	Huntsman	3,189,064	2,804,234
9-9-9 Fund	Cain	617,670	418,445

Source: The Campaign Finance Institute.

campaign. Ron Paul remained in the race, but because he had not won any primaries or caucuses, he did not pose a threat to Romney's eventual nomination.

The General Election Begins, While Outside Money Continues to Flow

After emerging from a long, acrimonious nomination campaign as the Republican presidential candidate, Mitt Romney turned in his worst fundraising numbers since January. The Romney campaign raised $11.7 million in April, less than the $12 million raised in February and the $13.1 million raised in March. Romney's relatively weak showing in April, his first month as the party's presumptive nominee, may have been a temporary side effect of the prolonged primary campaign. Indeed, many Republicans seemed to greet his nomination with relief rather than enthusiasm.

The April 2012 campaign finance reports for Mitt Romney and President Obama foreshadowed their fundraising strengths and weaknesses as they geared up for a general election in which, for the first time, both candidates rejected public financing (and the fundraising restrictions that come with it). Obama reported raising $26.6 million in April, bringing his cash on hand to $82 million—approximately ten times more than the $8.5 million Romney had in the bank. The president continued to rely heavily on small donors, collecting 43 percent of his April take from those giving $200 or less. Of the $11.7 million that Romney raised in April, only 10 percent came from small donors.

The level of small donor giving can be a proxy for voter enthusiasm, which is why Romney's failure to attract these donors was a concern. In the 2008 election, Obama was able to recruit thousands of his small donors to volunteer for his campaign. He was also able to "return to the well" multiple times with many of these donors, encouraging them to give more and get involved. In 2004, both President George W. Bush and Democratic presidential nominee John Kerry saw a spike in small donor contributions after Kerry became the presumptive Democratic nominee.[18] With the nomination behind him, Romney could return to donors who maxed out in the primary campaign and ask them to max out again, in the general campaign. But his continuing inability to build a broad network of enthusiastic small donors made it difficult for him to compete with Obama's extensive on-the-ground operation later in the campaign.

President Obama's potential vulnerabilities were tied to the fundraising ability of his party and supportive super PAC. The president's joint fundraising committee helped the Democratic National Committee (DNC) raise $185.8 million through April 30, 2012, which is more than twice as much as the DNC raised through April in 2004 and 2008.[19] Joint fundraising committees provide candidates with a way to raise money for both their campaigns and parties. Donors write one check, and then the money is divided between the candidate and various party committees. The Republican National Committee (RNC) reported raising $135.1 million. The problem was that the DNC had higher expenditures and more debt, leaving the committee with just $24.3 million in cash on hand, compared to the RNC's $34.8 million. And while the DNC included joint fundraising dollars in its report, the RNC did not; actually, the RNC had about $52 million in the bank. Party money matters because the party committees can spend unlimited amounts on independent campaigning, and on grassroots efforts.[20]

Romney's campaign also was set to benefit from a lot of super PAC spending. During the primary campaign, Restore Our Future raised a total of $56.5 million and spent $46.5 million. Once the general election got underway, a number of other super PACs stepped up to the plate and vowed to spend millions to help Romney get elected. Meanwhile, the pro-Obama super PAC, Priorities USA, reported raising only $10.6 million through April 30.

Because super PACs were a relatively new weapon in the campaign finance arsenal, candidates did not have a well-developed sense of how super PAC spending might help (or hurt) their campaigns. In the primaries, most super PACs went negative from the start and spent their money running attack ads. By allowing super PACs to do their "dirty work," candidates could remain above the fray and focus on more positive messages.

Having no control over the messages that super PACs broadcast can, however, present problems for candidates. Newt Gingrich went to great lengths to separate his campaign from the Sheldon Adelson–funded super PAC that ran erroneous attack ads against Mitt Romney in the South Carolina primary. And Romney publicly criticized a super PAC that planned to spend millions rehashing the controversy over President Obama's former minister, Jeremiah Wright. Because independent spending can be a mixed blessing, candidates prefer money they can directly control. By this measure, President Obama had an early advantage.

The May 2012 campaign finance reports contained no major surprises—President Obama continued to outraise Mitt Romney, and to collect more money from small donors than from large donors. Romney raised twice as much as he did in April, collecting $23.4 million, but did not come close to matching Obama's haul of $39.8 million. On the other hand, the DNC did not come close to matching the RNC's May fundraising total of $34.3 million. The DNC raised $20 million.[21]

The following month, Romney finally started to make some headway with small donors. Of the $33.8 million he collected in June 2012, 29 percent came from contributors who gave $200 or less. Romney's campaign reported an uptick in small donations right after the Supreme Court upheld the Affordable Care Act—President Obama's signature legislative achievement. While Romney welcomed the effect the Court's decision seemed to have on fundraising, so did President Obama. His campaign collected $18.6 million in small donations, and $49.2 million overall. Heading into the long summer months, though, Romney had more total cash on hand. Obama consistently outraised Romney, but the party committees and super PACs backing Romney were much more flush than those supporting the president.[22] How much of an advantage this would be for Romney was unclear because the "super PAC effect" was still a new phenomenon.

The fundraising patterns established early on by both candidates and their various support committees held for most of the general campaign. The small donor strategy that the Obama campaign first developed in the 2008 race, and further refined in 2012, paid off in the final months leading up to election day. By the end of August, Obama had collected $147 million (34 percent of his total receipts) in small contributions, $26 million more than he had raised from small donors through August 2008. Romney reported raising $39.5 million (18 percent of his total receipts) from small donors. Obama also did well with wealthy donors, collecting $66.2 million from contributors who maxed out. Romney reported total contributions from maxed out donors at $61 million.[23] Wealthy donors more or less split their support between the candidates while small donors clearly favored the president.

As in previous months, Romney continued to reap the benefits of RNC and super PAC fundraising and spending. The joint fundraising committee he established with the RNC raised \$67.4 million in August, much more than the \$39.5 million the president's joint committee raised. And the RNC raised \$17.3 million—almost four times more than the \$4.7 million raised by the DNC. At the end of August, the Romney campaign and affiliated committees had about \$46.5 million more in cash on hand than President Obama. In addition, Romney's super PAC, Restore Our Future, had about \$1.4 million more in cash on hand than Priorities USA Action, the pro-Obama super PAC.[24]

Moving into the final stretch, both candidates began a late push to raise tens of millions of dollars. Romney's team hoped to finance around-the-clock advertising in battleground states like Florida and Ohio, where Romney appeared to be surging. The president's campaign had bombarded the airwaves all summer. Picking up where Romney's primary opponents left off, the Obama team portrayed the Republican candidate as a wealthy, out-of-touch venture capitalist. A number of Republican strategists criticized Romney for not fighting back. They feared that his strategy of holding back on ad spending during the summer months was allowing the president to define Romney and the Republican agenda.

As the race grew closer, the Romney team's final-hour fundraising and spending frenzy seemed to pay off. Heading into the final month of campaigning, Romney and the RNC reported \$169 million in cash on hand. Perhaps due to his strong performance in the first presidential debate on October 3, Romney and his supporting committees raised a whopping \$112 million in the first two weeks of the month alone. Seeking to capitalize on this momentum, the campaign organized a three-day retreat for big-money donors at the Waldorf-Astoria hotel in New York City. The retreat was designed to recruit new donors, while encouraging old ones to give more. Participants were treated to a debate watching party, emceed by comedian Dennis Miller. As a follow-up to the New York retreat, the campaign held a star-studded "Republicanpalooza" in Park City, Utah, a center of Romney's support among fellow Mormons. The entrance fee of \$50,000 bought participants dinner and drinks with campaign and party officials, as well as access to a number of panel discussions and seminars.[25]

Meanwhile, the Obama campaign and the DNC reported \$104 million in cash on hand, with virtually all of it raised by the president. Romney had more total money on hand, but Obama had direct control over more dollars. More than half of the \$169 million the Romney team reported was raised (and controlled) by the RNC.[26]

Although the party committees and joint-candidate-party fundraising committees can accept much larger contributions than candidate campaign committees, they also have to pay more for advertising (candidate committees get a discount from television stations that other committees do not) and are obligated to disperse funds to a host of component committees. For example, the joint fundraising committee Romney operated with the RNC transferred $44 million to several state party committees, and another $12 million to the Republican congressional campaign committees.[27] The hope, of course, was that the state parties would use the money for get-out-the-vote efforts that would benefit Romney. But ultimately, the Romney campaign had no control over how that money was spent. The Obama team, by contrast, mostly relied upon money from the president's campaign committee for their "ground game" efforts. This meant they had much greater control over where money went and how it was spent.

In the final weeks of the general election, the Obama campaign was also getting much more bang for its buck where ad buys were concerned. Despite being outspent by the Romney campaign, the president was running a lot more ads because his campaign had reserved air time much further in advance, when the rates were cheaper. In the first two weeks of October, the Romney team spent about $32 million on ads while the Obama team spent about $28 million. But Obama's campaign ran about 5,000 more ads.[28] The president's campaign also continued to raise and spend money at an unprecedented rate: in the final three weeks of the campaign, Obama outspent Romney by $71 million.

As the candidates fought it out in the final days before the election, super PAC spending went through the roof. After months of sitting on the sidelines, a handful of million-dollar contributors jumped on board and made large donations to Priorities USA Action, Obama's super PAC. The committee finished September with $7.3 million in the bank and spent about $13 million in the first few weeks of October. But the committee was hardly finished: between October 18 and November 26, Priorities USA Action spent an astonishing $21 million. Restore Our Future, the pro-Romney super PAC, finished September with close to $15 million in the bank, but burned through its cash much quicker than Priorities USA Action. The pro-Romney super PAC raised a staggering $112 million through September, more than twice the $50 million that Obama's super PAC collected. However, Restore Our Future only spent $45 million attacking Obama; most of the remaining funds had been used to fend off primary challengers earlier in the year.[29]

The election came down to a handful of swing states, most of which broke for the president. Obama maintained most of the support he received in 2008 from the education and legal sectors, but he lost the support of the securities and investment industry to Romney. Wall Street support for the president dropped to less than half of what it was in the 2008 election. One of his largest contributors in 2008, Goldman Sachs, switched teams and gave $1 million to the Romney campaign. The computer industry, and the broader communications sector, favored Obama, as did government employees and women's issue groups. The health sector,

Table 6.4 Total Spending in 2012 Presidential Race

Obama	
Candidate spending	$683,546,548
National party spending	$285,801,769
Outside spending	$133,676,984
Total	$1,103,025,301
Romney	
Candidate spending	$433,281,516
National party spending	$378,828,234
Outside spending	$412,287,252
Total	$1,224,397,002

Numbers based on Federal Election Commission data released on December 10, 2012.
Source: The Center for Responsive Politics.

still divided over the president's health care reform bill, split their contributions and gave about evenly to the two candidates.[30] Both teams raised and spent over $1 billion each for what turned out to be a status quo election. Table 6.4 lists final spending figures for President Obama and Mitt Romney.

The Race for Majority Control: Spending in Senate and House Races

As with the presidential race, outside spending by super PACs was the big story in congressional campaigns. Even though the House was expected to stay in Republican hands, majority control of the Senate was up for grabs. Democrats were defending twenty-three Senate seats and Republicans were defending ten—an imbalance which gave Senate Republicans the advantage heading into the 2012 election. Incumbent Democratic senators like Claire McCaskill (MO), Jon Tester (MT), and Sherrod Brown (OH) faced tough races, and several of the open Senate seats either leaned Republican or were too close to call. On the House side, a number of the freshman Republicans elected in 2010 faced tough reelection campaigns, and post-census redistricting left some incumbent members, especially Democrats, fighting to hold on to their seats. In the end, the candidates who had the most money on their side, including candidate campaign money and outside money, won 93 percent of House races, and 64 percent of Senate races. Winning Senate candidates spent an average of $9.5 million, while winning House candidates averaged $1.2 million.[31]

Heading into election day, Democrats held fifty-three of the Senate's one hundred seats (fifty-one, plus two Independents who caucus with the

Democrats). Several months before the election, the conventional wisdom was that Republicans were poised to win majority control of the chamber. After the election, Democrats controlled fifty-five seats (fifty-three plus two Independents). Some of the most competitive Senate races demonstrated the limitations of outside spending. Experienced candidates who are well known in their states can raise a lot of money for their campaign committees—money that they control and can use to directly confront outside attacks.

Despite this reality, outside players were willing to roll the dice. In all, outside groups (excluding party committees) spent over $1 million in each of twenty-two Senate races; in eight of those races, spending topped $15 million. In the final week before election day, outside groups spent $6.6 million in the Indiana Senate race between open-seat candidates Joe Donnelly (D) and Richard Mourdock (R). In Virginia, where Republican George Allen and Democrat Tim Kaine were fighting for an open Senate seat, outside groups dropped $6 million in the final week of the campaign. More than 60 percent of the $82 million spent on the Virginia Senate race came from outside spenders. The Wisconsin Senate race attracted just under $6 million in the final week, and Senate races in Missouri and Arizona attracted about $2 million in the week leading up to election day.[32]

Most of the outside money groups that spent big in 2012 were funded primarily by large donations from a small number of wealthy contributors. Democrats were behind the curve in figuring out how to use super PACs to their advantage, but being "late to the dance" did not seem to cost them, electorally. Liberal super PACs and outside groups spent a fraction of what conservative ones did, yet their smaller investments seemed to yield bigger results.

Sheldon Adelson, the billionaire from Las Vegas, poured millions into outside groups backing Republican Senate candidate George Allen, who lost the Virginia Senate race. Harold Simmons, a Dallas billionaire, gave $24 million to super PACs that opposed Senate candidates Bill Nelson of Florida, Tammy Baldwin of Wisconsin, and Joe Donnelly of Indiana, all of whom won. Simmons also gave more than $1 million to a super PAC opposing Ted Cruz, who won the Texas Senate race. Another Texas billionaire, Bob Perry, gave millions to a super PAC supporting Republican Senate candidate, Connie Mack, who lost the Florida race to incumbent Bill Nelson.[33] Outside groups also spent $15.6 million in an unsuccessful attempt to defeat Democratic incumbent senator Sherrod Brown of Ohio; shadow money from Crossroads GPS and the U.S. Chamber of Congress accounted for $10.6 million of this spending. Liberal groups spent about $6.4 million in what turned out to be a successful attempt to defeat Brown's Republican opponent, Josh Mandel.[34]

Big donors to liberal outside money groups got a much better return on their investments. Newsweb owner, Fred Eychaner, was the biggest donor to pro-Democrat super PACs. Of the $12 million he contributed overall,

$3.8 million went to Majority PAC, which supported Democratic Senate candidates. All of the candidates Majority PAC supported won and all of the candidates they opposed lost. James Simons, the founder of Renaissance Technologies, also contributed to Majority PAC, giving $3 million to help Democrats keep majority control of the Senate.[35]

The most expensive Senate race of 2012 pitted Democrat Elizabeth Warren against Republican incumbent Scott Brown of Massachusetts. Candidate spending topped $70 million, with Warren raising $36 million to Brown's $30 million. Interestingly, both candidates requested that outside groups stay out of the race and for the most part, they did. Super PACs spent about $6.5 million on the Massachusetts Senate race, but limited their spending to get-out-the-vote efforts. Pledging to "take the high road" and shun super PAC-funded attack ads wound up hurting Brown more than Warren, however. Following President Obama's model, Warren went after small donors, collecting 44 percent of her overall funds from these contributors. Small donors only made up 16 percent of Brown's fundraising base, leaving him with fewer donors he could return to for help.[36]

Table 6.5 lists the top Senate races in which outside money either favored the winner or the loser. In only three races did the Senate candidate who was backed by more outside money actually win. Indeed, adding outside money to the mix actually lowered a Senate candidate's chances of winning.[37] Table 6.6 lists the most expensive Senate races.

The race for majority control of the House was hardly a nail-biter; the Republicans lost seven seats to the Democrats, but remained firmly in control of the chamber. Despite minimal change in the House's partisan balance, millions of dollars were spent. In keeping with this year's campaign finance theme, outside money dominated the story lines in House campaigns. And

Table 6.5 Top Races Where Outside Spending Favored the Winner/Loser

Race	Amount Spent	Bulk of Spending
Favored winner		
Wisconsin Senate	$28.9 million	Against Republicans
Nevada Senate	$19 million	Against Democrats
Arizona Senate	$12.7 million	Against Democrats
Favored loser		
Virginia Senate	$36.9 million	Against Democrats
Ohio Senate	$29.8 million	Against Democrats
Indiana Senate	$19.6 million	Against Democrats
Florida Senate	$17.5 million	Against Democrats
Montana Senate	$16.2 million	Against Democrats
North Dakota Senate	$8.7 million	Against Democrats

Source: The Center for Responsive Politics.

Table 6.6 Most Expensive Senate Races

Rank	Race	Total	Candidate	Outside Spending
1.	Virginia Senate	$80,076,095	$30,123,548	$49,952,547
2.	Massachusetts Senate	$72,219,027	$65,421,208	$6,797,819
3.	Ohio Senate	$69,166,469	$32,408,558	$36,757,911
4.	Wisconsin Senate	$55,937,963	$17,728,268	$38,209,695
5.	Connecticut Senate	$54,412,808	$44,683,588	$9,729,220
6.	Nevada Senate	$44,103,515	$17,834,885	$26,268,630
7.	Florida Senate	$41,441,741	$18,893,940	$22,547,801
8.	Montana Senate	$41,118,841	$18,898,760	$22,220,081
9.	Indiana Senate	$39,208,068	$10,581,346	$28,626,722
10.	Missouri Senate	$33,104,957	$22,041,609	$11,063,348

Based on data released by the FEC on November 26, 2012. General Election candidates only.
Source: The Center for Responsive Politics.

proving that no members were safe from outside attack, one super PAC—the Campaign for Primary Accountability—spent millions opposing incumbents, regardless of party affiliation. The PAC's goal is to make the electoral system more competitive, and Congress more accountable.

Although Congress's historically low public approval ratings undoubtedly fueled contributions to anti-incumbent groups like the Campaign for Primary Accountability, they did not deter big spenders who wanted to keep their favorite members in office. When Rep. Mike McIntyre (D-NC) first ran for a House seat in 1996, he raised and spent $450,000. In 2012, after redistricting made McIntyre's seat more competitive, nearly $9 million dollars were spent on the race that McIntyre ultimately won. He beat his Republican challenger, Dave Rouzer, by less than one thousand votes.[38]

Most of the money in the McIntyre-Rouzer race was spent by super PACs and party committees. In twenty-five toss-up House races (including that one), outside group spending was on par with party committee spending through the September 30 filing deadline.[39] But in the final weeks of the campaign, outside spending skyrocketed. Outside groups spent close to $70 million on House races in the week leading up to election day alone. The race for Pennsylvania's 12th District, which pitted Democratic incumbent Mark Critz against Republican Keith Rothfus, attracted over $10 million in outside spending—more than any other House contest. Critz ultimately lost his seat. When candidate and outside spending are combined, the race between incumbent Florida Republican Allen West and Democratic challenger Patrick Murphy was the most expensive, topping out at over $30 million. Despite outspending Murphy $13.8 million to $3.4 million, West lost.

Outside spending also played a major role in some of the chamber's other toss-up races. Minnesota Republican Chip Cravaack lost the seat he won two years earlier to Democratic challenger, Richard Nolan. After American Action Network, a super PAC run by former Republican senator Norm Coleman, spent $1.7 million on ads attacking Nolan, the House Majority PAC, a Democratic super PAC, fired back at Cravaack to the tune of $1.4 million. Outside groups spent close to $10 million in Ohio's 13th District, where Democratic incumbent Betty Sutton was defeated by Republican Jim Renacci. A super PAC affiliated with House Speaker John Boehner spent $3.1 million to help Renacci win the seat.[40] Table 6.7 lists the most expensive House races, in both money raised and spent.

In eleven of the twenty-five toss-up races, candidate spending accounted for less than 50 percent of the total money spent. Like their party counterparts in the Senate, Republican House candidates relied more heavily on financial support from outside groups. And like their Senate counterparts, Democratic House candidates raised more money from small contributors, compared to their Republican challengers.[41]

Although outside spending dominated the headlines on the campaign trail, the focus inside of Congress was somewhat different. Republican members vying for leadership posts within Congress were making their case with contributions to their colleagues and party committees. Representatives Cathy McMorris Rodgers (WA) and Tom Price (GA) each raised $2 million as they campaigned to become the next Republican Conference chair. Both Rodgers and Price gave heavily to their Republican colleagues in

Table 6.7 Most Expensive House Races

Rank	Race	Total	Candidate	Outside Spending
1.	Florida District 18	$24,599,316	$17,204,944	$7,394,372
2.	Minnesota District 06	$21,002,997	$20,812,657	$190,340
3.	Ohio District 08	$19,994,903	$19,992,465	$2,438
4.	California District 30	$15,157,057	$10,292,230	$4,864,827
5.	California District 52	$14,330,115	$5,564,145	$8,765,970
6.	Ohio District 16	$14,042,609	$4,121,211	$9,921,398
7.	Pennsylvania District 12	$13,825,316	$3,570,500	$10,254,816
8.	California District 07	$12,864,481	$4,411,276	$8,453,205
9.	Illinois District 17	$12,662,741	$3,343,671	$9,319,070
10.	Illinois District 08	$12,316,787	$5,493,628	$6,823,159

Based on data released by the FEC on November 26, 2012. General Election candidates only.

Source: The Center for Responsive Politics.

the House. Representative Martha Roby (AL) raised about $1 million in her quest to become the next Republican Conference vice chair; her challenger, Lynn Jenkins (KS) raised close to $2 million. And in the three-way race for Republican secretary, two of the challengers raised just under $1 million while the third raised over $2 million.[42]

Members who run for leadership posts within the chamber need to prove that they have the ability and the connections to raise and donate a lot of campaign money. This helps to explain why about seventy members who were elected to Congress in 2010 have already established leadership PACs. Members of Congress use leadership PACs to raise money for their party's candidates, and to build alliances and support networks with colleagues. Marco Rubio, the Republican freshman senator from Florida, raised over $1.5 million for Reclaim America, a leadership PAC he founded in 2012. Rubio is widely thought to have higher political ambitions. Senator Rob Portman (R-OH), who was considered a finalist as Romney's running mate, also raised around $1.5 million for his leadership PAC. Both Rubio and Portman spread the wealth to Republican colleagues, and to party committees. Representative Jeff Denham (R-CA) was the top freshman fundraiser in the House, bringing in over $125,000.[43] Of course, this amount hardly compares to the amounts House leaders typically contribute from their leadership PACs. House Majority Leader Eric Cantor (VA) gave over $2 million to federal candidates, while House Speaker John Boehner (OH), House Majority Whip Kevin McCarthy (CA), and House Minority Whip Steny Hoyer (MD) all contributed over $1 million. In all, 422 leadership PACs contributed over $37 million in the 2012 cycle.

Candidates running for Senate and House seats in 2012 spent a combined total of about $1.7 billion. Spending by outside group topped $1 billion. In the end, only a few seats shifted between the parties. The question of whether this was money well spent or money wasted is lost on the candidates, parties, and outside groups that have already moved on. Shortly after election day, Democrats held a three-day secret meeting of major donors and outside groups. The topic? Raising money for 2014.[44]

Conclusion

The morning after election day, Sheldon Adelson, the biggest single donor in political history, attended a post-election breakfast for Mitt Romney's supporters. Without us, he told them, the race would not have been as close as it was—little consolation for donors who had forked over hundreds of millions of dollars to support candidates who mostly lost. President Obama faced over $400 million in negative advertising paid for by outside groups—more than double what pro-Obama groups spent. And high spending by outside groups in several Senate races was offset with strong fundraising and smart spending by Democratic candidates. Rather than produce a wave election, massive spending resulted in a wash.[45]

Making sense of campaign spending and campaign outcomes in the 2012 elections is difficult without the benefit of more hindsight. National forces more important than money may have given Democrats a boost. Outside spending inundated the airwaves with more negative advertising than ever before, and this may have produced a backlash. Voters, especially those in swing states, who were already saturated with negative ads and phone calls may have just stopped paying attention in the final weeks of the campaign.

The 2012 elections demonstrated that the way in which candidates spend money matters just as much—and in some cases, more—than how much they raise. David Axelrod, one of President Obama's top campaign strategists, said that one of the best decisions the campaign made was to spend money early. Romney hoped that a lot of late spending would give him a boost at the polls, but the dye was already cast. President Obama's campaign also invested heavily in its ground game, while the Romney campaign focused primarily on television advertising. In the end, the Obama formula got more voters to the polls.

Many of the candidates who won congressional races proved that they knew their states and districts better than the outside groups that spent millions opposing them. Winning candidates were better attuned to where and how money would make a difference.[46] Put simply, they know who, what, and where they represent better than an out-of-state group run by partisan operatives. By this measure, outside spending in 2012 may have missed the mark.

Notes

1. Mike Allen, "Sheldon Adelson: Inside the Mind of the Mega-donor," *Politico,* September 23, 2012; Mark Fisher, "Sheldon Adelson: Casino Magnate, Mega-donor Is a Man of Many Motives," *Washington Post,* October 23, 2012; Thomas B. Edsall, "Embracing Sheldon Adelson," *New York Times,* August 6, 2012.
2. Center for Responsive Politics, www.opensecrets.org/pacs/superpacs.php?cycle=2012.
3. Megan Wilson, "Stephen Colbert Shuts Down His Super PAC," *The Hill,* November 13, 2012.
4. Eliza Newlin Carney, "Supreme Court Rejects Montana Case Challenging Campaign Finance Ruling," *Roll Call,* June 25, 2012.
5. Mike Allen, "Sheldon Adelson."
6. The figure does not include Fred Karger, a Republican political consultant who declared his candidacy and raised and spent a total of $600,000.
7. July 15, 2011 was the second campaign filing deadline of the year, but none of the Republican candidates had officially announced their candidacies until after the first filing deadline.
8. Campaign Finance Institute, "Three of This Year's Top Four Fundraisers So Far Are Relying on Small Donors," July 19, 2011, www.cfinst.org/press/preleases/11-07-19/Three_of_This_Years_Top_Four_Presidential_Fundraisers_So_Far_Are_Relying_on_Small_Donors.aspx.

9. Campaign Finance Institute, "Romney and Perry Financially Separate from the GOP Pack," October 17, 2011, www.cfinst.org/Press/PReleases/11-10-17/Romney_and_Perry_Separate_from_the_GOP_Pack_Obama_Raises_the_Bulk_of_His_Money_from_Small_Donors.aspx.
10. Dan Eggen, "Super PACs Dominate Republican Primary Spending," *Washington Post,* January 16, 2012.
11. Campaign Finance Institute, "President Obama Is Ahead of 2007 Pace, Romney Even. Corporations Supplied a Quarter of the Romney Super PAC Funds," February 2, 2012, www.cfinst.org/press/releases_tags/12-02-02/President_Obama_is_Ahead_of_2007_Pace_Romney_Even_Corporations_Supplied_a_Quarter_of_the_Romney_Super_PAC_Funds.aspx.
12. Campaign Finance Institute, "48% of President Obama's 2011 Money Came from Small Donors—Better than Doubling 2007. Romney's Small Donors: 9%," February 8, 2012, www.cfinst.org/Press/PReleases/12-02-08/Small_Donors_in_2011_Obama_s_Were_Big_Romney_s_Not.aspx.
13. Norman Ornstein, "Effect of *Citizens United* Felt Two Years Later," *Roll Call,* January 18, 2012.
14. Campaign Finance Institute, "88% of Obama's Itemized Donors in January Were Repeaters; 40% of Romney's Donors Have Maxed Out," February 22, 2012, www.cfinst.org/press/preleases/12-02-22/88_of_Obama's_Itemized_Donors_in_January_Were_Repeaters_40_of_Romney's_Donors_Have_Maxed_Out.aspx.
15. Campaign Finance Institute, "Obama's Small-Dollar Percentage Down Slightly in February; Santorum's Stayed High; Romney's Stayed Low," March 22, 2012, www.cfinst.org/Press/Releases_tags/12-03-22/Obama's_Small-Dollar_Percentage_Down_Slightly_in_February_Santorum's_Stayed_High_Romney's_Stayed_Low.aspx.
16. Nicholas Confessore, "Super PACs Supply Millions as G.O.P. Race Drains Field," *New York Times,* March 20, 2012.
17. Campaign Finance Institute, "Obama's Small-dollar Percentage."
18. Campaign Finance Institute, "Obama's and Romney's Reports Each Point Up Vulnerabilities as the Campaigns Turn toward the General Election," May 23, 2012, www.cfinst.org/Press/Releases_tags/12-03-22/Obama's_Small-Dollar_Percentage_Down_Slightly_in_February_Santorum's_Stayed_High_Romney's_Stayed_Low.aspx.
19. A joint fundraising committee allows a candidate to raise money for their candidacy and their party. Typically, donors will write one large check which is then distributed between a candidate's campaign and the party committee in accordance with predetermined formulas and contribution limits.
20. Campaign Finance Institute, "Obama's and Romney's Reports."
21. Campaign Finance Institute, "May Was the Presidential Candidates' Best Money Month So Far in 2012, with Obama Still Doing (Slightly) Better than Romney," June 22, 2012, www.cfinst.org/Press/PReleases/12-06-22/May_Was_the_Presidential_Candidates'_Best_Money_Month_So_Far_in_2012_with_Obama_Still_Doing_Slightly_Better_than_Romney.aspx.
22. Campaign Finance Institute, "Romney's Small Donor Pace Picked Up in June, But Still Has a Long Way to Catch Obama's," July 25, 2012, www.cfinst.org/Press/PReleases/12-07-25/Romney's_Small_Donor_Pace_Picked_Up_in_June_But_Still_Has_a_Long_Way_to_Catch_Obama's.aspx.
23. Campaign Finance Institute, "Obama's Long-term Small-donor Strategy Begins to Show Dividends against Romney in August," September 24, 2012, www.cfinst.org/Press/PReleases/12-09-24/Obama's_Long-Term_Small-Donor_Strategy_Begins_to_Show_Dividends_against_Romney_in_August.aspx.
24. Ibid.

25. Ashley Parker and Nicholas Confessore, "Romney Raises $170 Million to Finance Final Push," *New York Times,* October 15, 2012.
26. Matt Vasilogambros, "Romney Campaign Raises $111.8 Million in First Half of October," *National Journal,* October 25, 2012; Dave Levinthal and Tarini Parti, "Mitt Romney Has Cash Lead over President Obama," *Politico,* October 26, 2012.
27. Kenneth P. Vogel and Dave Levinthal, "2012 Campaign Cash: $1 billion vs. $1 billion," *Politico,* October 21, 2012.
28. Ibid.
29. Ibid; Tarini Parti, "Pro-Obama Super PAC Snares Big Guns," *Politico,* October 20, 2012.
30. Michelle Merlin, "Obama Keeps Most Major Contributors, Not Finance," Center for Responsive Politics, November 14, 2012, www.opensecrets.org/news/2012/11/obama-keeps-most-major-contributors.html.
31. Center for Responsive Politics, "Blue Team Aided by Small Donors, Big Bundlers; Huge Outside Spending Still Comes Up Short," November 7, 2012, www.opensecrets.org/news/2012/11/post-election.html.
32. Center for Responsive Politics, "Outside Groups Make Final Push in the Last Week," November 7, 2012, www.opensecrets.org/news/2012/11/outside-groups-make-final-push-in-t.html.
33. Center for Responsive Politics, "Blue Team Aided."
34. Ibid.
35. Ibid.
36. Ibid.
37. Ibid.
38. Kenneth P. Vogel, "The New Normal: $9 Million for a Rural House Seat," *Politico,* November 4, 2012.
39. Sundeep Iyer, "Election Spending 2012: 25 Toss-Up House Races," Brennan Center for Justice, www.scribd.com/doc/110792573/Election-Spending-2012–25-Toss-Up-House-Races.
40. Tom Hamburger, "Big Money from Super PACs Hits House Races," *Washington Post,* November 8, 2012.
41. Sundeep Iyer, "Election Spending 2012."
42. Daniel Newhauser, "GOP Leadership Candidates' Fundraising Helps Bolster Good Will," *Roll Call,* October 22, 2012.
43. Kevin Bogardus and Megan R. Wilson, "Freshmen Rake in Cash through PACs," *The Hill,* October 3, 2012.
44. Kenneth P. Vogel and Tarini Parti, "Democratic Super PACs Get Jump on 2014, 2016," *Politico,* November 26, 2012.
45. Nicholas Confessort and Jess Bidgood, "Little to Show for Cash Flood by Big Donors," *New York Times,* November 7, 2012.
46. Lee Drutman, "How Much Did Money Really Matter in 2012," *The Sunlight Foundation,* November 9, 2012.

7

Congress

Partisanship and Polarization

Gary C. Jacobson

The 112th Congress (2011–12) was the least productive and most contentious in living memory,[1] and during the year leading up to the 2012 elections, opinion surveys reported the most negative public evaluations of Congress ever recorded, with nearly four of five Americans typically disapproving its performance.[2] Yet voters ended up electing a new Congress that differed only marginally from the one they so roundly disdained. As in the presidential election, the more than $2.2 billion spent to sway the House and Senate elections ultimately left the status quo intact. Republicans easily retained control of the House of Representatives, and despite having to defend twenty-three of the thirty-three Senate seats at stake, Democrats added two seats to their Senate majority. House incumbents seeking reelection were only slightly less successful than average; aside from the thirteen who lost primary or general elections to other incumbents they faced because of redistricting, 92 percent of members pursuing reelection won.[3] Only two incumbent Senators were denied reelection, only one in the general election. Table 7.1 summarizes the results.

The most obvious reason that Congress's extraordinary unpopularity visited so little punishment on its members is that control was divided between the parties, inviting a highly partisan and polarized electorate to blame the other party for the Congress's failures and to vote loyally for their party's candidate, which is what the vast majority of voters did.[4] Unlike the three previous congressional elections in which one party was strongly favored by national conditions (the Democrats in 2006 and 2008, the Republicans in 2010), no clear national tide emerged in 2012. In the bitterly contested presidential contest neither Barack Obama nor Mitt Romney had much cross-party appeal, and their campaigns only reinforced the deep partisan divide inherited—and if anything, intensified—by the Obama administration. For a variety of reasons examined elsewhere in this volume, Obama ultimately won reelection despite the burden of lingering high unemployment and weak economic growth. His victory was helpful to his party's congressional candidates—the consistency between presidential and House and Senate election outcomes was extraordinarily high in 2012—but to an extent limited by its relatively narrow margin. Congressional Democrats bounced back from

Table 7.1 Membership Changes in the House and Senate, 2012

	Republicans	Democrats	Independents
House of Representatives			
At the time of the 2012 election	240	195	
Elected in 2012	234	201	
Incumbents reelected	199	152	
Incumbents defeated	16	4[a]	
Open seats retained	17	17	
Open seats lost	2	6	
New seats	8	14	
Senate			
At the time of the 2012 election	47	51	2[b]
After the 2012 election	45	53	2[b]
Incumbents reelected	6	16	
Incumbents defeated	1[c]		
Open seats retained	2	6[c]	
Open seats lost	2	1	

[a]Two additional incumbent Democrats lost to incumbent Republicans, and in California, two more lost to incumbent Democrats and two to Democratic challengers as a consequence of California's new top-two all-party primaries (treated here as "open seats retained").

[b]The two independents caucus with the Democrats.

[c]Incumbent Richard Lugar (R-IN) lost the primary; his seat is treated here as open; retired senator Joe Lieberman (I-CT) organized with the Democrats so his seat is considered a Democratic retention.

Source: Compiled by the author.

their "shellacking" (Obama's term) in 2010 and shared in the broad, if modest, national victory, for their party. Democratic candidates won a majority of major-party national votes cast for House candidates, their share rising from 46.6 percent in 2010 to 50.6 percent in 2012, not far below Obama's 52.0 percent. But their seat share grew only from 44.4 percent to 46.2, a consequence of the formidable advantage Republicans enjoy in the distribution of their regular voters across House districts, an advantage enhanced by redistricting after the 2010 census. Combined with a remarkably high level of consistency between underlying district partisanship and House election results, the configuration of House districts served to insulate the Republican House majority from the effects of the Democratic national victory.

Democratic Senate candidates, in contrast, faced no such handicap and collectively outdid Obama at the polls, managing to win five states that Obama lost decisively and strengthening their grip on the Senate. Still, the relationship between Senate and presidential results across states reached its highest level in at least sixty years. The two sets of election reproduced a Congress divided between the parties, not because voters preferred such an outcome, but because of the way the electoral system aggregated their votes. Why and how this happened, and what it portends for the new Congress and Barack Obama's second term, is the subject of this chapter.

The House Elections: Redistricting and Partisan Consistency

Redistricting

The decennial reallocation and redrawing of House districts is always destabilizing, and 2012 was no exception. The number of voluntary departures—forty-three—was typical (the average for the previous five reapportionment years ending in 2 is forty-one) and modestly above the average for non-reapportionment years (thirty-four over the same period). Thirteen incumbents lost primaries, about the average for the previous five reapportionment cycles (twelve, the average for other election years over this period is four). Of the thirteen, eight lost to other incumbents after their districts were combined. Another five incumbents lost to other incumbents in general election contests.[5] Turnover was slightly higher than usual in 2012; a total of eighty-four new members took office in 2013, compared to the average for the five previous reapportionment years of seventy-six and, for non-reapportionment years during this period, of sixty-two.

In addition to the normal shake-up occasioned by the shuffling of district lines, redistricting for 2012 enhanced the Republican Party's already impressive structural advantage in the House election. The advantage, which has existed for decades, lies in the fact that the party's regular voters are distributed more efficiently across House districts than are regular Democratic voters. Although previous Republican gerrymanders had contributed to the Republican advantage,[6] its main source is that Democrats win a disproportionate share of minority, single, young, and gay voters who are concentrated in urban districts that deliver lopsided Democratic majorities. Republican voters are spread more evenly across suburbs, smaller cities, and rural areas, so that fewer Republican votes are "wasted" in highly skewed districts. This structural advantage has grown more consequential over time with the increase in partisan coherence and consistency among district electorates, a trend that accelerated sharply in 2012.[7]

The Republicans' sweeping national victory in 2010 gave them an opportunity to strengthen this advantage though gerrymandering. They controlled the redistricting process in eighteen states with a total of 202 House seats, including nine states in which the allocation of seats changed (four losing seats, five gaining seats). Democrats controlled the process in only six states with a total of forty-seven seats, only two with a change in seat allocation. (In twelve of the remaining states, the parties shared control; seven were redistricted by commissions, seven were single-district states.) Republicans exploited this opportunity to shore up some of their marginal districts, adding Republican voters where their seats were most vulnerable. This is clear from an analysis of Charlie Cook's Partisan Voting Index (PVI), computed as the difference between the average district-level presidential vote in 2004 and 2008 and the national presidential vote averages for these elections.[8] For example, with the national average of the Democratic presidential vote in these two elections at 51.2 percent, a district in which the average was 54.2 percent would have a PVI of +3, whereas a district in which the average was 48.2 percent would have a PVI of –3.

As is evident from the data in Table 7.2, the Republicans already enjoyed a major advantage by this measure before the 2012 redistricting, with 210 Republican-leaning districts (defined here as having a PVI less than –2), compared with 175 Democratic-leaning districts (PVI greater than 2); the remaining 50 districts were balanced with PVIs between –2 and +2). After redistricting, there were eleven more Republican-leaning districts, five fewer Democratic-leaning districts, and six fewer balanced districts. This result was obviously intended; where Republicans controlled redistricting, the party gained sixteen favorable districts while the Democrats lost one and balanced districts were reduced by eleven. Where Republicans did not control the process, both parties lost a few favorable districts and the number of balanced districts increased by five.[9] The Republican gerrymanders improved the PVIs of their incumbents by an average of 5.3 points if they had represented Democratic leaning-districts (old PVI >2) and by 3.8 points if they had represented balanced districts. PVIs in Republican-leaning districts were on average left unchanged.[10] The current Republican structural advantage is illustrated in greater detail in Figure 7.1, which displays the number of House seats favoring each party at 4-point intervals of the PVI.[11] Plainly, Republicans hold a much larger proportion of seats with comparatively low PVI advantages, while the Democrats hold a larger proportion of the very lopsided seats in which many Democratic votes are wasted.

Democrats were able to overcome the Republicans' (then smaller) structural advantage in 2006 and 2008 to pick up enough Republican-leaning seats to reach a majority; after 2008, they held fifty-two districts where the PVI was –3 or less. But this required two strong and successive pro-Democratic national tides, and they lost forty-one of these seats in 2010 (plus another eighteen in balanced districts and five in Democratic-leaning districts), when national conditions swung strongly in favor of the Republicans. With the enhanced safety of some once-marginal Republican districts, Democrats could win all of the Democratic-leaning districts and all forty-four tossups, and still fall four seats short of a majority. Republicans could win the 218 seats required for a majority by winning only Republican-leaning seats. The Democrats' only hope lay in a powerfully favorable

Table 7.2 Control of Redistricting and Changes in District Partisanship, 2010–2012

Control of Redistricting		District Partisan Advantage		
		Democrat > 2	Balanced	Republican > 2
All districts	2010	175	50	210
	2012	170	44	221
	Change	–5	–6	+11
Republican control	2010	51	24	123
	2012	50	13	139
	Change	–1	–11	+16
Other control	2010	124	26	87
	2012	120	31	82
	Change	–4	+5	–5

Note: See text for a description of the Cook PVI.
Source: Compiled by the author.

Figure 7.1 District Party Advantage, 2012

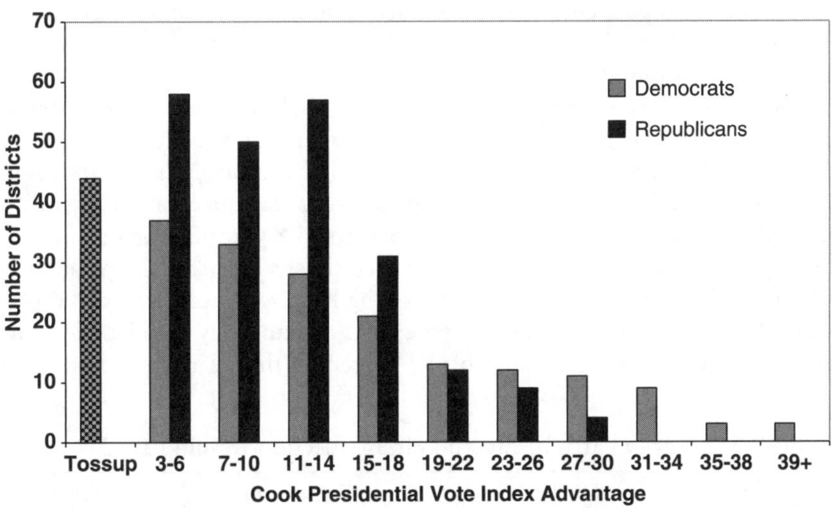

Source: Compiled by the author.

national tide, and none was in view for 2012. By the usual measures used to gauge partisan prospects early in the election year—the state of the economy and the president's approval ratings—neither party enjoyed any advantage. The economy was growing, but too slowly to reduce unemployment by much, and it remained over 8 percent until September. Real disposable income per capita was up, but only by about 1 percent for the year leading up to the election. During most of 2012, Obama's approval rating hovered in the high 40s, averaging about 48 percent until October, after which it rose to about 51 percent, safely above the level that guarantees defeat but not high enough to support a Democratic surge. Under these conditions, standard models predicted the Democrats would pick up a few House seats, as they indeed did, but nothing like the twenty-five they needed to reach a majority.[12]

Partisan Consistency

Once the votes were counted, House election results matched district leanings as measured by the PVI with astonishing consistency (Table 7.3). Only ten Democrats won Republican-leaning districts in 2012, and not a single Republican won in a Democratic-leaning district. The balanced districts were divided almost perfectly in half. For comparison, consider that in 2008, 14.8 percent of the results went against the partisan grain; in 2010, the proportion fell to 5.4 percent; in 2012, it was down to 2.5 percent. If we redefine partisan districts as those even the slightest bit partisan, with PVIs other than zero, which includes 426 of the 435 districts, 95.5 percent produced outcomes that were consistent with underlying district partisanship in 2012.

The PVI predicted not only winners but also vote shares very accurately in 2012, as the equations in Table 7.4 demonstrate. The first two are logit equations that estimate, respectively, the effect of the PVI, and of the PVI plus incumbency status, on the probability that the Democratic candidate would win the election. The PVI by itself correctly predicts 94.3 percent of the outcomes. Adding a measure of incumbency status, in recognition of the well-documented incumbency advantage in House elections,[13] increases the equation's predictive accuracy to 95.8 percent. The second two are regression equations estimating the Democrat's vote share as a function of the same two independent variables. The PVI alone accounts for 90 percent of the variance in the House vote; with incumbency status added, the equation accounts for a remarkable 93 percent of the variance. Incumbency

Table 7.3 District Partisanship and House Election Results, 2012

	Won by Democrat	Won by Republican	Number of Districts
Cook PVI advantage			
Democrat > 2	170	0	170
Republican > 2	10	211	221
Balanced	21	23	44
Total	201	234	435

Note: The Cook PVI advantage is described in the text.
Source: Compiled by the author.

Table 7.4 The Effect of District Partisanship and Incumbency on the House Vote in 2012

	Logit (Win/Lose)		Regression (Vote Share)	
PVI	.51***	.47***	1.20***	.97***
	(.06)	(.07)	(.02)	(.02)
Incumbency		2.14***		4.78***
		(.40)		(.36)
Constant	.43	1.31***	51.74***	52.34***
	(.24)	(.39)	(.27)	(.23)
Pseudo R^2/ Adjusted R^2	.78	.85	.90	.93
% Correctly predicted (Null=53.8)	94.3	95.8		
Number of cases	435	435	387	387

Note: Win/lose takes the value of 1 if a Democratic won, 0 if a Republican won; vote share is the Democrat's share of the major-party (candidates without major-party opposition are excluded from these equations); incumbency takes the value of 1 for a Democratic incumbent, –1 for a Republican incumbent, and 0 for all other candidates, including incumbents facing incumbents; standard errors are in parentheses.

***p<.001.

Source: Compiled by the author.

continued to have a significant effect on the House vote in 2012 and is estimated here to be worth about 4.8 percentage points.

Comparable data from previous elections underline just how extraordinary these results are. To make the comparison, the single-election presidential vote rather than the composite PVI is the measure of district partisanship, but these measures are so highly correlated (r = .99 between the current PVI and Obama's 2008 vote) that doing this makes no appreciable difference. Table 7.5 shows the results from the seven most recent elections.[14] The connection between presidential and House voting grew during the George W. Bush administration but has risen even more steeply during the Obama administration. The 2008 presidential vote in the district by itself correctly predicts the winner of 93.3 percent of the 2012 House contests. Also notice that as partisan coherence in voting patterns has risen, the value of incumbency (estimated as in Table 7.4) has fallen. Estimates of the incumbency advantage using the district presidential vote as the only control are always substantially higher than estimates for the same years produced by more elaborate methods. Unfortunately those methods are not applicable to years ending in 2 because they require inter-election comparisons across stable districts.[15] When the approach used here is applied to all thirty-three congressional election years going back to 1952, the estimated incumbency advantage for 2012 of 4.8 percentage points is the smallest in the entire series.

The district-level presidential vote for 2012 is still missing from twelve districts as of this writing, but the available data suggest that it will be at least as predictive of the House results as the PVI or the 2008 presidential vote (see the last row of Table 7.5). Thus it is highly likely that the data point for 2012 in Figure 7.2, which represents the correlation between the district-level 2008 presidential vote and the 2012 House vote, will remain at a record .95 when the complete 2012 presidential vote data can be analyzed.

Table 7.5 The District-level Presidential Vote and House Results, 2000–2012

House Election Year	Presidential Vote Year	House/President Vote Correlation	% Winners Correctly Predicted	Value of Incumbency
2000	2000	.80	80.4	12.1
2002	2000	.81	86.2	12.6
2004	2004	.84	86.4	11.3
2006	2004	.84	83.5	9.9
2008	2008	.85	80.7	9.6
2010	2008	.92	91.3	6.8
2012	2008	.95	93.3	5.1
2012	2012*	.95	94.6	4.8

*Based on the 423 districts for which the 2012 presidential vote is now available

Source: 2012 presidential vote data are from David Nir and reported at https://docs.google.com/spreadsheet/pub?key=0Av8O-dN2giY6dEFCOFZ4ZnlKS0x3M3Y0WHd5aWFDWkE&single=true&gid=0&output=html; the other data were compiled by the author.

Figure 7.2 Correlations between the Presidential Congressional Vote at the State and District Levels, 1952–2012

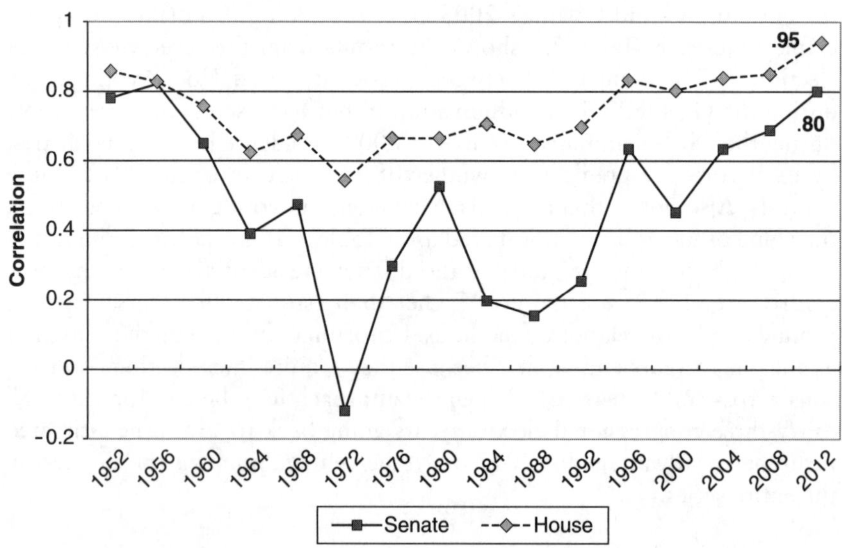

Source: Compiled by the author.

The clear implication of these results—namely, that the 2012 House elections were highly nationalized, president-centered events—is strongly supported by findings from the national exit poll data, a selection of which are presented in Table 7.6. First, at both the presidential and House levels, party loyalty was the highest and partisan defections the lowest ever recorded in an exit poll. Second, the parties' respective House electoral coalitions matched their presidential candidates' electoral coalitions almost perfectly. In particular, the much-discussed coalition that produced Obama's majority—women (especially single women), minorities, and younger voters—reappeared largely intact in the House electorate. Third, opinions of Obama predicted the vote at very high levels in both types of elections, although the consistency of opinions and vote was understandably higher for the presidential vote (94–95 percent) than for the House vote (90 percent). Finally the 2012 exit poll reports the lowest incidence of ticket splitting—voting for a Democrat for president and a Republican for U.S. representative, or vice versa—since exit polling began. Only 6.5 percent of the voters interviewed split their tickets in 2012; the previous low was 10.0 percent (in both 2004 and 2008); the 1976 to 2008 average was 14.6 percent. The aggregate data also show that the proportion of split districts—that is, districts that gave majorities to different parties' candidates in the presidential and House elections—reached its lowest level since the requisite data first became available in 1952. Only 6 percent of districts delivered split verdicts in 2012; the previous postwar low was 14 percent in 2004.[16] In sum, both survey and aggregate electoral data identify 2012 as the most partisan, president-centered House election in at least sixty years.

Table 7.6 The Electoral Coalitions of the Presidential and House Candidates, 2012 (Exit Poll Data)

		Percent Voting for			
		Barack Obama	House Democrat	Mitt Romney	House Republican
Party identification					
Democrat	(38)	92	94	7	6
Republican	(32)	6	5	93	94
Independent	(29)	45	44	50	51
Demographics					
Men	(47)	45	45	55	53
Women	(53)	55	55	44	44
Married	(31)	46	46	53	53
Unmarried	(22)	67	68	31	31
White	(72)	39	39	59	59
Black	(13)	93	91	6	8

(Continued)

Table 7.6 Continued

		Percent Voting for			
		Barack Obama	House Democrat	Mitt Romney	House Republican
Hispanic/Latino	(10)	71	68	27	30
Asian	(3)	73	73	26	25
18–29	(19)	60	60	37	38
30–44	(27)	52	51	45	46
45–64	(38)	47	47	51	51
65 or over	(16)	44	44	56	55
Under $30,000	(20)	63	63	35	35
$30,000–$49,999	(21)	57	56	42	42
$50,000–$99,999	(31)	46	46	52	52
$100,000–$199,999	(21)	44	43	54	55
$200,000–$249,999	(3)	47	43	52	56
$250,000 or more	(4)	42	39	55	59
Opinion of Obama					
Approve	(54)	89	86	9	12
Disapprove	(45)	3	7	94	91
Favorable	(53)	93	88	6	8
Unfavorable	(46)	3	11	94	90

Note: The percentage of respondents in each category is in parentheses.
Source: The 2012 National Exit Poll, www.foxnews.com/politics/elections/2012-exit-poll.

Money in the House Elections

The House campaigns that preceded these thoroughly party-driven results cost at least $1.35 billion, including $871 million spent by the candidates' campaigns, $116 million independently by national party committees, and $148 million spent independently by nonparty organizations.[17] As usual, campaign spending, especially independent spending by parties and groups, was heavily concentrated in the most competitive districts (Figure 7.3). Campaigns in the three most competitive categories (based on the PVI), comprising 138 districts, averaged nearly $4.5 million in total spending. The financial balance in districts leaning strongly to one of the parties favored its candidates overwhelmingly, mainly because even very safe incumbents now raise large sums, a portion of which they pass on to their parties' national committees and needier candidates in competitive races.[18] As in other recent elections, nearly every potentially viable candidate was amply funded, and no more than a couple of districts could be considered missed opportunities for the losing party.[19]

Figure 7.3 The Distribution to Campaign Money in House Elections, 2012

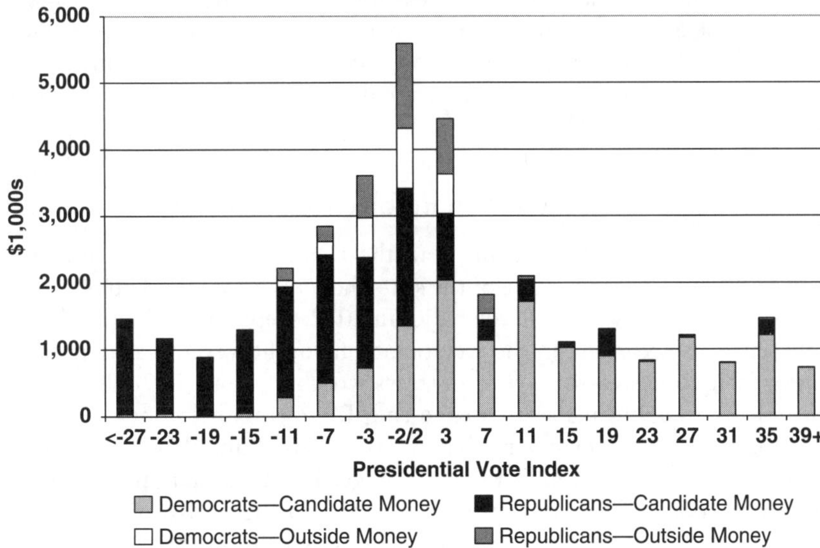

Source: Compiled by the author.

The huge investments by candidates and outside entities in the competitive districts basically produced a standoff. In the thirty-three closest races (those won with less than 53 percent of the vote) the winner outspent the loser in about half, seventeen to be precise. The ten Democrats who won Republican-leaning districts were amply financed, with an average of $3.9 million in support, 43 percent of it from outside sources, and most of them would have probably lost without such heavy investments. Still, in six of the ten races, the losing Republican opponent was the better funded candidate; these ten contests were not determined by the balance of finances. Why were these Democrats able to win against the partisan grain? Four were challengers who defeated Republican incumbents in Democratic-trending districts, where, despite PVIs of -3 or less, Obama had won between 50 and 53 percent of the vote in 2008.[20] Five were veteran incumbents with strong local ties and moderate voting records; for example, all five had identical 92 percent ratings from the National Rifle Association, and four had its endorsement.[21] Another was a former member of Congress, also with a moderate voting record, who won an open seat in 2012 after having lost to a tea party favorite in 2010.[22]

The most remarkable thing about these victories, however, is their rarity. At one time, centrist Democrats with moderate to conservative views on economic and social issues regularly won Republican-leaning districts. Not any more, and this may be the real effect of massive outside independent spending: it nationalizes campaigns, heightens partisanship, and undermines election strategies based on independence and soliciting the "personal vote." These effects are not invariably registered at the polls, however. Several of the 2012 Senate elections show that, under certain circumstances, local ties trump partisanship and nationalization even with huge infusions of outside money.

The Senate Elections

At the beginning of the election year, the Democrats' grip on the Senate seemed tenuous. Twenty-three of the seats that comprised their fifty-three to forty-seven majority were on the ballot in 2012; Republicans had to defend only ten seats. Working in the Democrats' favor, however, was that eighteen of their contested seats were in states won by Obama in 2008, as were four of the Republicans seats. In the end, Democrats held onto twenty of the twenty-one seats in states Obama won in 2008 and 2012, losing only in Nevada, where the Democratic challenger lost by a margin of only 1.2 percentage points. They also won seats in five of the twelve states holding Senate elections whose electoral votes went to Mitt Romney.

Table 7.7 displays the state-level election results, listing states in rank order of the total sum spent by outside entities—party and nonparty—in the campaigns.[23] This ordering highlights the major financial role that outside money played in the 2012 Senate campaigns. Democratic Senate candidates were helped by $48 and $118 million, respectively, in party and nonparty outside spending; the total was more than double the outside spending for Democratic candidates in 2010. The comparable figures for Republican candidates, $26 million and $148 million, amounted to a 65 percent increase over 2010. For seventeen candidates individually, and for both candidates combined in nine states, spending by outside groups exceeded spending by the candidates' campaigns (up from five candidates and three states in 2010). Virginia led the way, with an astonishing $50 million spent by outsiders along with the $36 million spent by the candidates, but on a per-voting-age-resident basis, the most extravagant races were in the low-population states of Montana ($22 million in outside spending, $43 million total) and North Dakota ($14 million in outside spending, $25 million total). Outside spending was, as always, concentrated in the most competitive races; 77 percent went to the eleven races won with less than 55 percent of the vote; nearly half the spending in these races came from outside sources. Also as usual, about 80 percent of the outside money was spent attacking the opponent rather than extolling the favored candidate.

Inspired by the high-stakes struggle for majority control, parties and their auxiliaries made huge investments in trying to sway the 2012 Senate elections. Did these investments tip the scales? The simple answer is no: the candidate supported by the larger share of outside spending won only about

Table 7.7 2012 Senate Election Results and Campaign Money ($1,000s)

State	Candidate	% Vote	Candidate Spending	Independent Spending		$ Per Voter	% Outside
				Party	Nonparty		
Virginia	Tim Kaine (D)	52.9	21,028	7,070	13,121	6.60	49.0
	George Allen (R)	47.0	14,126	5,682	23,999	7.02	67.8
Ohio	*Sherrod Brown* (D)	50.7	21,469	4,700	9,806	4.06	40.3
	Josh Mandel (R)	44.7	18,698	994	21,231	4.62	54.3
Wisconsin	Tammy Baldwin (D)	51.4	15,333	5,842	16,253	8.53	59.0
	Tommy Thompson (R)	45.9	9,654	4,876	13,666	6.43	65.8
Indiana	Joe Donnelly (D)	50.0	5,497	4,081	9,470	3.87	71.1
	Richard Mourdock (R)	44.3	8,699	3,132	13,891	5.23	66.2
Nevada	Shelley Berkley (D)	44.7	11,590	3,900	9,509	12.14	53.6
	Dean Heller (R)	45.9	9,102	2,773	10,018	10.63	58.4
Florida	*Bill Nelson* (D)	55.2	15,161	3,699	2,348	1.41	28.5
	Connie Mack IV (R)	42.2	7,268	0	16,150	1.55	69.0
Montana	*Jon Tester* (D)	48.6	12,233	2,959	8,772	30.89	49.0
	Denny Rehberg (R)	44.9	8,621	2,405	7,998	24.52	54.7
Arizona	Richard Carmona (D)	46.2	6,271	3,139	6,799	3.34	61.3
	Jeff Flake (R)	49.2	9,335	4,215	8,823	4.61	58.3
Texas	Paul Sadler (D)	40.6	498	0	11,299	0.63	95.8
	Ted Cruz (R)	56.5	14,188	0	4,038	0.97	22.2
Missouri	*Claire McCaskill* (D)	54.8	19,480	3,582	6,446	6.42	34.0
	Todd Akin (R)	39.1	6,099	0	3,097	2.00	33.7

(Continued)

Table 7.7 Continued

State	Candidate	% Vote	Candidate Spending	Independent Spending		$ Per Voter	% Outside
				Party	Nonparty		
North Dakota	Heidi Heitkamp (D)	50.2	5,320	3,362	4,323	24.41	59.1
	Rick Berg (R)	49.3	6,185	1,670	4,566	23.31	50.2
Nebraska	Bob Kerry (D)	42.2	5,616	20	3,155	6.36	36.1
	Deb Fischer (R)	57.8	5,059	4	4,066	6.60	44.6
Massachusetts	Elizabeth Warren (D)	53.7	41,212	240	3,797	8.73	8.9
	Scott Brown (R)	46.2	34,858	0	2,820	7.27	7.5
Maine	Cynthia Dill (D)	13.3	189	1,490	489	2.05	91.3
	Charles Summers (R)	30.7	1,225	1,309	2,689	4.93	76.5
	Angus King (I)	52.9	2,695	0	1,428	3.87	34.5
Connecticut	Chris Murphy (D)	54.8	10,306	2,603	5,080	6.48	42.7
	Linda McMahon (R)	43.1	49,973	0	1,022	18.36	2.0
New Mexico	Martin Heinrich (D)	51.0	6,679	292	2,050	5.77	26.0
	Heather Wilson (R)	45.3	7,086	0	3,345	6.67	32.1
Pennsylvania	*Bob Casey* (D)	53.7	12,136	30	1,232	1.34	9.4
	Tom Smith (R)	44.6	21,098	87	2,847	2.41	12.2
Hawaii	Mazie Hirono (D)	62.6	5,599	1	974	6.14	14.8
	Linda Lingle (R)	37.4	5,813	35	1,525	6.89	21.2
Michigan	*Debbie Stabenow* (D)	58.8	11,377	0	315	1.54	2.7
	Peter Hoekstra (R)	38.0	5,550	122	2,002	1.01	27.7
Utah	Scott Howell (D)	30.0	396	43	1,314	0.90	77.4
	Orrin Hatch (R)	65.3	10,534	0	518	5.71	4.7
New Jersey	*Bob Menendez* (D)	58.9	13,157	0	913	2.08	6.5
	Joe Kyrillos (R)	39.4	4,537	0	479	0.74	9.5

New York	*Kirsten Gillibrand* (D)	72.2	14,077	257	166	0.96	2.9
	Wendy Long (R)	26.4	718	91	990	0.12	60.1
West Virginia	*Joe Manchin* (D)	60.6	3,567	57	125	2.55	4.9
	John Raese (R)	36.5	1,574	0	139	1.17	8.1
Rhode Island	*Sheldon Whitehouse* (D)	64.8	3,967	0	0	4.77	0.0
	Barry Hinckley (R)	35.0	1,663	0	205	2.25	11.0
Maryland	*Ben Cardin* (D)	56.0	5,119	5	12	1.15	0.3
	Dan Bongino (R)	26.3	1,718	0	130	0.41	7.0
Delaware	*Tom Carper* (D)	66.4	3,277	3	90	4.80	2.8
	Kevin Wade (R)	29.0	172	0	10	0.26	5.5
California	*Dianne Feinstein* (D)	62.5	15,559	3	48	0.55	0.3
	Elizabeth Emken (R)	37.5	1,074	15	3	0.04	1.6
Minnesota	*Amy Klobuchar* (D)	65.2	6,879	0	11	1.69	0.2
	Kurt Bills (R)	30.5	952	0	22	0.24	2.3
Wyoming	Tim Chestnut (D)	21.7	0	0	0	0.00	0.0
	John Barasso (R)	75.7	2,054	0	11	4.77	0.5
Washington	*Maria Cantwell* (D)	60.5	8,922	163	7	1.73	1.9
	Michael Baumgartner (R)	39.6	1,022	0	0	0.19	0.0
Tennessee	Mark Clayton (D)	30.4	0	0	0	0.00	0.0
	Bob Corker (R)	64.9	4,965	0	7	1.01	0.1
Vermont	*Bernie Sanders* (I)	71.0	2,601	0	0	5.20	0.0
	John MacGovern (R)	24.9	129	0	0	0.26	0.0
Mississippi	Albert Gore Jr. (D)	40.6	0	0	0	0.00	0.0
	Roger Wicker (R)	57.2	1,463	0	0	0.66	0.0

Note: Incumbents are italicized.

Source: See footnote 23.

half the time (fifteen winners, fourteen losers). But this was because the Democrats were so successful; they won eleven of the thirteen contests with the balance of outside spending on their side, but they also won twelve of sixteen contests where the balance favored the Republicans. Looking only at the eleven contests won with less than 55 percent, Democrats won three of four where they had an outside spending edge and six of seven where they did not. If candidate as well as outside spending is included, the story is almost identical: Democrats won four of five races where they held an overall financial advantage and five of six where Republicans held the advantage. The resources devoted to these races were sufficiently balanced—and lavish—that that their effect was at best a wash, and the outcomes were determined by other factors.

The most important of these factors was, as in the House races, local partisanship. Despite the five Democratic victories in states won by Romney, the 2012 Senate elections, like their House counterparts, were on the whole highly partisan affairs. Notice that in Figure 7.2, the correlation between the votes for president and senator was .80, the highest since the 1950s. Moreover, as Figure 7.4 shows, in 2012 the share of Senate seats won by the party of the state's presidential winner reached its highest level in at least sixty years, as did the total share of seats held after the election by the party of the state's presidential winner.[24]

Figure 7.4 Consistency of Presidential and Senate Elections Results, 1952–2012

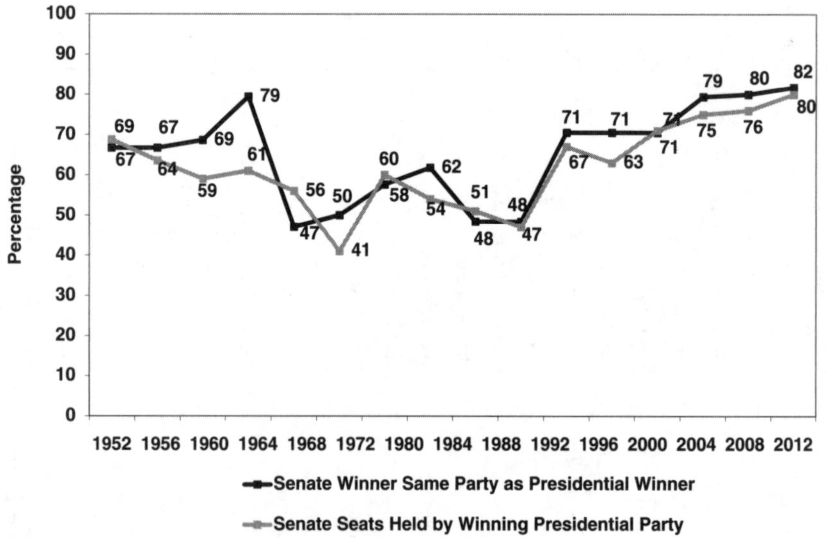

Source: Compiled by the author.

Winning against the Partisan Grain

The coincidence of state-level president and Senate outcomes would have been even greater had two candidates backed by the Republicans' Tea Party faction and other far-right groups not won nominations over more conventional conservatives favored by the party establishment. Richard Mourdock defeated veteran Republican incumbent Richard Lugar, a strong favorite for reelection, by attacking him from the right in the Indiana primary. Todd Akin, a member of the House's Tea Party Caucus, won the Missouri primary against a more mainstream Republican and another Tea Party favorite for the nomination to challenge Claire McCaskill, widely considered the most vulnerable Democrat running in 2012. McCaskill and Democratic committees actually funneled $1.5 million into independent campaign ads that subtly boosted Akin's appeal to conservative Republicans with the words it used to "attack" him.[25] It turned out to be a shrewd investment. Both Akin's and Mourdock's extreme views—exemplified but by no means exhausted by their arguments for forbidding women who become pregnant through rape to have abortions[26]—and their other shortcomings as candidates gave the Democrats two seats they would otherwise have gone to Republicans. The exit polls showed that in these two races, about 20 percent of Republican identifiers defected to the Democrat, twice the proportion of defectors in the other competitive states surveyed. By comparison, Republicans' defection rates in presidential voting were 6 percent in Indiana and 4 percent in Missouri; in the aggregate vote, Romney ran 8 points ahead of Mourdock, and 13 points ahead of Akin. Had these nominations gone to Lugar and Akin's mainstream rival, the coincidence of Senate and presidential outcomes would have been even higher, 88 percent.

The other three Democrats who won in Romney states did so without (inadvertent) Tea Party help. As noted earlier, two of these races generated by far the highest per-voter spending: Montana and North Dakota. Yet despite saturation advertising campaigns by national Republicans and allied super PACs devoted to tying them to Obama, who lost Montana by 13 points and North Dakota by 20, the Democratic candidates prevailed. One reason is that they, too, were supported by gushers of outside money. More important, however, was that they were effective campaigners competing in states ideally suited to personal politicking. Both states are lightly populated and accustomed to face-to-face, friends-and-neighbors politics. Moreover, both Democratic candidates had long political careers in their states (Heitkamp as North Dakota's attorney general, Tester as the president of the Montana senate and then a U.S. senator) and were already thoroughly familiar to their electorates. When they staked out conservative positions separating themselves from the president and national Democratic Party, they could do so credibly because they were well-known quantities. Tester was also helped by a Libertarian candidate who siphoned conservative votes from his Republican opponent.[27] Joe Manchin, the other Democrat who won a state that went to Romney, was a popular former governor of West Virginia elected to the Senate in 2010. He, too, had been careful to distance himself from the Obama administration, taking conservative positions on several salient issues,[28] and he won easy reelection against the Republican he had defeated two years earlier by much narrower margin, receiving 60.5 percent of the vote in a state that gave Obama only 35.5 percent.

Help from the Obama Campaign

The lone Republican victory in a state won by Obama belonged to Dean Heller, appointed in May, 2011, to replace Nevada senator John Ensign, who had resigned under pressure after involvement in a sex scandal. Heller won with 45.9 percent to Democrat Shelley Berkeley's 44.7 percent in a state Obama won with 53.4 percent of the vote. Berkeley, a member of the House, was hurt by ethics charges sufficiently credible to be taken up by the House Ethics Committee, and the Obama campaign's highly effective voter-mobilization operation, while delivering the president a comfortable majority, was unable to bring her along. In several other closely contested states, however, Obama's campaign effort and popularity clearly helped the Democrat to victory. Tim Kaine's margin over George Allen in Virginia's $86 million extravaganza, 4 percentage points, coincided with Obama's 3-point victory in this battleground state, a win attributed in no small measure to the Obama campaign's superior "ground game" for turning out the vote.[29] In Ohio, another battleground state featuring a major Obama mobilization effort, incumbent Democrat Sherrod Brown won the same share of votes as Obama (50.7 percent), although his margin in major-party votes was larger (6 points compared to Obama's 2 points) because a far-right independent took 4.6 percent of the Ohio Senate vote.

In Massachusetts, incumbent Republican Scott Brown, winner of the special election in January 2010, to replace Ted Kennedy, ran far ahead of Mitt Romney but still lost to Elizabeth Warren by 7 points in a state Obama won by 23 points. This was another wildly expensive contest, with spending exceeding $82 million, but uniquely for a highly competitive 2012 race, more than 90 percent came from the candidates' campaign committees. Scott and Warren had made a pact to reject help from outside spenders that had an enforcement clause: if an outside group broadcast an ad, the side benefiting from it had to pay a penalty equivalent to half the amount spent on the ad to a charity of the other's choosing.[30] Outside groups still managed to spend $7 million on other media, including mailings and telephone calls, but the national parties stayed out. Obama's popularity in Connecticut, which he won by 18 percentage points, also gave Republican Linda McMahon little chance to prevail against Democratic congressman Chris Murphy, even though by spending $42 million of her own fortune she secured a better than two-to-one financial advantage. Confirming that it is by no means easy for self-funded multi-millionaires to spend their way to victory,[31] McMahon has now personally invested an estimated $100 million in two Senate campaigns (she ran 2010 as well) without winning more than 43.1 percent of the vote either time.

In one other race of note, Angus King, twice elected governor of Maine as an independent (in 1994 and 1998) and running as one again in 2012, won more votes than both major-party candidates combined. According to the exit poll, Democratic identifiers preferred him over the Democratic candidate, 67 percent to 25 percent, and he announced after the election, to absolutely no one's surprise, that he would vote to organize with Senate Democrats, so this race can also be considered a Democratic victory. The same holds for the reelection of independent senator Bernie Sanders of Vermont with 71 percent of the vote against only Republican opposition.

Implications

The voters' endorsement of the status quo in the 2012 election incorporated a modest victory for the Democrats, but it did nothing to change the partisan configurations that made the 112th Congress so contentions and unproductive. With Obama as a touchstone, the congressional elections were nearly as partisan and polarizing as the presidential election. The partisan gap in presidential approval always expands when presidents are campaigning for reelection, but it reached a new high of 82 points in Gallup polls taken during the month preceding the 2012 election, with an average of 90 percent of Democrats but only 8 percent of Republican approving of Obama's performance.[32] Not surprisingly, party-line voting for president was correspondingly high, and with the extraordinarily strong linkage between presidential and congressional voting, it was also unusually high in the congressional contests, especially for House seats. Thus very few House candidates, and, by historic standards, comparatively few Senate candidates, won in places where the local partisan balance was unfavorable. The data displayed in Figures 7.2 and 7.4 show that this was not a one-off occurrence but rather the extension of a long-term trend. This trend, combined with other salient features of the current electoral environment, holds several important implications for congressional and electoral politics during Obama's second term.

An Even More Polarized Congress?

Although disdain for the polarized Congress was nearly universal in 2012, the election did nothing to mitigate the ideological differences between the congressional parties. The ranks of House moderates dwindled further. The Blue Dog Coalition of moderate Democrats lost nearly half its members through resignations, retirements, and primary and general election defeats, dropping from twenty-seven to fourteen.[33] (It already had dropped from fifty-four to twenty-seven in 2010.) On the Republican side, seven of sixteen defeated incumbents had been among the forty-eight members of the

Republican Main Street Partnership, a caucus of moderate conservatives.[34] Seven members of the Republican Tea Party Caucus also lost, including two of its most extreme and outspoken members, Joe Walsh (IL-8) and Allen West (FL-18), whose unalloyed extremism cost him his seat despite the more than $19 million spent to defend it.[35] The election's effect on the ideological gap between the House parties was not entirely one-sided; Keith Poole's prediction for the 113th Congress (2013–14) is that the gap will be about the same as in the 112th Congress, when it reached its all-time high.[36]

More important than this changing of the guard, however, is that the incoming party cohorts will be representing the most divergent sets of districts in at least sixty years. As Figure 7.5 shows, the 26-percentage-point difference in the underlying partisanship of the districts won by Republicans and Democrats in 2012 (measured by the 2012 presidential vote in the 423 districts for which data are currently available) exceeded the previous high reached in 2010. Party differences in electoral bases are strongly related to party differences in presidential support and roll call voting, so this difference is consistent with the projection that the House will be at least as polarized along party lines in the 113th Congress as it was in the 112th.[37] In particular, the electoral constituencies of the House Republicans—those constituents who actually voted for them—contain very few Obama supporters and thus provide very little electoral incentive for them to cooperate with the president. Although House Speaker John Boehner's claim that his Republican majority won a mandate as compelling as Obama's[38]

Figure 7.5 The Polarization of U.S. House Districts, 1952–2012

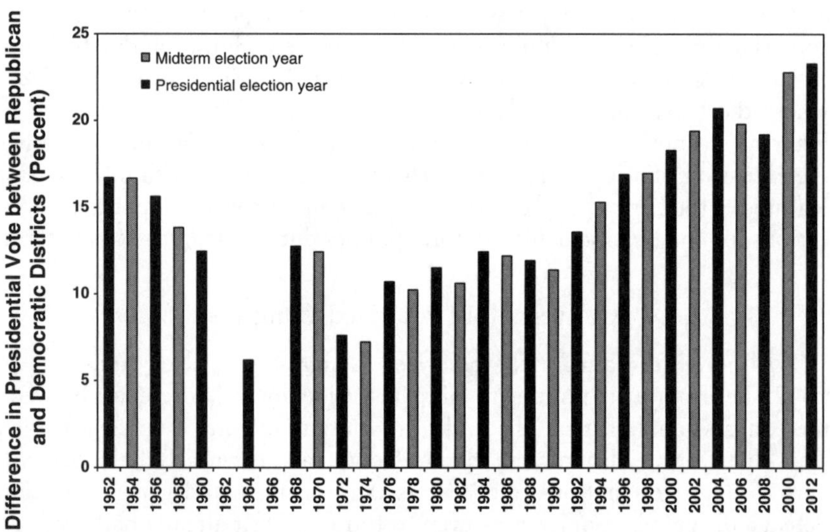

Note: Data for 1962 and 1966 are unavailable because of redistricting; entries for midterm elections are calculated from the previous presidential election; the entry for 2012 is calculated from the 2008 presidential vote in the district.

Source: Compiled by the author.

is overstated—Democrats won a majority of the national House vote, after all—he is in a practical sense correct, because the voters responsible for his Republican majority are far more likely to support his agenda than Obama's.

States tend to be more diverse politically and less lopsided in their partisanship than House districts, so the gap between the Senate parties' electoral constituencies is not as wide as in the House, but it reached a record level of more than 15 percentage points in 2012 (Figure 7.6). Only nine of the forty-five Republican senators in the 113th Congress represent states Obama won in 2012. The Senate did gain some likely moderate Democrats (Heitkamp, Donnelly, perhaps King) but lost an equal number through retirements (Kent Conrad, Ben Nelson, and James Webb). Republican departures included three of the party's more centrist members (Scott Brown, Olympia Snowe, and Richard Lugar), and all three of its newcomers, Deb Fischer (NE), and Ted Cruz (TX), and Jeff Flake (AZ) belong to the party's most conservative faction. In all, seven of the incoming senators are likely to be more extreme than the incumbents they replaced, and none of the remaining four are likely to be significantly more moderate than their predecessors. Thus the Senate is projected to be even more ideologically polarized than it was in the 112th Congress.[39]

In sum, the electoral underpinnings of the 113th Congress portend, if anything, even greater party polarization and greater difficulty for Obama in rounding up Republican votes for his initiatives than he experienced in the previous Congress. It remains to be seen if the political credit Obama

Figure 7.6 The Polarization of State Constituencies, 1952–2012

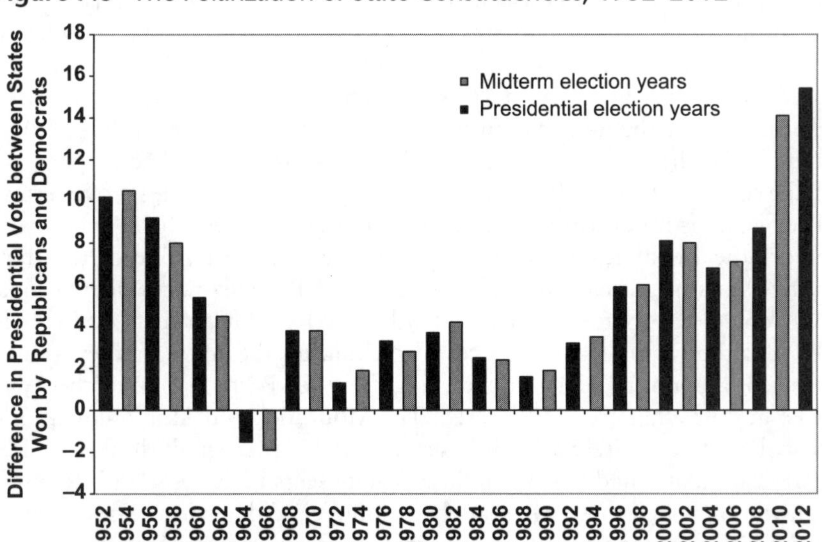

Source: Compiled by the author.

acquired by winning a narrow but surprisingly decisive victory over Mitt Romney will do anything to offset these electoral fundamentals.

Continuing Divided Government

The 2012 election also portends, for the near future at least, a stable pattern of divided government, with the House in Republican hands and the presidency (and most likely the Senate) in Democratic hands. The initial explanations of Obama's reelection, relying entirely on the national exit poll, have given great weight to his ability to attract the votes of growing segments of the electorate: young people, singles (especially single women), social liberals, the nonchurched, and ethnic minorities (see Table 7.6). Romney's coalition, in contrast, was overwhelmingly white, older, married, religiously observant and socially conservative, all shrinking demographic categories. The white share of the electorate, 88 percent when Ronald Reagan was elected in 1980, and 83 percent when George W. Bush won in 2000, was only 72 percent in 2012 and is projected to decline to less than two-thirds in a few more elections.[40] The implication is that unless the Republican Party broadens its appeal to young, minority, secular, and women voters, it will have a hard time competing for the presidency.

The Democrats, however, face an even greater barrier in trying to take control of the House. As noted earlier, they won 50.6 percent of the vote in 2012 but only 46.2 percent of the seats. The Republican's structural advantage, enhanced by recent gerrymandering (Table 7.2), means that Democrats will need a favorable national tide at least as powerful as the ones they rode to power in 2006 and 2008 to pick up enough seats to win a majority during the rest of the decade. Midterm elections rarely feature a national tide favoring the president's party, and it would be completely unprecedented for Democrats to gain the seventeen seats they currently need to attain a majority in 2014. Normally, the president's party loses House seats at the midterm; in the three historic exceptions (1934, 1998, and 2002), the most it gained was nine. It is also unusual for a party to make significant gains after holding the White House for at least two terms. The Senate is no lock for either party, and the lineup for 2014 once again favors the Republicans. Democrats must defend twenty-one of the thirty-five seats up for election, seven from states Romney won; Obama took only one of the fourteen states that will have Republican seats on the ballot. But the Republicans' chances of picking up the six seats they would need for a majority depend on keeping their Tea Party faction in check, at least in states that are not deep red. The Mourdock and Akin nominations cost them two entirely winnable seats in 2012 after similarly flawed Tea Party candidates had cost them three Senate seats in 2010.[41] Had Republicans not forfeited these five seats by fielding candidates too extreme (and, in several cases, too weird) for the states' electorates, the Senate partisan balance would be fifty-fifty for the 113th Congress, and Vice President Joe Biden would be spending a lot of his time hanging around Capitol Hill waiting to break ties.

It may not be easy for Republican officials to avoid such nominations, because Tea Party sympathizers make up a majority of Republican primary electorates in many states. The Tea Party faction's views on such issues as immigration, abortion, same-sex marriage, global warming, and taxation makes them resistant to changes in the party's message that might expand its appeal to growing segments of the electorate. The far right's demonstrated capacity to punish incumbent Republicans in primaries discourages straying from party orthodoxy. Unless national leaders find a way to avoid fielding candidates whose appeal is limited to the party's most conservative voters, Republicans will continue to lose winnable Senate seats.

The Future: A Question of Demography

The Republicans' nightmare demographic scenario played out in full view in 2012 in California. The state had given the nation Ronald Reagan, voted for George H. W. Bush in 1988, had Republican governors from 1982 through 1998, and as recently as 2004 elected twenty Republicans to its House delegation. After 2012, not a single Republican held statewide office, Democrats had greater than two-thirds majorities in both chambers of the state legislature, and Republicans won only fifteen of the state's fifty-three House seats, their smallest share of California's delegation, but for 1936, in more than a century. The party's decline coincided with an increase in the minority share of the electorate—between 1994 and 2012, the proportion of nonwhites grew from 27 percent to 40 percent, the proportion of Latinos growing from 15 percent to 23 percent[42]—and the spread of tolerant social attitudes while the state party stuck resolutely to its socially conservative, anti-immigrant, and anti-tax positions. The demographics of the newly elected California House delegation reflect the consequences. Among the thirty-eight Democrats are eighteen women, nine Latinos, five Asian Americans, three African Americans, four Jews, and at least one gay. Only twelve are non-Jewish white men. All fifteen Republicans are white, at least nominally Christian, presumably straight men.[43]

The full U.S. House is trending in the same demographic direction, although it has not gone nearly as far as California. In the 113th Congress, women and minorities will outnumber white males in the Democratic Caucus for the first time in history, while nearly 90 percent of the Republicans will be white Christian men. Of the record 102 women taking seats in the House and Senate in 2013, nearly three-quarters are Democrats, as are twenty-three of the twenty-eight Latinos, forty of the forty-one African Americans, all eleven Asian Americans, all six openly gay or bisexual members, and thirty-six of thirty-seven members who profess a religion other than Christianity. The incoming class of freshmen includes forty new members who are female, ethnic minority, non-Christian, or gay (some in multiples of these categories); only five of them are Republicans (all women).[44] The 2012 elections basically reiterated the partisan status quo, but the demographic mix of the incoming members points to a strong undercurrent of continuing and profound change in the makeup of Congress. Republicans may be able to hold onto the House (and compete for the Senate) with homogeneously white and overwhelmingly male delegation over the next few elections, but demographic and social trends threaten this coalition's long-term viability even if the Republicans' structural advantage remains robust. In the meantime, the glaring demographic differences between the party coalitions, embodied in their rival congressional delegations, can only add to ideological polarization in national politics.

Notes

1. Jennifer Steinhauer, "Congress Nearing End of Session Where Partisan Input Impeded Output," *New York Times,* September 18, 2012.
2. In the twenty-seven surveys that asked the question between January 2012 and election day, an average of 14 percent approved, and 79 percent disapproved, of how Congress was handling its job; see www.pollingreport.com/CongJob.htm.
3. The incumbent success rate was 89 percent if we include incumbents who lost to other incumbents.
4. In an October 2011 CNN survey, 68 percent of Democrats blamed congressional Republicans for doing nothing to solve the nation's problems, with 16 percent blaming both parties and only 13 percent blaming their own party; 52 percent of Republicans blamed the Democrats, 14 percent both, and 28 percent the Republicans.
5. Two of the five pitted incumbents from the same party in the general election, a consequence of California's new "top-two" primary which pits the two candidates with the highest vote totals against one another regardless of party. The two Republican incumbents who faced off in Louisiana's 3rd District runoff after the general election are included in this category.
6. Gary C. Jacobson, "Terror, Terrain, and Turnout: Explaining the 2002 Midterm Elections," *Political Science Quarterly* 118 (Spring, 2003): 9–10.
7. Gary C. Jacobson, *The Politics of Congressional Elections,* 8th ed. (New York: Pearson, 2013), 17–19.
8. David Wasserman, "Introducing the 2012 Cook Political Report Partisan Vote Index," *The Cook Political Report,* October 11, 2012, http://cookpolitical.com/house/pvi.
9. Democrats enjoyed favorable redistricting in Illinois (controlled by Democrats), California, and Arizona (done by commissions) or they would have been in even worse shape under the new configurations.
10. The difference between the first two categories and the third is significant at $p<.001$.
11. This is shown with the signs turned positive for Republicans to facilitate the comparison.
12. A model including as independent variables real income change, presidential approval, and the president's party's "exposure"—the percentage if seats it held above or below an eight-election moving average—predicted Democrats would pick up three seats in 2012; a model based on the relative quality of each party's

challengers—assumed to be both an indication of and contributor to the fulfillment of electoral expectations—predicted a thirteen-seat Democratic gain. The models are in Jacobson, *Politics of Congressional Elections,* 167 and 181.

13. Jacobson, *Politics of Congressional Elections,* 30–35.
14. For midterm elections, the presidential vote is from the immediately preceding presidential election; this relationship is in every case actually as strong or stronger at the midterm than it was two years earlier.
15. The two most widely used approaches are the "Slurge" (a combination of the "sophomore surge" and "retirement slump" and the Gelman-King regression model; for a description of these models and the estimates they generate, see Jacobson, *Politics of Congressional Elections,* 32–35.
16. Twenty-five of the 434 districts for which the presidential victor has been determined delivered split results (5.8 percent); even if the remaining district splits, the total proportion will be only 6.0 percent, less than half of the previous low. Data are from David Wasserman, Cook Political Report, reported at https://docs.google.com/spreadsheet/ccc?key=0AjYj9mXElO_QdHZCbzJocGtxYkR6OTdZbzZwRUFvS3c#gid=0.
17. These are estimates; final campaign finance are not yet available; see "2012 Election Will Reach $6 Billion, Center for Responsive Politics Predicts," www.opensecrets.org/news/2012/10/2012-election-spending-will-reach-6.html; Campaign Finance Institute, "Independent Spending Wars Fought to a Standstill in 2012," www.cfinst.org/press/preleases/12-11-07/Independent_Spending_Wars_Fought_to_a_Standstill_-_House_and_Senate_2012.aspx; Campaign Finance Institute, "Early Post-election Look at Money in the House and Senate Elections of 2012," www.cfinst.org/Press/PReleases/12–11–09/Early_Post-Election_Look_at_Money_in_the_House_and_Senate_Elections_of_2012.aspx.
18. Jacobson, *Politics of Congressional Elections,* 79–89.
19. Of the thirty-three losing candidates who won at least 47 percent of the vote, thirty had more than $2 million in support, one had $1.5 million, and two had less than this amount.
20. They are Ami Bera (CA-7, over Dan Lundgren), Raul Ruiz (CA-36, over Mary Bono Mack), Joe Garcia (FL-26, over David Rivera), and Pete Gellego (TX-23, over Quico Canseco).
21. The five are John Barrow (GA-12), Collin Peterson (MN-7), Mike McIntyre (NC-7), Jim Matheson (UT-4), and Nick Rahall (WV-2); only Matheson did not win the NRA's endorsement.
22. Ann Kirkpatrick (AZ-1).
23. Election results are based on final official data available from the states; candidate expenditures are as of the November 26, 2012 reporting date and were supplied by the Federal Election Commission, www.fec.gov/data/CandidateSummary.do?format=html&election_yr=2012; independent expenditure data are from Open Secrets, www.opensecrets.org/outsidespending/summ.php?cycle=2012&disp=R&pty=N.
24. Angus King, who won election from Maine as an independent but enjoyed wide Democratic support and organizes with the Senate Democrats, is treated as a Democrat in this analysis. If Maine is dropped, the percentage of consistent results drops from 81.8 to 81.2, still the highest for the period covered.
25. Sean Sullivan, "Why Todd Akin's Win Gives Democrats Hope in Missouri," *Washington Post,* August 8, 2012, www.washingtonpost.com/blogs/the-fix/post/why-todd-akins-win-gives-democrats-hope-in-missouri/2012/08/08/6e0246b8-e16c-11e1-ae7f-d2a13e249eb2_blog.html#pagebreak; "Missouri Senate 2012," *Cook Political Report,* http://cookpolitical.com/senate/race/1458, accessed November 23, 2012.

26. Akin explained that "if it's a legitimate rape, the female body has ways to try to shut that whole thing down," a piece of medical nonsense (The Fix, *Washington Post,* August 19, 2012, www.washingtonpost.com/blogs/the-fix/wp/2012/08/19/todd-akin-gop-senate-candidate-legitimate-rape-rarely-causes-pregnancy/); Mourdock expressed the view that "even when life begins in that horrible situation of rape, that is something that God intended to happen," (ABC News, "Mourdock Rape Comment Puts GOP on Defense," October 24, 12, http://abcnews.go.com/Politics/OTUS/richard-mourdock-rape-comment-puts-romney-defense/story?id=17552263#.UK1ak—cgld).
27. Tester won with less than a majority, 48.6 percent to 44.9 percent, with the libertarian taking 6.6 percent of the vote.
28. For example, he was the only Senate Democrat to vote against repealing "don't ask, don't tell," and thus against allowing gays to serve openly in the military.
29. Molly Ball, "Obama's Edge: The Ground Game that Could Put Him Over the Top," *The Atlantic,* October 12, 2012, www.theatlantic.com/politics/archive/2012/10/obamas-edge-the-ground-game-that-could-put-him-over-the-top/264031/,; Dana Davidsen, "McDonnell: 'They Beat Us on the Ground,'" CNN Politicalticker, www.theatlantic.com/politics/archive/2012/10/obamas-edge-the-ground-game-that-could-put-him-over-the-top/264031 (McDonnell is the Republican governor of Virginia).
30. Noah Bierman, "Warren, Brown's 'No Third Party' Pledge Holds, " *Boston Globe,* August 20, 2012, www.bostonglobe.com/news/politics/2012/08/19/surprise-brown-and-warren-truce-outside-spending-surviving-imid-hard-fought-campaign/OTbqEdGBT2u3rJDUH9QZpO/story.html.
31. Jennifer Steen, *Self Financed Candidates in Congressional Elections* (Ann Arbor: University of Michigan Press, 2006), 149–153.
32. Data reported at www.gallup.com/poll/124922/Presidential-Approval-Center.aspx?ref=interactive; averages are from the five weekly summaries of Gallup's daily tracking polls published between October 7 and November 4, 2012.
33. David Wasserman, "House Overview: How House Democrats Beat the Point Spread," *Cook Political Report,* November 8, 2012, http://cookpolitical.com/house, accessed November 10, 2012.
34. Doyle McManus, "The Death of the Moderate Republican," *Los Angeles Times,* November 18, 2012.
35. For example, he charged that "there are 78 to 81 members of the Democratic Party who are members of the Communist Party" ("Florida Rep Labels Congressional Democrats as Communists," CNN, April 11, 2012).
36. Keith Pool estimates that the ideological differences between the House parties, measured by DW Nominate scores, which take values from -1 to 1, will go from .909 to .911 in the new Congress; see his blog dated November 13, 2012, http://voteview.com/blog/.
37. Gary C. Jacobson, "Partisan Polarization in Presidential Support: The Electoral Connection," *Congress and the Presidency* 30 (Spring, 2003): 8–11.
38. Jonathan Weisman, "Boehner Digs in on Opposition to Tax Hikes for the Wealthy," *New York Times,* November 9, 2012, http://thecaucus.blogs.nytimes.com/2012/11/09/boehner-digs-in-on-opposition-to-tax-hikes-for-wealthy/.
39. Keith Poole estimates that the ideological differences between the Senate parties, measured by DW Nominate scores, will increase from .773 to .826 in the new Congress; voteview blog dated November 13, 2012, http://voteview.com/blog/.

40. Albert Hunt, "Republicans' Hispanic Problem Is with Party Base," *Bloomberg News,* November `18, 2012, www.bloomberg.com/news/print/2012–11–18/republican-hispanic-problem-is-with-party-base.
41. Gary C. Jacobson, "The Republican Resurgence in 2010," *Political Science Quarterly* 126 (Spring, 2011): 39.
42. Mark DiCamillio, "Post Election Analysis: The Growing Political Might of Ethnic Voters in the 2012 California Elections," Field Poll Release #2435, November 19, 2012.
43. These demographics were first identified by Harold Meyerson, "CA to GOP: Adios," *Los Angeles Times,* November 13, 2012.
44. From data reported by Scott Keyes, Adam Peck, and Zack Beauchamp, "Infographic: The 113th Congress Will Be the Most Diverse in History," http://thinkprogress.org/election/2012/11/13/1175491/113th-congress-diversity/.

8

The Presidency

No Exit from Deadlock

Bruce Nesmith and Paul J. Quirk

In the aftermath of the 2008 elections, some observers described Barack Obama's victory, in grandiose and celebratory terms, as *transformative.* The hoped-for transformation had to do mainly with the historic first election of an African American president, although also with the end of the widely disapproved George W. Bush presidency. In contrast, the 2012 elections have been described, lugubriously, as changing nothing—and doing so amid a national political crisis that, by most accounts, called desperately for changing *something*. The perception of sound and fury with no significance reflected the failure of the elections to effect any change in control of the nation's central policymaking institutions—that is, the retention of a Republican majority in the House of Representatives, a Democratic majority in the Senate, and the exact same Democratic president.

But there is more to an election than the sheer numbers of Democrats and Republicans installed in office, notwithstanding the obvious importance of those numbers. The campaign itself also matters, along with the individuals who participate. In this chapter, we take a broader look at the consequences of the election for the presidency and, more generally, for American government over the next four years. In view of the events and rhetoric of the campaign, as well as the results, what can we expect during President Obama's second term? Will the president and Congress deal effectively with the country's problems: the slow economic recovery and the long-term fiscal imbalances that threaten the nation's future, as well as other critical issues such as immigration and climate change? Or is the United States headed, as some fear, for sustained political incapacity and national decline?

We are also interested, in general, in the character of the electoral process as the source of these effects. Does the contemporary electoral process—with the multitude of primary elections, dense schedule of televised debates, massive spending on television advertising, among other features—promote successful presidencies and workable, responsive government? Or do contemporary methods of conducting and contesting elections themselves promote failure?

To organize the inquiry, we focus on three questions about the effect of elections on the presidency and government in the United States. First, does the presidential election *select for*—that is, favor candidates who actually possess—the character and skills that are important for a successful presidency? Second, do the discussion and debate of the campaign result in workable mandates, commitments, and expectations for the winning candidate? Third, do the presidential and congressional campaigns and elections, taken together, give the president a reasonable chance to lead Congress, or at least to work with it effectively?

Our account is on the whole far from reassuring. On the positive side, President Obama, after four years of generally successful experience in office, is likely to perform competently in his second term. The likelihood of a debilitating presidential scandal or a devastating policy mistake is relatively low.[1] Yet, we suggest, the election of this relatively competent president occurred despite a haphazard, if not perverse selection process—not because of a reliable one. Moreover, the election failed thoroughly to prepare the public for the hard choices that the country faces, or to sanction any credible plan for dealing with them. Finally, although the election persuaded some leading Republicans that the party needs to broaden its appeal, it left the ideological gulf between the Democrats and the increasingly extreme congressional Republicans even wider than in the preceding Congress. We expect, at best, limited improvement in the pathologically conflicted working relationship between the president and congressional Republicans that obtained during the 112th Congress—in short, no exit from deadlock. In the end, we suggest that the American political system is in trouble, and that the difficulty begins with contemporary elections.

Character and Skills

Regardless of party and ideology, a key function of the presidential election is to select an individual who is—by virtue of personality, experience, skills, and other traits—reasonably suited to the office of president. The campaign, therefore, should enable and encourage an attentive voter to assess the candidates as potential presidents. Did the 2012 election campaign, in fact, select for the attributes of a qualified president? We argue that it produced such a president largely by happenstance—without, in any reliable way, selecting for relevant attributes.

Elections and Presidential Character and Skills

No official or widely accepted statement of qualifications exists for the office of president. Presidential campaigns tout whatever arguably positive qualities their candidate appears to possess. Thus Republicans promoted honorable military service as a central qualification when their candidates were the militarily distinguished Bob Dole (1992) and John McCain (2008), but not when the indifferent reservist George W. Bush ran against the decorated war hero, John Kerry. In the same way, Democrats proclaimed the importance of executive experience when their candidates were former governors Michael S. Dukakis or Bill Clinton, but not when they were senators Kerry or Barack Obama.

In considering the important attributes the president should have, scholars have stressed such qualities as the ability to bargain with and persuade other policymakers,[2] the ability to lead the public through effective communication,[3] the ability to manage arrangements for advice and implementation,[4] and the possession of a well-adjusted personality, free of personality defects.[5] In an effort to sum up what he calls "the presidential difference," Fred Greenstein identifies six major factors: public communication, organizational capacity, political skill, vision, cognitive style, and emotional intelligence.[6] In part, scholars merely divide up the relevant attributes in different ways. But they also disagree—for example, about whether a president needs extensive knowledge of government and policy.[7]

To some degree, a presidential election campaign provides a test of the candidates' relevant political skills. Campaigns test a candidate's endurance in pursuit of the office, management of a large organization, strategic calculation, and ability to build coalitions and maintain public support.[8] Since the 1970s, the presidential election system has in effect been premised on this notion, as a long series of primary elections has replaced conventions dominated by party professionals as the central events in choosing the parties' nominees. In fact, however, some of the most effective campaigners for president have displayed major shortcomings once in office. Jimmy Carter and Bill Clinton struggled with managing the White House, particularly early in their presidencies, and compounded these struggles by relying on inexperienced subordinates. Ronald Reagan found that his bold campaign messages on economics and budgeting were no match for the constraints of reality.[9] In a cautionary tale of a candidate who did not become president, two lengthy presidential campaigns did not reveal serious flaws in the character of Democrat John Edwards. An appealing outsider approach in 2004 landed him on that year's ticket as John Kerry's vice presidential candidate. In 2008 he was well-funded and well-positioned for a second run for his party's presidential nomination, though he fell behind Hillary Clinton and Barack Obama. Only later did it become widely known that while his wife suffered from breast cancer, Edwards fathered a child with a campaign aide, and convinced another aide to claim paternity. Edwards's extravagant sleaziness was not exposed during two lengthy, competitive campaigns for president.

A plausible account, therefore, is that the campaign tests some relevant traits and skills, but not others. Most obvious, the campaign challenges a candidate's ability to form coalitions and build political support—skills that are important, though in different forms, in presidential policymaking. No one lacking in communicative and persuasive skills will be competitive. On the other hand, a presidential campaign provides only a limited test of policymaking ability. Campaigns need to have positions on major issues. To a great extent candidates compete at offering positions that will appeal to voters. But they do not need to demonstrate much specificity, planning for implementation, or making of hard choices. John F. Kennedy ran a splendid campaign in 1960 and almost immediately launched the disastrous Bay of Pigs invasion. Finally, the campaign provides only a weak test of emotional stability. Greenstein defines *emotional intelligence* as "freedom from distracting emotional perturbations significant enough to impair their leadership."[10] He cites Lyndon Johnson's mood swings, Richard M. Nixon's anger and suspiciousness, and Jimmy Carter's rigidity as cases of presidents who failed because of character defects. Bill Clinton's lack of impulse control also undermined his presidency—not only through the scandal that led to his impeachment and near removal from office, but also by causing him serious difficulties in making policy decisions.[11] Unfortunately, a successful presidential campaign can fail to reveal these defects—both because public discussion rarely explores significant episodes in the candidates' lives, and because personality defects are difficult to diagnose from secondhand accounts of past behavior.

Indeed, rather than trying to understand each candidate's character and skills, voters and the media pay attention to a very limited set of attributes. For at least three decades, the presidential candidate the public viewed as more likeable has won.[12] Communications scholar Leonard Steinhorn writes, "Political campaigns . . . have always been about using every possible media vehicle to create an iconic image of your own candidate and an unflattering impression of your opponent." As long ago as 1840, William Henry Harrison was elected by portraying himself as "a man of the people, a humble frontiersman who drank hard cider and hailed from log cabin roots."[13] Obama's advantage over Romney in likability through most of 2012 was seen as a protective firewall against negative assessments of his economic performance. "I'd rather have a beer with him than Romney," said Republican strategist Stuart Spencer. "Wouldn't you?"[14] Indeed, an NBC/*Wall Street Journal* poll in mid-October gave Obama a 57 to 25 percent advantage over Romney on "being easygoing and likeable" and a 53 to 29 percent advantage on "being compassionate enough to understand average people."[15]

Even more perverse, the voters may prefer certain candidates for having lesser, rather than greater, relevant experience. In parliamentary systems, candidates for party leader (and thus for prime minister) usually have served in the cabinet or in the leadership (sometimes called the *shadow cabinet*) of a nongoverning party. Either way, they have been centrally engaged in top-level national policymaking, along with campaigning for the party and winning election in their own districts.[16] In the United States, very few candidates for president have comparable experience. But the voters are not even looking for candidates who come relatively close. Jimmy Carter in 1976 may have been the first candidate in the modern era to proclaim a lack of any experience in the federal government as a virtue. The appeal has been a consistent theme in subsequent presidential campaigns. In 2008, the government experience of those in the second tier of Democratic candidates (Joe Biden, Chris Dodd, and Bill Richardson) vastly exceeded that of those who led the field (Hillary Clinton, Edwards, and Obama). The voters' preference for inexperience reflects their dim view of politicians and government: only 15 percent of respondents in a 2011 poll said they trusted the federal government "to do what is right" all or most of the time.[17] Voters apparently suppose that working in Washington ruins an elected official. As a result, they overlook the importance of learning about national issues, Washington policymaking, and the presidency through direct engagement and close observation.

The most important occasions for voters' assessment of candidate capabilities are undoubtedly the televised debates—of which the 2012 Republican nomination campaign featured more than twenty. Debates test certain kinds of information and mental agility. But doing well in a debate bears little resemblance to any activity required of the president. A debate requires listening to a question or an opponent's statement, often in the nature of an attack; taking no more than five to ten seconds to begin speaking; avoiding gross factual errors or unintended implications; and making an effective statement, based largely on well-rehearsed material. [18] By contrast, a president never has to make an important decision in ten seconds, or without assistance. Notoriously, voters' assessments of the candidates' performance turn heavily on matters of style. Democrat Al Gore performed poorly in 2000 by alternating between cordiality and toughness from one debate to another; George H.W. Bush hurt his chances during a 1992 debate by being caught on camera looking at his watch, evidently impatient with the proceedings.

Recent developments in campaign finance and the media have reduced the quality of the information that voters receive about the candidates' attributes. The Supreme Court's 2010 decision in *Citizens United v. FEC* facilitated an explosion in the campaign presence of super PAC groups unaffiliated with the candidates, with no contribution limits.[19] Negative, often salacious messages sponsored by these groups, with no accountability for their candidate, can dominate the campaign debate. At the same time, the news media have become more segmented and politically biased—with Fox News catering exclusively, and often recklessly, to a hard-line conservative audience; and MSNBC catering, with somewhat less inflammatory content, to a liberal audience; and numerous ideologically oriented Internet sites. Such sources trade in ideologically loaded and sensational content, and if anything, distract from sober consideration of candidates' character and skills.

The Nominations

In the general election, most voters have a strong preference for one party or the other, making the competing candidates' relative aptitude politically far less salient. If the overall presidential electoral process is to select individuals for character and skills, it has to do so in the selection of the two parties' nominees.

The Democrats' selection in 2012 occurred, in effect, four years earlier. As generally is the case with an incumbent president, Barack Obama was unopposed for the Democratic nomination. Obama had been nominated and elected president on the basis of scanty experience in 2008. Republican vice presidential candidate Sarah Palin had belittled his work as a community organizer, noting pointedly that when she was a small-town mayor, she had had "actual responsibilities." Nevertheless, Obama had demonstrated considerable effectiveness as president during his first term. According to most economists, his stimulus policy had prevented the economy from spiraling into depression.[20] Despite consistent and virtually unanimous opposition from Republicans in Congress, he had additional policy accomplishments in health care and financial reform. He also had a positive foreign policy record, including the formal end of the combat mission in Iraq, the commitment to a 2014 withdrawal of troops from Afghanistan, and above all the killing of the terrorist leader Osama bin Laden. Critical accounts of his economic leadership had alleged that he was not personally engaged in major policy decisions.[21] Liberals had complained that he was too passive in dealing with Congress, and too quick to make concessions to Republicans.[22] And the raid on bin Laden's suspected compound, deep in Pakistan, could have proved a fiasco.[23] In any case, Obama had served a term with significant achievements and neither a major scandal nor any widely perceived policy blunder.

With a potentially vulnerable Democrat in the White House, the Republican nomination contest attracted a large and diverse field of aspirants, thereby revealing more of the character of the selection process. At the outset, former Massachusetts governor Mitt Romney led the field, with name recognition from his competitive campaign for the 2008 nomination. His experience included four years as governor of a large state (2003–2007), heading the organizing committee for the 2002 Winter Olympics, and cofounding a successful private equity firm, Bain Capital.

In any process that seriously considered capabilities for presidential leadership, Romney's performance as governor of Massachusetts—by far the most pertinent evidence in his case—would have figured prominently in the discussion. But, caught in a monumentally perverse strategic bind, Romney found it awkward to bring up the subject of his governorship. He had had a substantial record of policy achievement. He had worked with, while sometimes bypassing, a state legislature that was firmly in control of the opposition Democratic party. In doing so, however, he had taken positions that, in 2012, were anathema to Republican primary voters. Most important, he had engineered the passage of a state-level plan for universal health care, with a requirement that all individuals purchase insurance. The Massachusetts plan was similar to the federal plan that Obama later pushed through Congress, and which nearly all Republicans, including Romney, vowed to repeal.[24] He had also taken moderate or liberal positions on social issues like abortion and gay rights. Romney usually avoided discussing his governorship, except to claim success in bipartisan leadership. Democratic legislators disputed that claim.[25] Nevertheless, his actual conduct as governor was never a major focus of discussion or debate.

The most consequential effect of Romney's Massachusetts political career was that he sharply reversed many of his prior policy positions—on health care, abortion, and gay rights, among other issues—in order to appeal to the conservative Republican primary electorate of 2012.[26] As the nomination season progressed, the *Economist* magazine called him "a dissembler prepared to tie [himself] in ever more elaborate knots."[27] From the standpoint of performance as president, there are far worse attributes than not having durable commitments to a set of ideological beliefs. Voters, however, generally regard such "flip-flopping" as evidence of poor character.

Romney was more vocal about his business experience. Unfortunately, discussion of that experience on all sides was relentlessly exaggerated and misleading. Romney had cofounded Bain Capital in 1984 and remained as chief executive officer until 1999, building a highly profitable partnership. He argued that running a successful company gave him insight into the workings of the economy—and especially into how to create jobs—that career politicians lacked.[28] As with his governorship, there was little discussion of his specific activities, roles, or decisions.[29] His opponents tried to use his business career against him. In January 2012, former Speaker of the House Newt Gingrich, who emerged as a leading rival for the Republican nomination, attacked Romney's business record in a series of speeches, characterizing Bain as "vulture capital" that profited from the assets of weak companies before killing them off: "Show me somebody who has consistently made money while losing money for workers and I'll show you someone who has undermined capitalism."[30] It was implausible to argue either that running a venture capital company gave Romney the ability to design effective economic policies or that his conduct indicated that he would lack the other Republicans' concerns for American workers and businesses. What Romney's business career demonstrated was high-level management skills in a context completely different from the presidency.

At least nine other nationally known candidates entered the Republican nomination contest, each vying to be the leading alternative to Romney, whose moderate past inspired a strong anybody-but-Romney sentiment among many Republican primary voters.[31] The outstanding characteristics of the field of rivals were the rigor of the selection for very strong, if not extreme, conservatives and the lack of much selection for other attributes, such as substantive competence or relevant experience.

The leading challengers to Romney included Gingrich, the architect of the 1994 Republican takeover of Congress; Rick Perry, governor of Texas since 2001; three other current or former Congress members known more for extreme views than for policy achievements (Michele Bachmann, Ron

Paul, and Rick Santorum); and Herman Cain, a business executive-turned-conservative commentator. Except for Gingrich and Perry, these candidates had few credentials as leaders. Perry's candidacy crashed and burned when—in an excruciating, prolonged moment during a televised primary debate—the Tea Party favorite could not remember which three federal departments he had proposed to abolish, suggesting that he had not given the dramatic proposal much thought. A number of more substantive, experienced candidates fell by the wayside early or chose to stay out of the race. Former governor Tim Pawlenty of Minnesota (2003–2011), seriously considered by John McCain as a potential running mate in 2008, dropped out in August 2011 after a disappointing finish in the Ames, Iowa, straw poll. Several prominent governors with pragmatic policy records considered running but stayed out of the race.[32] The *Economist* observed, "As the Republican base has become ever more detached from the mainstream, its list of unconditional demands has become ever more stringent."[33]

Despite his advantages over the other Republicans in money and organization, Romney stumbled to the nomination. He suffered embarrassing gaffes. During a televised debate, he offered to bet Perry $10,000 about a factual disagreement—both an ostentatious display of wealth and an offhand endorsement of gambling, strongly disapproved by Christian conservatives. He pointed out his loyalty to American cars by noting that his wife Ann owned two Cadillacs. And he tried to claim solidarity with victims of the recession by saying, "I'm also unemployed."[34] Such episodes—largely devoid of significance for government or policy—received widespread attention because television and Internet audiences would understand them and find them amusing. An observer of the discussions of Romney's gaffes might have inferred that the main requirement for an effective president is not to say something stupid.

The General Election Campaign

With the choices narrowed after the conventions to the Democrat Obama and the Republican Romney, questions of character, skills, and suitability were important mainly for the less partisan, less ideological, and less engaged independent or undecided voters. The televised debates, watched by huge audiences, had major effects on the campaign.

Romney trounced Obama in the first debate, on October 3 in Denver, although partly by means that proved costly later. In addition to giving crisp, coherent responses, he caught Obama off guard by repositioning himself as, once again, a moderate, after his strident conservatism in the nomination campaign. Asked in the first question about his approach to the economy, Romney said "[We're] going to take a different path. Not the one we've been on, [and] not the one the President describes as top-down, cut taxes for the rich. We're not going to do that."[35] In his response, Obama aimlessly mentioned several unrelated proposals. His remarks were disorganized and ineffective throughout the debate. He did not launch any strong attacks on Romney. Liberal commentator Chris Matthews said on MSNBC, "What was he doing tonight? He went in there disarmed."[36] Comedian Bill Maher quipped, "I can't believe I'm saying this, but Obama looks like he *does* need a teleprompter."[37] Subsequent news accounts solved the mystery of his weak performance: In addition to Romney's surprise strategy, Obama had taken the debate lightly and failed to prepare seriously. (He had spent the day before the debate sightseeing with his family in Colorado.) As a result of his decisive victory, Romney's standing in the polls improved markedly and he drew roughly even with Obama.

Obama recovered in the remaining two debates by preparing thoroughly, going on the attack, and exploiting Romney's eleventh–hour policy repositioning.[38] Early in the second debate, Obama challenged the honesty of Romney's new position on taxes for the wealthy: "And when Governor Romney stands here, after a year of campaigning, when during a Republican primary he stood on stage and said 'I'm going to give tax cuts'—he didn't say tax 'rate cuts,' he said 'tax cuts to everybody,' including the top 1 percent, you should believe him because that's been his history."[39] Using these methods, Obama by all nonpartisan measures clearly won the second and third debates, as Vice President Biden won his single debate with his Republican counterpart, Paul Ryan. On the campaign trail, Obama started referring to "Romnesia," suggesting that Romney was trying to forget positions he had taken earlier.

To a great extent, the advertising campaign focused on similar issues of character, values, and suitability. Beginning in the spring, Obama sought to "define" Romney's character with a barrage of advertising that attacked his role with Bain Capital—highlighting cases where Bain takeovers had led to layoffs. One inflammatory ad essentially blamed a woman's death from cancer on Bain Capital, alleging that when Bain put her husband out of work, they were unable to obtain the health care she needed.[40] Republicans complained about the implication that Romney's business practices caused the woman's death—after all, all businesses lay off employees—but a pro-Obama super PAC continued to run ads blaming Bain and Romney for causing hardship among American workers.[41]

Democrats also pounced on Romney's long refusal—against the advice of most Republican commentators—to release more than one year's worth of his income tax returns. Democratic critics suggested that Romney apparently had something to hide, perhaps that he had managed to avoid paying any taxes at all.[42] Belatedly, three weeks after the Republican convention, Romney released his returns for 2011 along with summaries for the years from 1990 to 2009. (He had released his 2010 return in January.) The summary showed that Romney had a very large income—an average $13.7 million per year—and had paid a moderately low effective tax rate of 14 percent, despite foregoing some deductions for which he was eligible.[43] Considering the pressure to disclose that he had resisted, the inference that

Romney had had something to hide was probably warranted. But there was no reason to suppose that it was anything illegal, or beyond the ordinary in the financial affairs of the very wealthy.

Romney harmed his own image as presidential material through an additional series of errant statements. On a summer international tour intended to bolster his foreign policy credentials, he told an interviewer that he doubted London organizers were adequately prepared to host the Olympic Games. British prime minister David Cameron, a presumed ideological ally, angrily belittled Romney's accomplishment of managing a Winter Olympics in the serene location of Salt Lake City, Utah, while the British press dubbed him "Mitt, the Twit."[44] At subsequent stops, Romney caused controversy with remarks insulting to Palestinians, Mexicans, and the government of Poland.[45]

Romney suffered by far the most important blow to his public image, however, when a video, recorded at a fundraising dinner in May and leaked to news organizations, showed him speaking in September to wealthy contributors. "All right," he said, "there are 47 percent who are with [Obama], who are dependent on government, who believe that . . . they are victims, who believe that government has the responsibility to care for them, who believe that they are entitled to health care, to food, to housing—you name it."[46] The remark was widely deplored as pandering to wealthy donors and disparaging veterans, the elderly, the unemployed, and many others who receive help from government programs.[47] In the same video, Romney told the audience that if his father (who was born in Mexico) had been Latino, "I'd have a better shot of winning this."[48] Obama and the Democrats seized on the remarks as showing Romney's contempt for large categories of citizens and reminded audiences of them at every opportunity until the election. Romney's poll standing sunk sharply after the revelations, which bore primarily on matters of values and character, as opposed to policy.

Apart from his desultory performance at the first debate, Obama largely avoided episodes that cast doubt on his character or skills for the presidency. (In 2008, in contrast, he had been caught making patronizing remarks about working-class people "clinging to their guns and religion.") The Romney campaign, however, took one of Obama's statements out of context to suggest that he did not respect the efforts or accomplishments of small business. At a rally, Obama had reminded the audience that any business depended on government to create conditions necessary for its success, such as education and infrastructure. His conclusion, "You didn't build that"—meaning, for example, that a given business owner had not built roads and bridges—was construed by the Romney campaign as saying that the business owners had not built their businesses. The distortion was widely recognized, and the attack probably had minimal effect on Obama's support. Nevertheless, the Republicans did not abandon it, and the Republican convention and Romney rallies featured audience chants of "You built it."

In the last week of the campaign, Obama received the political benefit of an "October surprise" from Mother Nature when Hurricane Sandy caused devastation along the East Coast, especially in New York and New Jersey. As president, Obama had the responsibility and the politically priceless opportunity to display compassion and effective leadership in bringing federal assistance to the millions of victims. Republican governor Chris Christie of New Jersey, setting aside partisan politics in favor of a more urgent local politics, gave the president fulsome credit for an effective and helpful response.

Results and Assessment

The election offered voters a choice between two candidates with credible-to-superior credentials for the office of president. Romney was the weaker in a few respects—lacking spontaneous comfort with ordinary people; ability to self-censor awkward or embarrassing remarks; and, probably, to the extent it matters, genuine commitment to an ideological position. None of these weaknesses were of central importance for the presidency.[49] And he probably offered a compensating advantage of exceptional management skill. In the final polls, voters gave Romney the higher ratings in ability to control the budget deficit (50–42 percent) and to create jobs (51–37 percent), the two areas where Obama's record was obviously vulnerable. But they gave Obama the edge on "a strong leader" (48–43 percent), "more moderate" (50–38 percent), working with the other party (47–41 percent), honest and truthful (46–40 percent), and consistent positions (51–46 percent).

At the same time, the availability of even one presumably competent, experienced leader was at bottom almost accidental. Obama, selected with the advantage of incumbency, had originally been nominated on the basis of virtually no record of political leadership in 2008. Romney had squeaked through a Republican nomination contest in which the party's primary voters had cared almost exclusively about the candidates' ideology and had seriously entertained several candidates with virtually no credentials at all. The campaign had drawn voters' attention largely to trivial episodes and misleading attacks. The actual conduct of the two candidates as leaders was rarely mentioned.

Commitments, Mandates, and Expectations

The consequences of an election depend in large part on what the candidates say the election is about, and how they discuss policy during the campaign. As research shows, presidents as well as members of Congress make serious efforts to make good on their campaign promises.[50] But the practices surrounding campaign promises and appeals are often problematic. In the idealized scenario of democratic theory, the contending parties present distinctly different platforms or sets of policies. They argue the merits of the opposing platforms during the campaign. Voters attend carefully to the debate, make up their minds which platform they prefer, and determine policy by casting their ballots.[51]

In fact, however, this idealized process describes the decisions of very few voters. Most people do not pay enough attention to policy debates to make informed choices about specific policies.[52] Accordingly, political scientists have identified two methods of voting that are arguably rational, yet less demanding. In what Paul Sniderman calls *fixed-choice* decisions, voters know simply which general direction of policy they prefer—more governmental effort to solve problems and help the less well-off, or less such effort, more individual freedom, and lower taxes—and which party promotes that general direction. When choosing a candidate or answering an opinion poll about an issue, they can use the cues from the parties and rely on that simple preference of one direction or the other.[53] Alternatively, in what scholars term *retrospective voting,* voters can ignore policy entirely and just decide whether the president has improved the condition of the country. As candidates often suggest, voters can ask themselves, "Am I better off now than I was four years ago?"[54] Such voting undoubtedly occurs—for example, the electorate strongly rewards the incumbent party for a strong economy, and punishes it for a weak one. Either of these patterns will often produce a reasonably constructive form of popular control.

Another sort of relationship between politicians and voters, however, is less benign. Opposing candidates may appeal for support on the basis of specific policies, not just general directions; but in doing so they may exploit the responses of uninformed, inattentive voters—especially independent and swing voters—by making attractive-sounding promises that in truth can never be kept, or would have very serious hidden costs. Put simply, politicians compete at manipulating unsophisticated voters by covering up unpleasant realities. One version of such campaigning is simply to overlook crucial problems, acting as if they did not exist—like an auto repair shop proposing an affordable list of repairs for a car while ignoring that the engine is about to fail. Another version is to make claims that are simply false about the causes or solutions of real problems—like promising to fix the failing engine with nothing more than an oil change. Still another is to promise results without identifying specific means—"just bring it in; we'll get you back on the road in half a day." What is most important, these misleading appeals will promote perverse conduct by the winning candidate after the election. There will be strong pressure to try, or at least pretend, to make good on the promises of the campaign. Politicians in democracies are prone to promise lower taxes, more generous benefits, easier solutions to problems, more decisive defeat of enemies, fewer casualties, and more wealth and security, among other things, than real-world policies can deliver. George H. W. Bush, for example, promised in his 1988 campaign to create thirty million jobs. Despite generally sound economic policies, the four years of his administration saw only three million jobs added. Barack Obama's 2008 promise to cut the budget deficit in half in his first four years was similarly doomed. Politicians love to promise to cut budgets, in the abstract, because many Americans believe federal spending is replete with waste, fraud, and abuse. The tendency toward campaign appeals that pander to voters by ignoring or denying crucial realities—and toward policies that reflect those appeals—is probably the central vulnerability of democratic political systems.

By comparison to past presidential campaigns, Obama and Romney both were unusually rigorous in avoiding specific positions on public policy issues. They had strong incentives to withhold such positions. Obama faced public skepticism about his stewardship of the economy, as well as about his signature policy achievement, health care reform. Romney had few options that appealed both to the intensely conservative core Republican constituencies and to more moderate independents and swing voters. So each candidate's campaign kept the focus on its respective opponent: Romney stoked dissatisfaction with the economy while Obama pushed suspicion of Romney's personal values and policies. Neither candidate talked at length about his own qualifications or plans for office. Both campaigns were at once exceptionally negative and exceptionally light on public policy.

Apart from offering general slogans, the campaigns notably avoided the main issues of the time—the state of the economy and the government's budget deficit. Former Rep. Mickey Edwards commented, "In most elections, especially for president, what you get is: Here is my vision, here's where I'm going to take the country. And [this time] there's none of it."[55] *Washington Post* columnist Robert J. Samuelson suggested a title for a book on the campaign, "Profiles in Expedience."[56] Romney pointed to persistent high unemployment rates to charge that Obama had failed to boost the economy. He touted a low-tax, low-regulation approach as the formula for growth, but avoided calling it a return to the policies of previous Republican administrations. In fact, given widespread disdain for the most recent Republican president, George W. Bush, Romney tried to distinguish his proposals from Bush's policies. "President Bush and I are different people, and these are different times," he said during the second presidential debate. He criticized Bush for increasing the budget deficit, without saying how his policies would depart from Bush's.[57]

Romney's catering to different audiences resulted in an unusual array of positions. During the primary campaign he promised to stimulate the economy through various tax cuts: reducing payroll taxes and corporate taxes, ending taxation of income earned outside the United States, and eliminating taxes on financial earnings for anyone making less than $200,000.[58] Toward the end of the general election campaign, Romney abruptly backed away from some of his conservative views, stating in the first debate that "high-income people are doing just fine in the economy" and didn't need their taxes cut, and that "regulation is essential."[59] His final economic pitch was based on his business success: "I've got a policy for the future and agenda for the future. And when it comes to our economy here at home, I know what it takes to create 12 million new jobs and rising take-home pay."[60] He did not, however, offer details about his business activities, nor explain how they would translate into policy in the White House.

As we have noted, Obama could justifiably claim to have prevented economic collapse. His proposals for further stimulus had been blocked by congressional Republicans. But Obama did not even try to explain the obstruction by Congress, and settled for noting the grim situation he had inherited and the economy's improvement since early 2009. Unemployment had dropped more than 2 percentage points, but remained at a distressing 7.9 percent on the eve of the election. Obama argued mainly that his policies needed more time to work, and that Romney represented a bottom-line oriented capitalism and a return to the failed policies of the Bush administration. In the words of Republican strategist John Feehery, "Romney wants to make this a referendum on Obama's last four years while Obama wants to make it a referendum on Romney's last 14 years. There are no easy choices to make looking forward, so both campaigns are probably more comfortable relitigating the past."[61]

An enormous budget deficit complicated the candidates' economic proposals. The recession, following the fiscally extravagant policies of the Bush administration, produced large immediate deficits and added to a long-term imbalance in retirement programs. Romney promised to balance the budget by 2020 through better fiscal practices as demonstrated in his business career. He promised to reduce the budget deficit through unspecified spending cuts that would not affect the military—capping spending at 20 percent of national income and cutting the federal workforce by 10 percent. He also proposed turning Medicare into a voucher system and Medicaid into a block grant to states.[62] Romney strictly foreswore any tax increases; during a Republican primary debate on February 22, he promised, "We're going to cut taxes on everyone across the country by 20 percent, including the top 1 percent [of earners]."[63]

Romney's budget policy was widely criticized as unrealistic. While proposing to raise tax revenues and avoid increasing budget deficits by ending some tax expenditures, he declined to specify which ones he had in mind.[64] Most analysts contended that long-term deficit reduction required tax increases as well as spending cuts, and no plausible program of loophole-closing would even come close to matching the revenue that would be lost with Romney's the proposed tax cuts.[65] When Obama cited such findings by the nonpartisan Tax Policy Center at their October 3 debate, Romney tried to turn the tables, "There are six other studies that looked at the study you describe and say it's completely wrong." In fact, five of the six were publications—including two blog posts—by Romney's own advisers; the sixth was by a Princeton economics professor who had advised George W. Bush and who used an unorthodox assumption that the tax cuts would produce a large upsurge in economic growth.[66] Apparently recognizing the difficulties of his overall position, Romney promised at the next debate that he would not reduce the share of taxes paid by top earners, although he did not specify even preliminarily how he would adjust his plans to avoid it.

Obama was only somewhat more responsible on budget issues than Romney. He also promised spending reductions, mostly unspecified, including adjustments to entitlement programs and efficiencies supposedly to be achieved through health care reform. He claimed $716 billion in future Medicare savings from negotiations with health care providers to cut reimbursements; Romney, assuming the worst, charged that Obama was slashing benefits to the elderly to pay the costs of the reform.[67] Obama's repeated claim that his plan would reduce the deficit by $4 trillion was widely panned as a gimmick.[68] His signature proposal, repeated throughout the campaign, was to raise income taxes on the top 2 percent, restoring the rates that had prevailed prior to the 2001 Bush tax cut. Such a narrowly based tax increase would raise some revenue, but not remotely enough to bring the budget into balance.

Obama made the top 2 percent tax-increase proposal often enough that his reelection could be seen as an electoral mandate for this position. He took it into deficit-reduction negotiations with the lame-duck Congress in late 2012, while the top-ranking Republican, Speaker of the House John Boehner, reiterated the Romney campaign position as that of the House majority, which after all had been returned to power in the elections, too.[69] The negotiations were necessitated by the provisions of a 2011 agreement to extend the government's borrowing limitation; the law stated that, barring enactment of a major deficit-reduction package before December 31, 2012, massive across-the-board spending reductions would ensue automatically. At the same time, numerous temporary tax cuts also were due to expire. Economists warned that so much fiscal retrenchment, imposed suddenly, would endanger the already shaky recovery. Economist Mark Zandi said, "We would be stepping into an economic netherworld of slow growth and high unemployment that would leave us very vulnerable to anything else that goes wrong."[70] Nonpartisan commentary suggested that either candidate's positions, if maintained in office, would do serious damage to the economy.

Other important issues were also either avoided or else discussed with minimal regard for real-world constraints. On immigration, Romney had supported Bush's balanced, bipartisan reform proposal in 2005, but had abandoned that approach during his 2008 campaign, when he advocated deporting all illegal immigrants.[71] By the fall of 2012 he promised to "work with Republicans and Democrats to permanently fix our immigration system" but did not say how he would deal with undocumented immigrants already in the country.[72] Obama issued an executive order in June 2010 to allow some illegal immigrants to apply to defer deportation, and he called for enactment of the "Dream Act" to allow them a path to citizenship. But neither candidate addressed immigration issues as broadly as, for example, New York City mayor Michael Bloomberg, who called for allowing more immigrants with technical expertise and business plans, as well as a guest-worker program for temporary labor.[73] Romney promised to repeal Obama's order, as well as "supersede" it with another policy which he did not specify.[74]

Both candidates poked their heads firmly into the sand in dealing with climate change. Romney had written in his book *No Apology* that climate change was occurring and human activity was contributing to it. In the nomination campaign, he shifted his position in order to advocate removing limits on energy exploration and production. He criticized Obama as waging a "war on carbon dioxide," and pronounced, contrary to the scientific consensus as well as his book, that "we don't know what's causing climate change on this planet."[75] In his acceptance speech at the Republican convention, Romney ridiculed concerns about climate change, quipping, "President Obama promised to begin to slow the rise of the oceans. And to heal the planet. My promise is to help you and your family."[76] Obama prominently included the issue in his victory speech on election night: "We want our children to live in an America that isn't burdened by debt; that isn't weakened by inequality; that isn't threatened by the destructive power of a warming planet."[77] Before that safe moment, he had steadfastly ignored the issue throughout the campaign. In his first post-election news conference, Obama clearly indicated that any action on climate change would have to wait until the economy and budget were solved: "I think the American people right now have been so focused and will continue to be focused on our economy, jobs and growth that if the message is somehow that we're going to ignore jobs and growth simply to address climate change, I don't think anybody's going to go for that. I won't go for that."[78]

Romney twisted himself in knots to avoid candid discussion of health care. In campaigning for the nomination, he abandoned the policy approach that he had helped enact as governor of Massachusetts, and called for the outright repeal of the quite similar national reform enacted under Obama. He argued for cutting health costs by limiting malpractice suits, and for increasing access to care through tax deductions for health insurance and health savings accounts—standard Republican positions.[79] Toward the end of the campaign, however, he changed course again to deal with the popularity of parts of the Obama reform and the increasing public acceptance of the entire measure. He promised to require coverage of preexisting health conditions, but only for people who already had insurance coverage.[80]

Although Romney tried to portray fundamental differences with Obama over foreign policy—attacking him as "apologizing for the United States" around the world—the two actually had few substantive differences on foreign policy issues. In the October 22 foreign policy debate, Romney repeatedly acknowledged agreeing with Obama's major decisions—such as his 2011 call for Egyptian president Hosni Mubarak to resign, and his plan to withdraw the last American combat troops from Afghanistan in 2014.[81]

They disagreed on certain points as well. Romney wanted to increase the defense budget while Obama wanted to cut it. Romney went out on a limb promising to declare China a currency manipulator; Obama said he would work with China through diplomatic channels. Romney expressed firm solidarity with Israeli prime minister Benjamin Netanyahu and his hard-line positions on Palestine and Iran. Obama took roughly the same positions, although with more cautious rhetoric and a willingness to criticize Israeli settlements in disputed areas.[82] For the most part, voters would have seen little to choose between the two candidates on foreign policy based on what they said, although after four years as president Obama clearly had experience that Romney lacked. Nor did Obama, as the winning candidate, acquire any problematic commitments or mandates in this area.

If Romney had won the election, he would have had a major challenge adjusting his campaign positions to arrive at workable policies in a number of areas, especially those where he had bent over backwards to satisfy core Republican constituencies during the nomination process. Obama, having had no challenger for the nomination, and focused largely on attacking Romney's extreme positions, faced fewer such problems. In one, very serious exception, his campaign made it difficult to deal with the reforms of entitlement programs, especially Medicare and Social Security, that will be needed to make possible serious progress on budget deficits.

Support and Cooperation

Citizens and journalists often assume that skilled presidents can achieve their policy goals through sufficient applications of effort and skill.[83] In fact, a president's opportunities to shape public policy depend on the political circumstances. In making decisions on legislation, members of Congress look mainly to their own policy views and their own constituencies.[84] They regard the president's preferences as distinctly secondary. A president can sometimes induce the public to pressure Congress in support of a bill—but usually only if the public already supports the bill's purpose.[85]

Presidential success in policymaking depends above all, therefore, on the relative strengths of the two political parties and of the associated ideological factions in Congress.[86] Including the current 113th Congress, President Obama has faced three distinct balances of partisan and ideological power in Congress. Unfortunately, from Obama's standpoint, the latter two have been roughly similar and have amounted to a recipe for presidential frustration, policy deadlock, and governmental failure.

Obama and the 111th and 112th Congresses

In many respects, the 2008 elections gave Obama generous opportunities to set policy. In addition to his own decisive victory—in itself a modest advantage—the partisan and ideological makeup of the 111th

Congress placed him in a commanding position. The Democrats began Obama's presidency with a 257 to 178 advantage in the House of Representatives and a 59 to 41 majority in the Senate, which became 60 to 40 when Sen. Arlen Spector, a veteran Pennsylvania Republican, switched parties in 2009. These were the largest majorities held by one party in both chambers in thirty years.

But the ideological makeup of Congress complicated the picture. For the most part, ideology is the force driving presidential support in Congress.[87] And since the 1970s the two parties have been growing further apart, more polarized, ideologically.[88] Recent Congresses have been the most polarized in more than a century—with even the most conservative Democrat in the House now more liberal than any House Republican.[89] At the same time, there has been a steep decline in the size of the centrist group. This alignment gave Obama a somewhat larger base of support, when he sought to promote a liberal measure. But it also ensured a larger and more devoted opposition. And it left Obama without an automatic base of support if he tried to promote a moderate bipartisan measure.

Congressional polarization has reflected basic forces in American politics. One is a realignment of the party system that has made conservative southern Democrats an endangered species and virtually eliminated liberal Republicans from the Northeast—two groups that were enduring relics of the Civil War and Reconstruction. The other contributing force has been the increasingly influential role played by ideologically motivated activists in the politics of congressional nominations.[90] Importantly, the trend toward polarization has not affected the two parties equally or in the same way. On the Democratic side, the source of polarization has been simply the disappearance of white southern Democrats, which has made the party as a whole more liberal; northern Democrats themselves—the core of the party—have not moved significantly along the ideological scale since the 1970s. In contrast, Republicans in all regions have moved sharply to the right.[91]

In 2009–10, Obama leveraged his partisan and ideological advantages in Congress to enact an imposing set of landmark policies. The American Recovery and Reinvestment Act—the economic stimulus plan—was a $787 billion package of federal spending, aid to states, and tax cuts intended to stop and reverse the rapid economic deterioration that Obama inherited. The Affordable Care Act—so-called Obamacare—provided, for the first time, nearly universal health care in the United States, while making a start at controlling the growth of health care costs. The Wall Street Reform and Consumer Protection Act ("Dodd-Frank") reregulated the financial services industry to control the fast-and-loose financial practices that had led to the economic crisis. The combination of these measures—along with a bailout for the auto industry—made the 111th Congress the most productive of major policy action of any Congress since the 1960s.

Yet, the legislative process by no means worked smoothly during Obama's first two years in office. Each of these measures was enacted over intense Republican opposition. Obama was able to get only three Republican votes—all from senators—for the economic stimulus package, and the same for Dodd-Frank. He got no Republican votes in either chamber for the health care bill. Republicans, sometimes with support from the few remaining moderate Democrats, had used the filibuster to hold up action in the Senate, and had forced important concessions on every one of his major reform measures. Notwithstanding its productivity, the 111th Congress was also extraordinarily divided and disaffected, with many Republicans charging that Obama and the Democrats were imposing socialism.

The 2010 congressional elections brought Obama's reform agenda to a screeching halt. In a sweeping victory at all levels of the political system, Republicans picked up sixty-three House seats to win solid majority control in the House and six Senate seats, narrowing the Democratic majority to fifty-three to forty-seven.[92] In their campaign, the Republicans capitalized on disappointment with the slow economic recovery, anxiety about the health care law, and widespread anger about the huge budget deficits. With Tea Party–supported candidates forming a powerful faction among congressional Republicans, partisan conflict became even more intense than in the preceding Congress. The Republicans, with control of the House and enough members to sustain filibusters in the Senate, adopted obstruction of Obama's agenda as their stated mission.[93] The result was the least productive Congress in modern history—not only in the number of bills enacted, but also in the ability to adopt essential measures.

Despite grave danger to the economy, Republicans and Democrats played chicken over stimulus measures and the deficit, leading to paralyzing uncertainty in the business sector, and disgust among the general public. Public approval of Congress fell, for the first time, below 10 percent.[94] An apparent agreement in July 2011 between Obama and House Speaker John Boehner over raising the debt ceiling—which was needed to avoid default on government bonds, among other things—and reducing long-term budget deficits collapsed when the House Republican rank-and-file rejected the revenue increases in the agreement, thereby embarrassing their Speaker and bringing the country to the brink of economic disaster.[95] A short-term debt-limit increase without deficit reduction was passed the following month, "kicking the can down the road" until after the 2012 election. Congress's inability to deal responsibly with the country's long-term fiscal problems, and near failure even to avoid immediate calamity, led commentators to wonder whether the United States was in decline.

The 2012 Election Results and the New Congress

The 2012 presidential and congressional election results generally favored Democrats, but not decisively enough to indicate a clear path out of the stalemate that plagued policymaking in the 112th Congress. Obama won twenty-six states and 332 electoral votes, decisive but less than the twenty-eight and 365 he had won in 2008; his percentage of the popular vote also decreased, from 53 to 51 percent. Democrats added two seats to their majority in the Senate, and though they gained eight in the House, Republicans remained firmly in control of that chamber. Some of the more outspoken congressional ideologues departed, but so did the four most centrist members of the Senate and five of the eighteen most centrist members of the House.[96] With Obama's narrow reelection margin, and ideological balances in Congress only slightly altered, the pieces were in more or less the same places as in the preceding, 112th Congress. One could only speculate whether this would lead to more of the same, or whether the parties would see the need for some policy accomplishment as sufficiently compelling that they would be willing to compromise.

Early indications of the potential for cooperation were at best mixed. The first test came immediately after the election. Members of the lame-duck Congress were compelled to enter deficit-reduction negotiations with the White House to avert a so-called fiscal cliff looming at the end of the year. The 2011 agreement to increase the federal debt limit stipulated that unless substantial long-term deficit reduction was enacted by the end of 2012, massive across-the-board spending reductions would ensue automatically. At the same time, major tax cuts were about to expire—in effect, automatic tax increases. Economists warned that the sudden drop in fiscal stimulation—like falling off a cliff—would sink the economic recovery.[97] Democrats and Republicans needed to agree on a major deficit-reduction package, or at least postpone the automatic spending cuts and tax increases, to avoid serious harm.[98]

Both Obama and the Republican leaders acknowledged the need for compromise, yet they mostly stood firm on their earlier positions. Obama had campaigned on his intention to raise tax rates on the highest incomes to the pre-2001 levels, and he argued that his reelection was a mandate for such change: "If we're serious about reducing the deficit, we have to combine spending cuts with [increased] revenue—and that means asking the wealthiest Americans to pay a little more in taxes."[99] The president made his first formal proposal in a meeting with Speaker Boehner at the end of November. He offered only modest spending cuts. He called for tax increases on dividends and inheritances, and proceeded to make several assertive speeches promoting his positions. Republicans complained that Obama was trying to bully them.[100] Senate Democrats laid down some markers of their own, partly to make room for later concessions. They demanded that any deal include increases in tax rates (not just elimination of exemptions and deductions) and a long-term increase in the debt limit (ending the need for frequent short-term measures). Obama's press secretary said the administration would rule out reductions in Social Security benefits.[101]

Speaker Boehner was the principal public face of House Republicans, who had also retained power in the elections, and were inclined to make only minor concessions. Following Romney's approach in the presidential campaign, Boehner agreed to entertain proposals for revenue increases, but only if they were achieved by ending loopholes rather than raising rates.[102] In a gesture of compromise, several Republican legislators withdrew their commitment to an absolute anti-tax pledge that had hampered earlier negotiations. But Republicans, like Obama, were more specific about the limits of their flexibility than about what they were willing to concede. Besides rejecting tax-rate increases, Boehner demanded that the 2010 health care reform be "on the table" during the budget negotiations.[103] He categorically rejected the administration's first formal offer in late November. Senate Republican leader Mitch McConnell added that Obama "took a step backward, moving away from consensus and closer to the fiscal cliff."[104]

The fiscal cliff was averted, with House Republicans severely divided and in tactical retreat. As the end of the year approached, Republicans blocked Democratic proposals from floor votes in the Senate. But they were unable to unite around their own plan. When Speaker Boehner could not find the Republican House votes to pass a leadership proposal that gave ground on tax revenue, he was forced to withdraw it and, in effect, declare House Republicans unable to act.[105] In what was likely the last chance to reach a timely agreement, Biden and McConnell met repeatedly for lengthy bargaining sessions and worked out a deal, including a compromise on tax rates. The Biden-McConnell proposal easily passed the Senate, 89-8. But the House remained sharply divided, with the conservative wing of the Republicans unwilling to endorse the only remaining vehicle for avoiding the fiscal cliff. To prevent both economic and political disaster, Boehner broke with longstanding party practice and brought the bill to the House floor to pass with mostly Democratic votes while a majority of Republicans voted against it. Within days, he used the same strategy to pass a Hurricane Sandy relief bill for New York and New Jersey. Recognizing the political costs the party had incurred in prior episodes of economic brinkmanship, the Republicans also acceded to Obama's demand for a new debt-limit increase without conditions.

In the aftermath of the Republican retreat, Obama commenced his second term with an inauguration address that rejected "absolutism" and "name-calling" in an implicit appeal for greater bipartisan cooperation; but it firmly asserted a liberal agenda on health care, poverty, civil rights, the elderly, immigration, climate change, and gay rights.[106] Obama made few gestures toward Republicans, and showed little deference to conservative concerns. "One thing is clear from the president's speech," McConnell said, "the era of liberalism is back." McConnell pronounced the president's agenda, as described in the speech, "not designed to bring us together, and certainly not designed to deal with the transcendent issue of our era, which is deficits and debt."[107]

The drama over the fiscal cliff showed that the President and Congress, and Democrats and Republicans, were able to act together, at least temporarily, to avert catastrophe. But the means of doing so—with Republican

House leaders relying on Democratic members to pass a bill—created no expectation that such feats could be repeated. Certainly, the Republican leadership's bypassing of the party's hard-line conservative rank-and-file would not become the *modus operandi* of a functioning government. At the outset of Obama's second term, therefore, it was unclear whether his ambitious legislative agenda would get beyond square one in Congress, especially in the House. And it was very unclear whether the president and Congress would be capable of the cooperation needed to keep the economic recovery on a solid footing, much less to accomplish the more difficult task of putting the country's fiscal house in order.

Conclusion

To borrow a phrase from the title of a famously bleak play, the 2012 elections offered *no exit* from the polarized conflict and institutional deadlock of recent American politics.[108] In the aftermath of their party's losses in the 2012 election, some Republicans have argued that the party needs to mount more moderate campaigns if it expects to remain competitive, especially in presidential races. For the immediate future, however, the congressional Republican Party remains dominated by possibly the most conservative membership it has ever had. President Obama and the congressional Democrats have been measurably less extreme and rigid. But they too press narrow ideological and constituency interests—in particular, resisting cuts in costly entitlement programs to the detriment of long-term fiscal balance. The resulting conflicts are likely to dominate Obama's second term, and produce much the same frustration, deadlock, and governmental incapacity that they did in the second half of his first term.

Why is the country that has the oldest written constitution, and that was the most successful, powerful, and admired country on earth for most of the last century, now apparently failing? The answer seems to lie in broad developments in American electoral politics, and in the relation between electoral politics and the structures of policymaking institutions.[109] Three developments have changed the conduct of American elections. First, since the early 1970s, ordinary voters have played an enlarged role in selecting not only the holders of elective office, but also the parties' nominees for those offices—including, most importantly, the presidency. Nomination processes dominated by ordinary voters do not provide the peer review—that is, evaluations of potential nominees by political professionals—that existed prior to the 1970s.[110] As a result, the United States faces a chronic risk of electing a president who lacks the character, experience, or skills to perform effectively in the office. By the time Obama and Romney had wrapped up their parties' respective nominations, the country had dodged this bullet, this time around. But the 2012 Republican nomination process illustrated the risks—the possibility, for example, of electing a president who would propose to abolish several federal departments so casually that he might not remember the list.

Second, the conditions of electoral competition increasingly have favored relatively extreme politicians—liberal Democrats and conservative Republicans—and disfavored moderates of either party. This tendency pertains less, or not at all, to general elections for the presidency, where appealing to independent voters in swing states remains crucial to success.[111] But the advantage for candidates holding strong ideological positions certainly describes primary elections for both the presidency and Congress, as well as general elections for Congress in most states and districts.[112] Scholars have identified a variety of causes of electoral polarization—among them, party realignment (the abandonment of the Democratic Party by conservative white Southerners and of the Republican Party by liberal Northeasterners), redistricting in the House, and a sorting of the population into states and districts with increasingly homogeneous cultural, religious, and political values.[113] The most fundamental source of polarization in our view, however, is that a growing proportion of voters—especially, the core constituencies of the two parties—have strong ideological beliefs, consistent with their partisan attachments.[114] Politically active citizens are either liberal Democrats or conservative Republicans. In particular, highly committed activists—from the Tea Party to members of MoveOn.Org—are increasingly influential in primary elections.[115]

Third, campaign discourse is increasingly superficial, uninformative, and misleading. Again, several factors contribute. But the most fundamental is that citizens increasingly get their news from politically biased, cable TV, radio, and internet news sources that reinforce their existing political positions.[116] Increasingly, the purveyors of political news are in the business of telling a certain audience (liberal or conservative) whatever it wants to hear about politics.[117] For the contestants in election campaigns, the potential costs of straying from the path of truth and accuracy are therefore diminished.

Several organizations—FactCheck.org, PolitiFact.com, and others—try to expose the false and misleading claims. To all appearances, however, the fact checkers are losing the battle. Increasingly, the politicians and others whose misleading statements they expose are not deterred from continuing to use them, let alone from concocting new ones. Democrats continued to blame Romney for destroying jobs at companies that were failing before Bain Capital took them over. The Republicans continued to push "you didn't build that," long after their distorted interpretation had been discredited. A Romney campaign official was forthcoming on the matter of strategy, "We're not going to let the fact-checkers dictate our campaign."[118]

As a consequence of these three developments, the population of elected officials in the United States—especially, though not only, a sizable group of Republicans—is increasingly responsive to activist constituents, committed to an extreme ideological position, and indisposed toward study, deliberation, or compromise.[119] Such politicians do not fit well with two permanent and central features of the American constitutional system: First, the three federal elective offices (president, senator, and representative) are elected at different times, for terms of different length, and thus will often have occupants or majorities from different parties. Second, the three corresponding institutions (the presidency, Senate, and House) must reach agreement for the constitutional system to work effectively. The new, more ideological species of elected politician, when required to sacrifice ideological goals and cooperate across party lines for government to work, is quite likely to refuse. The challenge facing the political leaders and citizens of the United States is somehow to bring the conditions of electoral politics back into harmony with the working requirements of the constitutional system.

Notes

1. Paul C. Light, *The President's Agenda: Domestic Policy Choice from Kennedy to Clinton* (Baltimore: Johns Hopkins University Press, 3rd ed., 1998); compare, however, Michael Nelson, "Bill Clinton and the Politics of Second Terms," *Presidential Studies Quarterly* 28, no. 4 (Fall 1998): 786–792.
2. Richard Neustadt, *Presidential Power and the Modern Presidents: The Politics of Leadership from Roosevelt to Reagan* (Macmillan, 1990); Barbara Kellerman, *The Political Presidency: Practice of Leadership* (New York: Oxford University Press, 1984).
3. Samuel Kernell, *Going Public: New Strategies of Presidential Leadership*, 3rd ed. (Washington, D.C.: CQ Press, 1997).
4. James P. Pfiffner, *The Managerial Presidency*, 2nd ed. (College Station: Texas A & M University Press, 1999).
5. James David Barber, *The Presidential Character: Predicting Performance in the White House*, 4th ed. (Englewood Cliffs, N.J.: Prentice Hall, 1992).
6. Fred I. Greenstein, *The Presidential Difference: Leadership Style from FDR to George W. Bush* (Princeton, N.J.: Princeton University Press, 2004).
7. Paul J. Quirk, "Presidential Competence," in *The Presidency and the Political System,* 9th ed., ed. Michael Nelson (Washington, D.C.: CQ Press, 2010), 108–141.
8. Stephen Hess, "'Why Great Men Are Not Chosen President:' Lord Bryce Revisited," *Brookings Review* 5, no. 3 (Summer 1987): 34–39.
9. David A. Stockman, *The Triumph of Politics: How the Reagan Revolution Failed* (New York: Harper & Row, 1986).
10. Greenstein, *Presidential Difference,* 221.
11. Greenstein, *Presidential Difference,* 221–222; on Clinton's characteristic indecisiveness, see John Brummett, *Highwire: From the Backwoods to the Beltway—the Education of Bill Clinton* (New York: Hyperion, 1994).
12. Ruth Marcus, "Is Romney Likeable Enough to Win?" *Washington Post,* August 28, 2012, www.washingtonpost.com/opinions/ruth-marcus-is-mitt-romney-likable-enough-to-win/2012/08/28/5ae5d4f4-f144–11e1–892d-bc92fee603a7_story.html.
13. Leonard Steinhorn, "The Selling of the President in a Converged Media Age," in *Campaigns and Elections American Style: Transforming American Politics,* 3rd ed., ed. James A. Thurber and Candice J. Nelson (Boulder, Colo.: Westview, 2010), 140.
14. Lou Cannon, "Obama and Reagan: The Likability Factor," *Real Clear Politics,* September 14, 2012, www.realclearpolitics.com/articles/2012/09/14/obama_and_reagan_the_likability_factor_115445.html.

15. "Campaign 2012," *PollingReport,* http://pollingreport.com/wh12.htm.
16. Nelson W. Polsby, *Consequences of Party Reform* (New York: Oxford University Press, 1983); Richard Rose, *The Postmodern President: George Bush Meets the World,* 2nd ed. (Chatham, N.J.: Chatham House, 1991), ch. 6.
17. "Government," *Pollingreport.com,* www.pollingreport.com/institut.htm#Government; 54 percent of respondents in an NBC News-Wall Street Journal poll would vote to replace the entire U.S. Congress if they could (L. Sandy Maisel, "The Negative Consequences of Uncivil Political Discourse," *PS: Political Science and Politics* 45, no. 3 (July 2012): 408.
18. See, for example, Jeff Zeleny and Ashley Parker, "8 from G.O.P. Trade Attacks at Iowa Debate," *New York Times,* August 11, 2011.
19. Nicholas Confessore, "Campaign Aid Is Now Surging into 8 Figures," *New York Times,* June 14, 2012, A1, 20.
20. Betsey Stevenson and Justin Wolfers, "The U.S. Economic Policy Debate Is a Sham," *Bloomberg View,* July 23, 2012; see also Michael Grunwald, *The New New Deal: The Hidden Story of Change in the Obama Era* (New York: Simon & Schuster, 2012); Eduardo Porter, "Stimulus Is Maligned, but Options Were Few," *New York Times,* February 29, 2012, B1, 4; for an argument about why the stimulus was inadequately large, see Noam Scheiber, *The Escape Artists: How Obama's Team Fumbled the Recovery* (New York: Simon & Schuster, 2012).
21. Ron Suskind, *Confidence Men: Wall Street, Washington, and the Education of a President* (New York: Harper, 2011); Scheiber, *The Escape Artists.*
22. Scott Wilson, "Obama, the Loner President," *Washington Post,* October 7, 2011, www.washingtonpost.com/opinions/obama-the-loner-president/2011/10/03/gIQAHFcSTL_story.html; for an alternative view of Obama as skillful political manipulator, see David Corn, *Showdown: The Inside Story of How Obama Battled the GOP to Set Up the 2012 Election* (New York: William Morrow, 2012).
23. People involved in the decision to order the operation against Osama bin Laden were assuming about a 50 percent probability that he was in the targeted house at all; see Mark Bowden, *The Finish: The Killing of Osama bin Laden* (New York: Atlantic Monthly, 2012).
24. See Louis Jacobson, "Krugman Calls Senate Health Care Bill Similar to Law in Massachusetts," *PolitiFact,* February 4, 2010, www.politifact.com/truth-o-meter/statements/2010/feb/04/paul-krugman/krugman-calls-senate-health-care-bill-similar-law-/.
25. See Ben Adler, "Romney's False Claims of Bipartisanship in Massachusetts," *The Nation,* October 17, 2012, www.thenation.com/blog/170637/romneys-false-claims-bipartisanship-massachusetts#; David Welna, "Romney as Governor: 800 Vetoes and One Big Deal," *All Things Considered,* June 13, 2012, www.npr.org/2012/06/13/154583216/romney-as-governor-confrontation-one-big-deal.
26. Olga Belogolova et al., "Romney's Policy Positions: Changing with the Times," *National Journal,* November 12, 2011, 2.
27. "The Right Republican," *Economist,* December 31, 2011, 7.
28. Tom Hamburger, Melanie Mason, and Matea Gold, "A Closer Look at Mitt Romney's Job Creation Record," *Los Angeles Times,* December 3, 2011, http://articles.latimes.com/2011/dec/03/nation/la-na-romney-bain-20111204; Marc Maremont, "Tally of Job Creation by Bain Proves Vexing," *Wall Street Journal,* July 11, 2012, http://online.wsj.com/article/SB10001424052702303292204577519293959381060.html.
29. Maggie Haberman, "The Hidden Mitt Romney," *Politico,* July 24, 2012, www.politico.com/news/stories/0712/78878.html; he also was vague about his role

as CEO of the 2002 Olympics, the internal records of which have mostly been destroyed (Maureen Dowd, "Hiding in Plain Sight," *New York Times,* July 25, 2012, A23).

30. Jonathan Easley, "Newt Gingrich: Bain Capital 'Undermined Capitalism,' Killed Jobs," *The Hill,* January 10, 2012, http://thehill.com/video/campaign/203265-gingrich-romney-firm-bain-capital-undermined-capitalism.
31. Others were concerned about his lack of personal touch or his Mormonism; for an argument that Romney's Mormonism was testament to presidential character, see Michael Kinsley, "Playing the Mormon Card," *Los Angeles Times,* July 19, 2012, http://articles.latimes.com/2012/jul/19/opinion/la-oe-kinsley-column-romney-mormonism-20120719.
32. "The Right Republican."
33. Ibid.
34. Reid J. Epstein, "Mitt Romney's 'Cadillac' Flub One of Many," *Politico,* February 24, 2012, www.politico.com/news/stories/0212/73258.html.
35. Commission on Presidential Debates, "October 3, 2012, Debate Transcript," www.debates.org/index.php?page=october-3–2012-debate-transcript.
36. Brian Stelter, "No Kind Words for Obama at His Friendliest Network," *New York Times,* October 3, 2012, http://elections.nytimes.com/2012/debates/presidential/2012–10–03.
37. Michael D. Shear, "Debate Praise for Romney as Obama Is Faulted as Flat," *New York Times,* October 4, 2012, www.nytimes.com/2012/10/05/us/politics/after-debate-a-torrent-of-criticism-for-obama.html?hp.
38. Jim Rutenberg and Jeff Zeleny, "Rivals Bring Bare Fists to Rematch," *New York Times,* October 16, 2012, www.nytimes.com/2012/10/17/us/politics/obama-and-romney-turn-up-the-temperature-at-their-second-debate.html?pagewanted=all&_r=0.
39. Commission on Presidential Debates "October 16, 2012, Debate Transcript," http://debates.org/index.php?page=october-1–2012-the-second-obama-romney-presidential-debate.
40. "Understands," *The Living Room Candidate,* www.livingroomcandidate.org/commercials/2012/understands#4587; see also "The Cheaters," on Bain and offshoring, www.livingroomcandidate.org/commercials/2012/the-cheaters#4593.
41. Ashley Killough, "Pro-Obama Super PAC Brings Back Bain in New TV Ad," *Political Ticker,* October 23, 2012, http://politicalticker.blogs.cnn.com/2012/10/23/pro-obama-super-pac-brings-back-bain-in-new-tv-ad/.
42. Sam Stein and Ryan Grimm, "Harry Reid: Bain Investor Told Me that Mitt Romney 'Didn't Pay Any Taxes for Ten Years,'" *Huffington Post,* July 31, 2012, www.huffingtonpost.com/2012/07/31/harry-reid-romney-taxes_n_1724027.html.
43. Nicholas Confessore and David Kocieniewski, "Under Pressure, Romney Offers More Tax Data," *New York Times,* September 21, 2012, www.nytimes.com/2012/09/22/us/politics/under-pressure-romney-offers-more-tax-data.html?pagewanted=all.
44. Ashley Parker, "A Visitor's Questions on Readiness for Games Prompt a Curt Response," *New York Times,* July 27, 2012, A12.
45. Terence Burlij and Katelyn Polantz, "Romney's Comments in Israel Overshadow Visit to Poland," *The Rundown,* July 31, 2012, www.pbs.org/newshour/rundown/2012/07/weekend-in-israel-hangs-over-romney-speech-in-poland.html.
46. The remark conflates a number of categories. The 47 percent figure is approximately the number who are not required to pay individual income taxes, although many pay a sizable fraction of their income in payroll and other taxes.
47. Julie Hirschfield Davis and John McCormick, "Romney Seeking to Regain Control, Allies Bemoan Lost Days," *Bloomberg.com,* September 18, 2012,

www.bloomberg.com/news/2012–09–18/full-romney-fundraising-tape-to-be-released-today-by-magazine.html.

48. Bryan Llenas, "Mitt Romney: If I Was Latino, I'd Have Better Chance of Winning," *Fox News Latino,* September 18, 2012, http://latino.foxnews.com/latino/politics/2012/09/18/mitt-romney-if-was-latino-id-have-better-chance-winning/.
49. It would be important to know if a president would be willing to do what he or she believed was best for the country even if it was politically difficult. However, firm commitment to a particular ideological position is not implied by that willingness.
50. Jeff Fishel, *Presidents and Promises* (Washington, D.C.: CQ Press, 1994); Tracy Sulkin, *Issue Politics in Congress* (Cambridge, U.K.: Cambridge University Press, 2005).
51. Cf. Robert A. Dahl's description of "populistic democracy" in *A Preface to Democratic Theory* (Chicago: University of Chicago Press, 1956), ch. 3.
52. See Bernard Berelson, Paul F. Lazarsfeld, and William N. McPhee, *Voting* (Chicago: University of Chicago Press, 1954); Angus Campbell, Philip E. Converse, Warren E. Miller, and Donald A. Stokes, *The American Voter* (New York: Wiley, 1960); but also Norman H. Nie, Sidney Verba, and John R. Petrocik, *The Changing American Voter* (Cambridge, Mass.: Harvard University Press, 1976), ch. 10.
53. Paul M. Sniderman, "Taking Sides: A Fixed-Choice Theory of Political Reasoning," in *Elements of Reason: Cognition, Choice and the Bounds of Rationality,* ed. Arthur Lupia, Mathew D. McCubbins, and Samuel L. Popkin (Cambridge, U.K.: Cambridge University Press, 2000), 67–84.
54. Morris P. Fiorina, *Retrospective Voting in American National Elections* (New Haven, Conn.: Yale University Press, 1981).
55. Peter Baker, "Candidates Racing for the Future, Gaze Fixed Firmly on the Past," *New York Times,* July 13, 2012, A1, 12.
56. Robert J. Samuelson, "The Disconnect of 2012," *Washington Post,* November 4, 2012.
57. Jim Rutenberg and Jeff Zeleny, "Rivals Bring Bare Fists to Rematch," *New York Times,* October 16, 2012.
58. "Romney's Policy Positions: Changing with the Times," *National Journal,* November 12, 2011, 2ff.
59. Michael Cooper, David Kocieniewski, and Jackie Calmes, "Entering Stage Right, Romney Moved to Center," *New York Times,* October 4, 2012.
60. Commission on Presidential Debates, "October 22, 2012 Debate Transcript."
61. Baker, "Candidates Racing," A12.
62. "Romney's Policy Positions."
63. Cooper, Kocieniewski, and Calmes, "Entering Stage Right."
64. Michael Cooper, "Some Romney Proposals Await Fuller Detail," *New York Times,* September 14, 2012; his unwillingness to specify which loopholes would be closed enabled Obama to claim the burden would fall mainly on middle class families claiming deductions for home mortgage interest and child care.
65. Stevenson and Wolfers, "The U.S. Economic Policy Debate"; Eugene Kiely, "Romney's Impossible Tax Promise," *FactCheck.org,* August 3, 2012 www.factcheck.org/2012/08/romneys-impossible-tax-promise/.
66. Brooks Jackson, "Dubious Denver Debate Declarations," *FactCheck.org,* October 4, 2012, http://factcheck.org/2012/10/dubious-denver-debate-declarations/.
67. Sarah Kliff, "Romney's Right: Obamacare Cuts Medicare by $716 Billion. Here's How," *Wonkblog,* August 14, 2012, www.washingtonpost.com/blogs/wonkblog/wp/2012/08/14/romneys-right-obamacare-cuts-medicare-by-716-billion-heres-how/; Lori Robertson, "Medicare's 'Piggy Bank,'" *FactCheck.org,* August 24, 2012, www.factcheck.org/2012/08/medicares-piggy-bank/; none of the savings

affected patient benefits, and the savings were also included in the House Republicans' budget proposals authored by vice presidential candidate Paul Ryan.

68. Jackson, "Dubious Denver Debate Declarations."
69. "Remarks by the President," *Whitehouse.gov,* November 9, 2012; "Speaker Boehner Responds to President Obama's Fiscal Cliff Statement," *Speaker.gov,* November 9, 2012.
70. Lori Montgomery, "On Edge of Brutal 'Fiscal Cliff,' Some See an Opportunity to End Debt Paralysis," *Washington Post,* November 11, 2012; Alister Bull, "Republicans Say Deal Can Be Done on U.S. 'Fiscal Cliff,'" *Chicago Tribune,* November 12, 2012.
71. "Romney's Policy Positions."
72. Seema Mehta, "Romney Campaign Promises New Specifics, But He Offers None," *Los Angeles Times,* September 17, 2012.
73. David Rohde, "Why Immigration Is the Most Important Debate the Presidential Campaigns Aren't Having," *Atlantic Monthly,* August 2012.
74. Cooper, "Some Romney Proposals."
75. "Romney's Policy Positions."
76. Transcript is available at www.nytimes.com/interactive/2012/08/29/us/politics/annotated-republican-convention-speeches.html#romney.
77. "Remarks by the President on Election Night," *Whitehouse.gov,* November 7, 2012.
78. Andrew Restuccia, "President Obama Says Climate Change to Take Back Seat to Economy," *Politico,* November 14, 2012, www.politico.com/news/stories/1112/83865.html.
79. "Romney's Policy Positions."
80. Cooper, Kocieniewski, and Calmes, "Entering Stage Right."
81. Peter Baker and Helene Cooper, "Sparring Over Foreign Policy, Obama Goes on the Offense," *New York Times,* October 22, 2012.
82. "Obama and Romney: Where They Stand on the Issues," *New York Times,* November 2, 2012, www.nytimes.com/aponline/2012/11/02/us/politics/.
83. For a careful analysis of the president's influence, see Matthew N. Beckmann, *Pushing the Agenda: Presidential Leadership in US Lawmaking, 1953–2004* (New York: Cambridge University Press, 2010).
84. Jon R. Bond and Richard Fleisher, *The President in the Legislative Arena* (Chicago: University of Chicago Press, 1990); George C. Edwards III, *At the Margins: Presidential Leadership of Congress* (New Haven, Conn.: Yale University Press, 1989); and Brandice Canes-Wrone, *Who Leads Whom? Presidents, Policy, and the Public* (Chicago: University of Chicago Press, 2006).
85. Canes-Wrone, *Who Leads Whom?;* George C. Edwards, *On Deaf Ears: The Limits of the Bully Pulpit* (New Haven, Conn.: Yale University Press, 2003).
86. Andrew Rudalevige, "The Executive Branch and the Legislative Branch," in *The Executive Branch,* eds. Joel D. Aberbach and Mark A. Peterson (Oxford, U.K.: Oxford University Press, 2005), 433; Rudalevige also cites Paul C. Light, *The President's Agenda,* 3rd ed. (Baltimore: Johns Hopkins University Press, 1999), 281; Edwards, *At the Margins,* 172–173; Bond and Fleisher, *President in the Legislative Arena,* chap. 4; Steven A. Shull and Thomas C. Shaw, *Explaining Congressional-Presidential Relations: A Multiple Perspective Approach* (Albany: State University of New York Press, 1999), 84ff.; and George C. Edwards III and Andrew Barrett, "Presidential Agenda Setting in Congress," in *Polarized Politics: Congress and the President in a Partisan Era,* eds. Jon R. Bond and Richard Fleisher (Washington, D.C.: CQ Press, 2000), 128.
87. Rudalevige, "Executive Branch," 434; Rudalevige also cites Bond and Fleisher, *President in the Legislative Arena,* 87; Richard Fleisher and Jon R. Bond, "Partisanship and the President's Quest for Votes on the Floor of Congress," in *Polarized Politics,* 154–185.

88. Keith T. Poole and Howard Rosenthal, "The Polarization of the Congressional Parties," *Voteview.com,* http://voteview.com/political_polarization.asp.
89. Paul J. Quirk, "The Legislative Branch: Assessing the Partisan Congress," in *A Republic Divided,* Annenberg Democracy Project (Oxford, U.K.: Oxford University Press, 2007): 121–156.
90. Richard Fleisher and Jon R. Bond, "The Shrinking Middle in the U.S. Congress," *British Journal of Political Science* 34, no. 3 (July 2004): 429–451.
91. Poole and Rosenthal, "Polarization."
92. Republicans had also gained one Senate seat in a January 2010 special election.
93. Robert Draper, *Do Not Ask What Good We Do: Inside the U.S. House of Representatives* (New York: Free Press, 2012); Thomas E. Mann and Norman Ornstein, *It's Even Worse Than It Looks* (New York: Basic Books, 2012).
94. Lucy Madison, "Congressional Approval at All-time Low of 9%, According to New CBS News/New York Times Poll," *CBSNews.com,* October 25, 2011, www.cbsnews.com/8301-503544_162-20125482-503544/congressional-approval-at-all-time-low-of-9-according-to-new-cbs-news-new-york-times-poll/?tag=contentMain;contentBody; the low point in the Gallup poll was 10 percent, in February and August 2012 (Jeff Jones and Lydia Saad, "USA Today/Gallup Poll December Wave 1," 14–17 December 2012, www.gallup.com/file/poll/159404/Congress_approval_121219.pdf, 2–4).
95. Boehner was challenged by House Republican leader Eric Cantor, who was skeptical of the talks with Obama and who spoke for more of the rank-and-file; see Matt Bai, "Obama vs. Boehner: Who Killed the Deal?," *New York Times Magazine,* April 1, 2012, www.nytimes.com/2012/04/01/magazine/obama-vs-boehner-who-killed-the-debt-deal.html?pagewanted=all#7; Peter Nicholas and Lisa Mascaro, "How the Obama-Boehner Debt Talks Collapsed," *Los Angeles Times,* July 22, 2011, http://articles.latimes.com/2011/jul/22/nation/la-na-obama-boehner-20110723.
96. Jeremy W. Peters, "113th Congress: This Time, It's Out with New," *New York Times,* December 10, 2012, A1, 17; "Rank Orderings of All Houses and Senates," *Voteview.com,* http://voteview.com/senrank.asp.
97. Quoted in Lori Montgomery, "'Fiscal Cliff' Already Hampering U.S. Economy, Report Says," *Washington Post,* October 25, 2012, www.washingtonpost.com/business/economy/fiscal-cliff-already-hampering-us-economy-report-says/2012/10/25/45730250–1ecf-11e2-ba31–3083ca97c314_story.html.
98. Lori Montgomery, "On Edge of Brutal 'Fiscal Cliff,' Some See an Opportunity to End Debt Paralysis," *Washington Post,* November 11, 2012; Alister Bull, "Republicans Say Deal Can Be Done on U.S. 'Fiscal Cliff,'" *Chicago Tribune,* November 12, 2012.
99. "Remarks by the President," *Whitehouse.gov,* November 9, 2012, www.whitehouse.gov/the-press-office/2012/11/09/remarks-president.
100. Caitlin Huey-Burns and Erin McPike, "GOP Leaders Pan White House's Budget Plan," *Real Clear Politics,* November 30, 2012, www.realclearpolitics.com/articles/2012/11/30/gop_leaders_pan_white_houses_fiscal_cliff_plan_116289.html.
101. Jonathan Weisman, "Democrats Vow Not to Take Deal without Extension of Debt Ceiling," *New York Times,* November 28, 2012, A18; Robert Pear, "Efforts to Curb Social Spending Face Resistance," *New York Times,* November 27, 2012, A1, 20.
102. "Speaker Boehner Responds to President Obama's Fiscal Cliff Statement," *Speaker.gov,* November 9, 2012, www.speaker.gov/speech/full-text-speaker-boehner-calls-bipartisan-action-avert-fiscal-cliff.
103. John Boehner, "House GOP Is Angling to Repeal Health Care," *Cincinnati Enquirer,* November 21, 2012, http://news.cincinnati.com/article/20121121/

EDIT02/311210016/House-GOP-angling-repeal-health-care?nclick_check=1.
104. Jonathan Weisman, "G.O.P. Balks at White House Plan on Fiscal Cliff," *New York Times,* November 30, 2012, A23.
105. Jonathan Weisman, "Boehner Cancels Tax Vote in Face of G.O.P. Revolt," *New York Times*, December 21, 2012, www.nytimes.com/2012/12/21/us/politics/house-moves-toward-vote-on-boehners-backup-plan.html.
106. "Inaugural Address by President Barack Obama," January 21, 2013, www.whitehouse.gov/the-press-office/2013/01/21/inaugural-address-president-barack-obama.
107. Alan Silverleib and Tom Cohen, "After Inauguration, Political Reality Returns to Washington, *CNN,* January 22, 2013, www.cnn.com/2013/01/22/politics/pol-back-to-reality/?hpt=hp_t2.
108. Jean-Paul Sartre, *No Exit: A Play in One Act,* trans. Stuart Gilbert (New York: A.A. Knopf, 1948).
109. Paul J. Quirk, "Public Opinion: Polarized Populism and Policymaking," in *New Directions in American Politics*, ed. Raymond J. La Raja (New York: Routledge, forthcoming 2013), ch. 9; compare, Morris P. Fiorina and Samuel J. Abrams, *Disconnect: The Breakdown of Representation in American Politics* (Norman: University of Oklahoma Press, 2009).
110. Nelson W. Polsby, *Consequences of Party Reform* (Oxford, U.K.: Oxford University Press, 1983); compare Marty Cohen, David Karol, Hans Noel, and John Zaller, *The Party Decides: Presidential Nominations Before and After Reform* (Chicago: University of Chicago Press, 2008).
111. Samuel L. Popkin, *The Candidate: What It Takes to Win—and Hold—The White House* (Oxford, U.K.: Oxford University Press, 2012).
112. Gary C. Jacobson, "The Electoral Basis of Partisan Polarization in Congress," paper presented at the Annual Meeting of the American Political Science Association, Washington, D.C., August 31–September 3, 2000.
113. Paul J. Quirk, "A House Dividing: Understanding Polarization," *The Forum* 9, no. 2 (2011): article 12; Sean Theriault, *Party Polarization in Congress* (Cambridge, U.K.: Cambridge University Press, 2008); Matthew Levendusky, *The Partisan Sort: How Liberals Became Democrats and Conservatives Became Republicans* (Chicago: University of Chicago Press, 2010).
114. Alan I. Abramowitz, *The Disappearing Center: Engaged Citizens, Polarization, and American Democracy* (New Haven, Conn.: Yale University Press, 2010).
115. Seth Masket, *No Middle Ground: How Informal Party Organizations Control Nominations and Polarize Legislatures* (Ann Arbor: University of Michigan Press, 2011).
116. W. Lance Bennett and Shanto Iyengar, "A New Era of Minimal Effects? The Changing Foundations of Political Communication," *Journal of Communication* 58 (2008): 707–731.
117. James T. Hamilton, *All the News That's Fit to Sell: How the Market Transforms Information into News* (Princeton, N.J.: Princeton University Press, 2004).
118. Michael Cooper, "Campaigns Play Loose with Truth in a Fact-check Age," *New York Times,* August 31, 2012, www.nytimes.com/2012/09/01/us/politics/fact-checkers-howl-but-both-sides-cling-to-false-ads.html?_r=0.
119. Mann and Ornstein, *It's Even Worse than It Looks.*

9

The Meaning of the 2012 Election

David R. Mayhew

The nation's fifty-seventh presidential election has come and gone. What are we to make of it? This chapter addresses the shape of the election, the political context surrounding it and brought by it, and its policy implications. Election patterns for the House and Senate as well as the presidency are taken up.[1]

The General Shape of the Election: Incumbency Prevails

Overwhelmingly, 2012 was a personal incumbency election. Possibly it set a new standard in that respect. In all the elective institutions, if you held an office and ran for it again on the November ballot you were exceedingly likely to keep it.[2] It was like a Wall Street firm at Christmas: bonuses for virtually everybody. There was little "edge" to the 2012 election. It was not driven by background forces like the Iraq war in the midterm of 2006,[3] the Wall Street crash (and Iraq, still) in the contest of 2008,[4] or a blowback against unpopular legislative enactments, notably Obamacare, in the midterm of 2010.[5] (The term *Obamacare* started out as invidious, but the president himself warmed to it.) That is, those three elections had edge. But in 2012 the voters seemed to recede into a stance of default, exhausted perhaps, by the policy extravagance of both the in-office Democrats in 2009–10 and the in-office congressional and state-level Republicans in 2011–12. In an edgeless environment, personal incumbency can play out.

Let us tackle this feature of incumbency institution-by-institution, at the national level along with a word on the state governors.

The Presidency

Presidents running for reelection can lose. Bad luck or hammered performance can do them in. The losers include both Adamses, William Howard Taft, Herbert Hoover, James Carter, and George H. W. Bush. Incumbents can even lose big. But generally speaking, sitting American presidents win if they run. This is not a fluke: personal incumbency is a plus in the elections of other presidential systems, not just those of this country.[6] One test of the

American propensity can be seen in Table 9.1. It asks the question, based on fifty-five presidential elections going all the way back to 1792: has a party running an incumbent presidential candidate—as opposed to in-office parties running open-seat candidates—kept the White House in an election? [7] The party keep rate is 69 percent, or twenty-two of thirty-two, for the personal incumbency elections, now including Barack Obama's victory in 2012. It is only 48 percent, or eleven out of twenty-three, basically a toss-up, for the open-seat elections. We see in this gap a pattern that basically trumps other interpretations of U.S. presidential history such as whether "party eras" have existed.

Table 9.1 Has the Party Holding the Presidency Kept It?

Elections with an Incumbent Candidate Running (with winners named)	
Yes, party kept the presidency (N = 22)	No, party lost the presidency (N = 10)
1792—Washington	1800—J. Adams lost to Jefferson
1804—Jefferson	1828—J. Q. Adams lost to Jackson
1812—Madison	1840—Van Buren lost to W. H. Harrison
1820—Monroe	1888—Cleveland lost to B. Harrison
1832—Jackson	1892—B. Harrison lost to Cleveland
1864—Lincoln	1912—Taft lost to Wilson
1872—Grant	1932—Hoover lost to F. D. Roosevelt
1900—McKinley	1976—Ford lost to Carter
1904—T. Roosevelt	1980—Carter lost to Reagan
1916—Wilson	1992—G. H. W. Bush lost to Clinton
1924—Coolidge	
1936—F. D. Roosevelt	
1940—F. D. Roosevelt	
1944—F. D. Roosevelt	
1948—Truman	
1956—Eisenhower	
1964—L. B. Johnson	
1972—Nixon	
1984—Reagan	
1996—Clinton	
2004—G. W. Bush	
2012—Obama	

(Continued)

Table 9.1 Continued

Elections without an Incumbent Running (with winners named)	
Yes, party kept the presidency (N = 11)	No, party lost the presidency (N = 12)
1796—J. Adams	1844—Polk
1808—Madison	1848—Taylor
1816—Monroe	1852—Pierce
1836—Van Buren	1860—Lincoln
1856—Buchanan	1884—Cleveland
1868—Grant	1896—McKinley
1876—Hayes	1920—Harding
1880—Garfield	1952—Eisenhower
1908—Taft	1960—Kennedy
1928—Hoover	1968—Nixon
1988—G. H. W. Bush	2000—G. W. Bush
	2008—Obama

Note: Omitted from the calculations are 1788, when the presidency was new, and 1824, when all the serious contenders for the office were of the same hegemonic party.

Source: Compiled by the author.

Somehow, as a statistical matter, the playing field is tilted. But it is a good deal easier to discern the pro-incumbent tilt than to figure out why it exists. Many theories or hunches have been posed for the presidency or other offices such as senator and representative in which a pro-incumbent tilt also has existed.[8] At the presidential level, voters may be risk-averse. We know we have endured the current incumbent. Given among other things the start-up costs a new person in office faces, as classically instanced in John F. Kennedy's botch of the Bay of Pigs invasion in early 1961, who knows what rookie mistakes a successor might make? On-the-job experience may thus bring appreciation as well as upgraded political skill.

Also, an incumbent president may manage to keep a campaign apparatus in good tune and raise ample campaign money when needed. And, in a different vein—at issue is a statistical pattern—politicians who have won an earlier presidential election may on average be better politicians than their challengers. An incumbent has already defeated a big-league opponent in at least one election;[9] a challenger has not.[10] Further still, an incumbent president can often campaign on "valence issues," basically ones of managerial performance, untroubled by any need to appease a party's base on position issues in order to win a nomination—even at the cost of later November embarrassment.[11] Remember Romney on the stage in those Republican primary debates of early 2012 withstanding Rick Santorum, Herman Cain, and the others before a large television audience. Imagine Obama on a stage like that needing to outpoint week after week the rhetoric of other liberals on issues like card-check unionization. Finally in this grab bag of considerations, an incumbent president can obviously just plain do things—emit executive orders at the right time, postpone troubles until December, or preside over crises or disasters. In the latter vein, Obama in emollient appearances with Republican governor Chris Christie of New Jersey in the wake of hurricane Sandy in October 2012 is on par with George W. Bush personally dispensing ice to people after a rugged Florida hurricane in the election season of 2004.[12] Of such threads can history be spun.

In terms of popular vote share, there is econometric time-series analysis. Ray C. Fair, covering most of the past century, has clocked the vote bonus for White House incumbents at approximately 4 percent. That is controlling for the condition of the economy.[13] Perhaps that figure has dipped in very recent times since a hardening of party allegiances among voters has narrowed the range of quadrennial vote outcomes. Blowout elections are less common. One estimate of the incumbency bonus for recent times is 2.5 percent.[14] Yet on average there is a bonus. Obama won 51.8 percent of the two-party popular vote in 2012. We will never know for sure, but a not easily unpackable incumbency bonus might have made the difference in the election. A similar instance would be George W. Bush's narrow reelection victory in 2004.

Governors and Senators

Six governors, including four Democrats and two Republicans, ran for reelection in 2012. All of them won. In the five open-seat contests, the Republicans gained one state—North Carolina.

In the Senate, twenty-two incumbents including fifteen Democrats, six Republicans, and one Democratic-leaning Independent—Bernie Sanders of Vermont—ran on the ballot in November 2012 to keep their jobs. Of these, twenty-one won. That is a keep rate of 95 percent. Only two of these twenty-two had never faced an even-year November electorate before. One of the two, Republican Scott Brown of Massachusetts, the surprise victor of a relatively low-turnout special election in January 2011, lost this time. The other, Republican Dean Heller of Nevada, a recent appointee to the Senate, won the squeakiest victory.

Of the eleven open seats (that is, no incumbents running in November), the Democrats lost one in Nebraska, gained one in Indiana, and sort of gained one in Maine as the winner there, Independent Angus King, declared his Democratic allegiance on Capitol Hill.[15] Eight of the open seats went to Democrats (including King). This was a very bad showing for the Republicans. Overall, the party ran into an unexpected wall in trying both to defeat incumbent Democrats and capture open seats. As in 2010, they fielded certain candidates who positioned themselves at a remarkable ideological distance from the median voters of their states. In 2010, that happened in Colorado, Delaware, and Nevada. In 2012, it was Indiana—owing to veteran senator Richard Lugar's defeat in a primary—and Missouri. At the Senate level, the Republicans suffered what seems a systematic nominating difficulty during the Tea Party context of Obama's first term. There were at least five lost opportunities. Thanks to the 2012 election, the Democratic share of Senate seats rose from fifty-three to fifty-five (including Sanders and King) in the one hundred–seat chamber.

The House of Representatives

The House elections were murkier. Many House seat losses or gains by members or parties in 2012 need an asterisk attached to them because of the census of 2010. In consequence of that decennial process, several House seats were reapportioned, and probably every House district in a state possessing more than one district had its map changed at least a bit.

Of the 162 Democrats running again on the November ballot, 152 kept their seats. That is a keep rate of 94 percent.[16] A few others lost their seats earlier in primaries. The ten losses were a varied lot. Two members lost to Republican incumbents in new districts where two incumbents were thrown in together. Four lost to Democrats (two of them other incumbents) in the new California jungle-primary system that can advance two contenders from the same party onto the November ballot. Three lost to Republican challengers in redrawn districts now more Republican in texture.[17] Probably only one Democratic member—Ben Chandler (KY)—can be said to have lost to a Republican challenger in a contest not seriously clouded by remapping.

As for the Republicans, 216 of them ran again, and of these 199 kept their seats. That is a 92 percent keep rate.[18] The seventeen Republican losses were a varied lot, too. One election was not yet decided on November 7—a Louisiana race between two Republican incumbents. Twelve Republican losers seem to have been nontrivially inconvenienced by new district maps.[19] Some of those races might have drifted Democratic anyway, but it is hard to tell. That leaves four Republicans who lost to Democratic challengers in more or less straight-out contests not levered by redistricting difficulties—Frank Guinta (NH), Charlie Bass (NH), Chip Cravaack (MN), and David Rivera (FL). Rivera had trouble with corruption allegations.

For the 378 House incumbents of both parties running again in November 2012, the keep rate was 93 percent. In the sixty-two open seats, the Democrats won thirty-one contests, the Republicans thirty-one.[20] In the nationwide popular vote cast for the House in November 2012, the Democrats secured about 50.4 percent—a sizable gain of roughly 4 percent over the party's embarrassing share in 2010.[21] And the Democrats did gain a net of some eight seats, growing in membership from 193 to 201 in the House chamber of 435.[22] Perhaps that was an Obama coattails gain, short as those coattails may have been. But the gain is slight. The question is: how could a Congress so unpopular in the polls (which do not ordinarily distinguish between House and Senate) not get pounded in an election? There is nothing new in this nonpounding. Overwhelmingly, voters vote for Congress on the basis of partisanship, the standing of the White House party, and regard for particular congressional candidates—notably incumbents—not on the basis of appraisals of Congress as a whole or its individual chambers or majority parties. Also, on casual inspection there is no sign that Republican House members associated with the Tea Party, a connection much noted in the media and in general political discourse, registered any special gain or loss in November 2012.

House Redistricting

But how, it is asked of the House elections, could a 50.4 percent Democratic edge in votes generate a 234–201 Republican edge in seats? One answer is that the Republicans controlled a great many state governments in consequence of the 2010 election, and they did their Machiavellian best when reconfiguring the district lines. In North Carolina, an aggressive party scheme drew targets on the backs of several Democratic incumbents. In Ohio, Pennsylvania, Virginia, Michigan, Georgia, and several smaller states, maps of a defensive aim shored up Republican incumbents, many of them newcomers. The Democrats did their best, too, but their venues of control were few—in Illinois a full-scale assault against several Republican incumbents (who lost), and in Maryland an astonishing map aimed at incumbent Republican Roscoe Bartlett (it defeated him). Unquestionably, given the arithmetic of party control in the states, the Republicans enjoyed a considerable advantage in this coast-to-coast game of geographic overhaul.

But does redistricting explain the Republican retention of the House? On that, considerable doubt arises. The hitch, once again, is that incumbents running for reelection tend to win anyway. The question is complex. But see Table 9.2, which zeroes in on a particular subset of House incumbents running again: the sixty-six Republicans who captured Democratic seats in the election of November 2010—an immense, historic gain that did much to shape the Washington, D.C. politics of 2011–12.[23] Of those sixty-six victors, sixty-three ran again in November 2012 against Democratic challengers.[24] The table thus illustrates the electoral fortunes of the sixty-three Republican House freshmen, Tea Partiers and otherwise, who captured Democratic-held seats in November 2010 and then faced Democratic challengers in November 2012.

In Table 9.2, the districts of the sixty-three Republican freshmen running again are divided into three categories, reading down. In the top category are districts in states where the redistricting process was controlled by the Republican Party during 2011–12. That is, the states' elected institutions—governor, assembly, and senate—had sovereignty over redistricting and all three institutions were Republican-controlled or else a state had a Republican legislature facing a veto-less governor (as in North Carolina) or possessing veto-proof

Table 9.2 Redistricting Politics, the Freshman Republicans, and 2012

State Redistricting Politics in 2011–12	*N* Districts ($N = 63$)[a]	N Who Lost Seats	% Who Lost Seats	Median Change in *R*% of Popular Vote[b]	Mean Change in *R*% of Popular Vote[c]	% Who Beat National 4% *D* Swing in Popular Vote[d]
Controlled by Republicans[e]	28	2[f]	7%	+2.5%	+2.1%	89%
Driven by divided party control, courts, commissions, or other tight constraints[g]	27	5[h]	19%	+4.4%	+3.3%	82%
Controlled by Democrats[i]	8	2[j]	25%	+4.7%	+3.2%	75%
Total seats	63	9[k]	14%	+3.7%	+2.6%	84%

[a]This excludes three Republican capturers of Democratic seats in 2010. In 2012, Rick Berg (ND) ran for the Senate, Sandy Adams (FL) lost a throw-in primary to another (nonfrosh) Republican incumbent, Jeff Landry (LA) faced another (nonfrosh) Republican incumbent in the November election.

[b]The major-party popular vote.

[c]This calculation omits four instances in which the freshman Republican incumbents were not challenged by Democratic candidates in November 2012: Austin Scott (GA), Kevin Yoder (KS), Diane Black (TN), and Bill Flores (TX).

[d]Nationwide, the Democratic share of the House popular vote rose roughly 4% between 2010 and 2012. This entry tracks the share of Republican candidates who either won their seats again or fell by less than 4% in 2012.

[e]AL, GA, IN, MI, NH, NC, OH, PA, SC, TN, VA, WI.

[f]Charlie Bass (NH) and Frank Guinta (NH)

[g]AZ, CO, FL, ID, KS, MN, MS, MO, NV, NJ, NM, NY, SD, TX, WA. Included here is the one-district state SD where no party discretion was available.

[h]Chip Cravaack (MN), Nan Hayworth (NY), Ann Marie Buerkle (NY), Allen West (FL), and Francisco Conseco (TX).

[i]AR, IL, MD, WV.

[j]Joe Walsh (IL) and Bobby Schilling (IL).

[k]Actually six of the nine losers seem to have been seriously hurt by new districting maps—Hayworth, Buerkle, West, Conseco, Walsh, and Schilling.

Source: Compiled by the author.

two-thirds majorities in both legislative chambers (as in New Hampshire). In the bottom category are the Democratic-controlled states. In the middle category are states where a single-party remap was not possible: party control was divided, or commissions did the redistricting, or the courts intruded, or a state had only one district (no party leeway there), or in one case (Florida) the voters had applied tight constraints to the legislature's discretion.[25]

First to be noticed in Table 9.2 is the high keep rate of these sixty-three Republican freshmen—86 percent. Only nine of them lost, and, of those, six had been poleaxed or at least burdened by redistricting. This success rate is extraordinary. November 2010 was a decisively off-normal election, yet, generally speaking, its winners came and have stayed. Beyond that, reading down in the table, there is not a lot of outcome differentiation across the three categories of districting control. Generally speaking, the Republican freshmen did well in all three kinds of line-drawing politics. Note one summary result at the bottom of the next-to-last column: On average, the sixty-three incumbents ran 2.6 percent better than they had in 2010. Since the country as a whole (including the terrain of the sixty-six freshmen) shifted about 4 percent Democratic between 2010 and 2012 in its House voting, these freshmen as a class bucked the trend by some 6.6 percent. The three redistricting categories allow an additional analysis—this one involving the full House and a counterfactual probe. Of all 435 House districts in November 2012, 143 were in states where the Republicans had controlled the districting, 42 in states where the Democrats controlled it, and 250—the bulk of the seats—in neutral territory where neither party had the reins.[26] Between 2010 and 2012, the Republican seat share fell 4 percent in the neutral category—from a party edge of 125-121 to a party deficit of 117-133. Now for the counterfactual. Suppose that the Republicans' same 4 percent loss in seat share had occurred in both the other categories—the states of Republican districting control (that would mean a drop there from 68.3 percent of seats in 2010 to a counterfactual 64.3 percent in 2012) and the states of Democratic control (a drop from 40.9 percent to 36.9 percent).[27] In this imaginary scenario, the party would have shed eighteen seats in November 2012, not the eight seats that it apparently lost. Republican control of the new House would be 224-211, not 234-201. Going by this particular counterfactual test, the Republicans did rack up a seat advantage through redistricting in 2011–12, but they probably did not need it to keep House control. It is good bet that the working of personal incumbency advantage otherwise was sufficient.[28]

Continuing Context: Divided Party Control

The keep rates for reelection-seeking incumbents in 2012 were 100 percent for the president and vice president, 100 percent for governors, 95 percent for senators, and 93 percent for House members. Not least of the static outcomes of the election is that divided party control of the government continues: as in 2011–12, so in 2013–14, a Democratic presidency, a Democratic Senate, and a Republican House. The Democrats may enjoy a small political and policy premium given their presidential victory and their gain of two seats in the Senate and eight in the House. But the basics remain. Not only that, power is likely to stay divided after the 2014 midterm. In midterms, a party possessing the White House routinely loses seats in the House. Exceptions have occurred. During Franklin D. Roosevelt's first term in 1934, a zooming economy helped loft the president's party.[29] For the Democrats, a similar economic surge in 2013–14 would be great luck. But such favorable midterms are rare. The odds are that the Obama White House saw the last of a Democratic-controlled Congress at the close of calendar 2010.

In historical context, divided party control in Washington has become usual, if not exactly normal. Coalition government, so to speak, is the statistical mode. As of December 2014, divided party control will have prevailed 62 percent of the time since 1946. (See Table 9.3.)[30] The House of Representatives' status as the party outlier of the three institutions, the current configuration, is not unprecedented. In addition to 2011–12, that was the pattern from 1981 to 1986 when Democratic House Speaker Tip O'Neill faced the Reagan administration and a Republican Senate. Taking in a longer historical frame, there is one wrinkle of note. In November 2012, the same national electorate simultaneously chose a president of one party and a House majority of the other party. Before the mid-1950s, that particular juxtaposition of results almost never happened. But starting then it has happened, counting 2012, slightly over half the time. The personalizing of both presidential and congressional candidates through the coming of television, at the price of party regularity in voter behavior, may have been the chief cause of this development.[31]

So what? Here is food for thought. The parties have always liked to use the momentum of presidential election victories to press their legislative programs. "Honeymoons" are the familiar dynamic. But the chance for honeymoons, given the split election outcomes, has become rarer since the mid-1950s. It is less common for a newly elected president to have a friendly Congress. That rareness may be raising the political stakes when a party does strike it rich, or may be about to, with a big across-the-board election victory, spurred for whatever reasons. Gifted with such a victory, a party may expeditiously clean out its files to enact every policy its activists have been fancying for decades. Given a plausible companion psychology, both accentuated hope and accentuated fear may come to invest the public in the run-up time to any new presidential election.

Table 9.3 Unified and Divided Control of the U.S. National Government Since World War II

			Divided		
Years	President	Unified	Pres	Sen	House
1947–48	Truman		D	R	R
1949–50	Truman	D			
1951–52	Truman	D			
1953–54	Eisenhower	R			
1955–56	Eisenhower		R	D	D
1957–58	Eisenhower		R	D	D
1959–60	Eisenhower		R	D	D
1961–62	Kennedy	D			
1963–64	Kennedy/Johnson	D			
1965–66	Johnson	D			
1967–68	Johnson	D			
1969–70	Nixon		R	D	D
1971–72	Nixon		R	D	D
1973–74	Nixon/Ford		R	D	D
1975–76	Ford		R	D	D
1977–78	Carter	D			
1979–80	Carter	D			
1981–82	Reagan		R	R	D
1983–84	Reagan		R	R	D
1985–86	Reagan		R	R	D
1987–88	Reagan		R	D	D
1989–90	Bush 41		R	D	D
1991–92	Bush 41		R	D	D
1993–94	Clinton	D			
1995–96	Clinton		D	R	R
1997–98	Clinton		D	R	R
1999–2000	Clinton		D	R	R
Jan–June 2001	Bush 43	R			
June 01–2002	Bush 43		R	D	R
2003–04	Bush 43	R			
2005–06	Bush 43	R			
2007–08	Bush 43		R	D	D
2009–10	Obama	D			
2011–12	Obama		D	D	R
2013–14			D	D	R

Source: Compiled by the author.

An Evolving Context: Demographics and Opinion

The philosopher Heraclitus said: "You can never step in the same river twice." Thus it is with political parties: They can never step in the same electorate twice. Through coming of age, death, immigration, expatriation, suffrage, or turnout shifts, not to mention changes of view among the persisting voters, every four years brings a fresh electoral environment.[32] What does this mean for the parties? One view is a kind of demographic determinism. A rise in demographics favoring a party's cause can elevate it to success permanently, or at least for a very long time.[33] But that is not the way politics has worked in the two-party systems of the Anglophone world—at least not in the medium or long run. Bad luck, for one thing, is bound to drive any party from power after a while. But also, the parties, whether winners or losers, do not just sit there. They strategize. They tinker with the rules. They ride the waves of demographics and opinion. They update their appeals to stay even with the median voter. Thus historically the Democrats, fresh from levering the disfranchisement of African Americans in the South in the late nineteenth century, much to their electoral advantage, gravitated 180 degrees to a pro–civil rights stance in the late 1940s. The Republicans used a "southern strategy" to attract southern whites in the 1960s. Both parties are perpetually on the lookout for newly envisioned categories they can appeal to—the "silent majority" in Richard Nixon's time, "soccer moms" in Bill Clinton's. To be sure, blunders are common and mispositioning has a long history. But, generally speaking, the American parties adapt. Over the very long haul, partly as a consequence, they each have won power and held office about equally.[34]

The demographics or the opinion distributions of the 2012 election will not be emphasized in detail here, for they are amply addressed elsewhere in this volume. But two mentions are on point. First, the issue of same-sex marriage offers a perfect example of fast-moving opinion change that the two presidential parties, while staying apart, adapted to in 2012. The Democrats moved from waffling to support. The Republicans moved from opposition to, more or less, silence. In general, the two parties can very importantly ratify or legitimize opinion change even if they do not say much or clash much in an election. Behavior like this can be a key aspect of policy evolution. Thus there is good reason to believe that the gay marriage issue will keep evolving and drop out of presidential elections in future years.

Second, the Republican showing among Hispanic American voters was abysmal in 2012. Chalk it up to a base-induced blunder in positioning. But there is good reason to believe that the Republicans will learn from the returns of 2012 and adjust their actions and positions accordingly. In the wake of the election, they are already doing so. Reversion to the reach-out strategies of George W. Bush and Karl Rove is an obvious move. Of similar texture, instructive although forgotten now, was the coalitional strategy of the unbeatable William McKinley over a century ago in slapping down the Republican Party's nativists by way of a stance of "cultural harmony."[35]

A Vexed Context: Party Polarization

The parties may move in parallel on issues, but that is not their only option. They can polarize. Today, party polarization is loud background music to elections and policymaking. The subject is devilishly difficult to get a handle on, but one excellent source is a report issued by the Pew Research Center in mid-2012.[36] It enables us to ask: Who has been doing the polarizing? Is it Republicans or Democrats? In the report, we are afforded responses to survey questions asked a quarter century ago in 1987 and asked again with identical wording in 2012 (and at certain times in between). Let us zero in on all the questions of at least tangential relevance to domestic policymaking on which the identifiers of either party shifted more than 10 percent in any direction during the intervening quarter century.[37]

As Table 9.4 shows, there are six such shift questions for each party, with some overlaps. Today's Republican and Democratic identifiers are further apart from each other on all these questions than were their predecessors in 1987—a plain picture of growing polarization. As for who has been doing the position shifting, and on what, the two parties have contributed about equally to the mix. As shown at the top of the table, the Republicans have lurched in a more conservative direction on the social safety net (the first two questions), environmental protection, labor unions, government competence, and regulation of business—all of which have a flavor of economics. The Democrats, shown at the bottom of the table, have lurched more liberal on religion, family and marriage, minority preferences, immigration, government competence (in the direction opposite to the Republicans), and regulation of business (also in the opposite direction). These have more the flavor of social issues. Jibing with these party drifts, not surprisingly, are some of the hot policy confrontations of recent times—for example, the controversy over Obamacare, Wisconsin Republican governor Scott Walker disempowering of the state's public sector unions, and the Obama White House stiffing the Catholic bishops on contraception policy.

Each of the parties has lurched or drifted a good deal. Yet, interestingly, in the cases of all twelve questions, the parties' departures from their earlier 1987 benchmarks crossed the 10 percent point only recently, during the presidencies of George W. Bush and Obama. In fact, on nine of the twelve questions—all but environmental protection for the Republicans, religion and family for the Democrats—*most* of the statistical distancing from the 1987 benchmarks has taken place since 2007, which means chiefly under Obama. This has been a truly polarizing time—a period of policy action and policy reaction.

That was the opinion context of 2012. It framed, or was spurred by, the policy wrangling of Obama's first term. It infused the parties' debt-deficit showdown in the summer of 2011. For the Republicans, it underpinned the eruptive, base-driven nominating politics of 2012 that brought Romney difficulties in the fall. In 2013–14 it will be as a continuing source of toxic policy

Table 9.4 Issue Evolution Within Each Party: Policy-relevant survey questions on which identifiers of each party in 2012 differed more than 10 percentage points from their predecessor identifiers in 1987.

Change among Republicans	
From 62% to 40% (minus 22%)	Government should take care of people who can't take care of themselves.
From 39% to 20% (minus 19%)	Government should help more needy people, even if it means going deeper in debt.
From 86% to 47% (minus 39%)	There needs to be stricter laws and regulations to protect the environment.
From 58% to 43% (minus 15%)	Labor unions are necessary to protect the working person.
From 59% to 77% (plus 18%)	When something is run by the government, it is usually inefficient and wasteful.
From 57% to 76% (plus 19%)	Government regulation of business usually does more harm than good.
Change among Democrats	
From 88% to 77% (minus 11%)	I never doubt the existence of God.
From 86% to 60% (minus 26%)	I have old-fashioned values about family and marriage.
From 33% to 52% (plus 19%)	We should make every effort to improve the position of minorities, even if it means preferential treatment.
From 74% to 58% (minus 16%)	We should restrict and control people coming into our country more than we do now.
From 59% to 41% (minus 18%)	When something is run by the government, it is usually inefficient and wasteful.
From 57% to 41% (minus 16%)	Government regulation of business usually does more harm than good.

Note: In all twelve instances cases it was change during the last decade under George W. Bush and Obama that brought the results above 10 percent.

Source: Pew Research Center, Partisan Polarization Surges in Bush, Obama Years: Trends in American Values, 1987–2012. Released June 4, 2012.

dissensus in Washington. On the other hand, there is something time-specific about it. On many topics on the Republican side, it has the aspect, as does the Tea Party, of a one-off reaction to the specific Democratic policy drives of 2009–10, and could moderate as those drives fade in memory.

Policy and Governing Prospects

What will happen in an Obama second term that is hemmed in by divided party control? For one thing, the politicians and the country will start by taking a deep breath. At presidential inauguration time, conflicts are closeted, past sins are remitted, hope is recharged, and a new beginning is announced and in some degree enacted. The winner is given a break, even if not a honeymoon. That is the tradition. Yet how about the particulars of this time and president?

Even before the January inauguration, looming in late 2012 was the large omnibus question of taxes, spending, debt, deficit, and the so-called fiscal cliff. Could sense be made out of all this under continuing conditions of divided party control? In the summer of 2011, the government had stuttered. Now, after the 2012 election, here it all was again. Could the leaders make a deal? Alternatively, could Obama go to the country like Ronald Reagan in 1981 and pry loose a couple of dozen House Republican defectors into a president-led coalition? The auguries are clouded.

In general, across the broad sweep of U.S. history, there is no explicit evidence of better fiscal management by the government under unified party control than under divided party control. The last balanced budgets were arranged across party lines by President Clinton and Speaker Newt Gingrich. During recent times of unified control under George W. Bush in 2003–06 and Obama in 2009–10, the government's attitudes toward debt and deficits were, well, casual. Teeth-gnashing, unpopular settlements involving big money have been struck in divided party circumstances in the past. Under Herbert Hoover in 1932, at the depth of the Great Depression, the two parties joined to enact the steepest tax increase of the 1930s, in accordance with expert opinion at the time. Under George H. W. Bush in 1990, just days before a midterm election, an unpopular half-trillion-dollar deficit-reduction measure won approval from a Democratic Congress.[38] Under George W. Bush in October 2008, a $850 billion deal bailing out the banks went through the House and Senate, both controlled by the Democrats. But these days the polarization is wide, the two sides' positions are stubbornly staked out, and the policy problems are immense.

Ongoing conflict is also a good bet for Obamacare. This program racked up two major victories in 2012 through a positive Supreme Court ruling (except on features of Medicaid) and the president's reelection. But it remains unpopular. No other major U.S. welfare-state expansion has stayed so unpopular so long after enactment (although that could change as the benefits flow). Damage to the program's implementation, which is a gigantic task, could still issue from Congress, the courts, private industry, the state governments, and public opinion. Generally speaking, major federal programs are not formally repealed. But they can suffer enfeeblement through attrition as happened to the ambitious public housing program enacted in the 1940s and the antipoverty program enacted in the 1960s.

On the proaction side is immigration. With the Republicans burned by Hispanic American voters in the election, and immigration from Mexico tailing off, the stage seems set for "comprehensive immigration reform," a recurrent aim of the last quarter century sometimes emanating in laws.

That achievement could come to pass. Also stemming from the election we may see a drive to repeal the Defense of Marriage Act (DOMA), which may indeed succeed in coming years if the courts do not get there first.

Otherwise, the crystal ball is cloudy. In general, presidential "mandates" are a dubious matter,[39] and it is hard to spy one in the 2012 election any more than in, say, the George W. Bush reelection of 2004. As for presidential second terms, none of the last century has been judged especially innovative or successful in the sphere of domestic policymaking,[40] although some have seen the achievements of a first term consolidated. That latter story may be Obama's. To that end, or to the end of further innovation, we may see a good deal of conflict over executive orders. We can expect the White House to issue directives that do not have a clear warrant in law. It is a good bet that the newspapers, magazines, blogs, and law journals will balloon with constitutional interpretations of what a president can do and not do absent a law.

How about process reforms in light of the 2012 election? It is possible that two reform aims often favored by liberals and the media have suffered setbacks. One is campaign finance reform. Tighter disclosure rules may win acceptance, but anything beyond that seems questionable. It is pretty clear that big-bucks corporate or personal money did not buy the 2012 election, that the Democrats had ample money when they needed it, and that labor unions used the leeway offered them by the Supreme Court's ruling in *Citizens United.* As a consequence, steam may hiss out of this reform drive. Similar facts and reflections may set back the faint, but persisting, drive to reform the Electoral College. Still in mind is the searing memory of 2000 when Democrat Al Gore won the popular vote but lost the Electoral College. But now, for the third presidential election in a row, the Democrats have enjoyed a slight statistical edge in the Electoral College. That edge has not tipped any of these elections as it did for the Republicans in 2000, but there it is. The idea is available in counterfactuals. Consider this one for 2012: Slice about 2 percent off Obama's popular vote in each of the fifty-one units of the Electoral College (that includes the District of Columbia). Doing that takes the president below 50 percent of the two-party popular vote nationwide, but he stills wins the White House with a majority of electoral votes. Democratic Party activists are bound to notice statistics like these.

Finally, it should not be overlooked that the presidency is primarily a managerial office. First in the job description is management. Chiefly that means foreign policy and the macro-economy. As much as anything, voters might have reelected Obama on managerial grounds. On foreign policy: pretty good. On the macro-economy: generic, given the circumstances. A dash of voter risk averseness could have done it. Obama's second term might be very dominantly a management term. That can entail crisis management. In roughly half of all the presidential terms (first or second) of the last century, large crises have struck. Black swans, to use the locution for unpredictable disasters, have flown in. It is in handling crises that presidents and their cabinets earn much of their pay.

As for future elections, on current theory and experience the best bet for 2014 is Republican gains. The best bet for 2016 is a toss-up open-seat presidential election.

Notes

1. Thanks to Eleanor Powell for advice on this paper.
2. In the House of Representatives, the share of members running again tends to dip in elections that occur just after a census has forced a remapping of districts.
3. Gary C. Jacobson, "Referendum: The 2006 Midterm Congressional Elections," *Political Science Quarterly* 122 (Spring 2007): 1–24.
4. James E. Campbell, "The Exceptional Election of 2008: Performance, Values, and Crisis," *Presidential Studies Quarterly* 40, no. 2 (June 2010): 225–246; Robert S. Erikson, "The American Voter and the Economy, 2008," *PS: Political Science and Politics* 42, no. 3 (July 2009): 467–471; Gary C. Jacobson, "George W. Bush, the Iraq War, and the Election of Barack Obama," *Presidential Studies Quarterly* 40, no. 2 (June 2010), 207–224.
5. David W. Brady, Morris P. Fiorina, and Arjun S. Wilkins, "The 2010 Elections: Why Did Political Science Forecasts Go Awry?" *PS: Political Science and Politics* 44, no. 2 (April 2011): 247–50; Gary C. Jacobson, "The Republican Resurgence in 2010," *Political Science Quarterly* 126, no. 1 (Spring 2011), 27–52.
6. David Samuels, "Presidentialism and Accountability for the Economy in Comparative Perspective," *American Political Science Review* 98 (August 2004): 425–436, at 428–429.
7. Table 9.1 is an update of Table 2 in David R. Mayhew, "Incumbency Advantage in U.S. Presidential Elections: The Historical Record," *Presidential Studies Quarterly* 123, no. 2 (Summer 2008): 201–228, at 212. Table 9.1 here accommodates fifty-five elections, not the full historical roster of fifty-seven. Excluded are 1788 and 1824 for which it is not apt, or does not seem so, to ask whether the party holding the White House kept it. Included as incumbents running again are the vice presidential succeeders: Theodore Roosevelt, Calvin Coolidge, Harry S. Truman, Lyndon Johnson, and Gerald Ford. The Whigs are credited with holding the White House going into the 1844 election, and the Republicans going into 1868, impeachable judgments both, although the summary numbers of the table do not change if both those judgments are reversed.
8. Across a wide range of U.S. elections, the statistical advantage of incumbency seems to have grown appreciably in the generation after World War II. See Stephen Ansolabehere and James M. Snyder Jr., "The Incumbency Advantage in U.S. Elections: An Analysis of State and Federal Offices, 1942–2000," *Election Law Journal* 1, no. 3 (September 2002), 315–338.
9. Excepting the vice presidential succeeders.
10. For this argument, see John Zaller, "Politicians as Prize Fighters: Electoral Selection and Incumbency Advantage," ch. 6 in *Politicians and Party Politics,* John G. Geer (ed.) (Baltimore: Johns Hopkins University Press, 1998).
11. For this argument, see Timothy Groseclose, "A Model of Candidate Location When One Candidate Has a Valence Advantage," *American Journal of Political Science* 45 (October 2001): 862–886.
12. This is not an exhaustive rendition of theories about the statistical advantage of personal incumbency at the presidential level. See also Mayhew, "Incumbency

Advantage," at pp. 214–28, where among things the possibility of strategic behavior in the selection of candidates is taken up.

13. Ray C. Fair, *Predicting Presidential Elections and Other Things* (Stanford, Calif.: Stanford University Press, 2002), pp. 46–51. The dates are 1916 through 1996.
14. Alan Abramowitz, "Forecasting in a Polarized Era: The Time for Change Model and the 2012 Presidential Election," *PS: Political Science and Politics* 45, no. 4 (October 2012): 618–619.
15. This account scores the retiring Joseph Lieberman of Connecticut, technically an Independent, as a Democrat.
16. The Democratic membership late in the Congress of 2011–12 was 193. Thirty-one of these members did not appear as candidates on the November ballot. What was the story of these thirty-one disappearances? There was one death. There were two preelection resignations—one spurred by a bid for higher office, the other by a redistricting misfortune. Seven members ran for Senate seats or in one case the San Diego mayoralty; six of these won their quests. Two lost nominations to nonincumbent Democratic challengers. Five lost nominations to other Democratic incumbents in throw-in primary contests. Fourteen flatly retired, although one of these partly because the decennial reapportionment demolished his district and another five or so because remapping had brought more difficult districts. In some cases the reason is blurry. In all the thirty-one instances, probably only one Democratic member—Silvestre Reyes (TX)—can be said to have lost a reelection bid in a straight-out Democratic primary contest not seriously clouded by remapping.
17. Those were Mark Critz (PA), Kathy Hochul (NY), and Larry Kissell (NC).
18. The Republican membership late in the Congress of 2011–12 was 242. Twenty-six of these members did not appear as candidates on the November 2012 ballot. There were two preelection resignations. Seven members ran for other offices, of whom only two won. Three lost nominations to other Republican incumbents in throw-in primary contests. Three lost primaries to nonincumbent Republican challengers—a key factor in the case of Cliff Stearns (FL) was new and unfamiliar district territory. Eleven members flatly retired, although two of these because their districts had been disassembled and possibly one or two more partly due to redistricting inconvenience. In all the twenty-six departure instances, probably only two members—Jean Schmidt (OH) and John Sullivan (OK)—can be said to have failed of renomination in straight-out primary contests unvexed by remap difficulties.
19. Those were Mary Bono Mack (CA), Dan Lungren (CA), Brian Bilbray (CA), Robert Dold (IL), Joe Walsh (IL), Judy Biggert (IL), Bobby Schilling (IL), Roscoe Bartlett (MD), Allen West (FL), Francisco Conseco (TX), Nan Hayworth (NY), and Ann Marie Buerkle (NY). The five Illinois and Maryland losers had been targeted in Democratic remaps, although one or more might have lost anyway. The rest were discommoded by nonpartisan or court-induced remaps. Whether those remaps offer smoking-gun explanations of the losses is not easy to say in several cases. At least Buerkle was thought to be in trouble anyway. Lungren had been slipping in previous elections apparently through demographic change.
20. The House incumbents running again in November 2012 numbered 378. The open seats numbered 62. Those two figures do not sum to 435 because in five instances pairs of incumbents ran against each other in November.
21. I arrived at the 50.4 percent figure quickly myself after the election by adding up, twice, district by district, the votes cast in all the 435 districts for Democratic and Republican House candidates. Doing this posed coding nightmares at the edges as always: how to deal with the California and Louisiana election

systems, the dozen districts with unreported totals, and so on. I came up with a figure of 49.9 percent for the Democrats, but that was almost certainly an underestimate. Two years earlier in November 2010, the Democratic percentage of the national House vote that I calculated immediately after the election rose roughly half a point as late-counted votes straggled in across the weeks from chiefly the Democratic-leaning states of California and Washington. In 2012, Arizona joined the list of late counters.

22. The House seat calls were not entirely finished at the time of this writing.
23. The gross Republican gain of seats in 2010 was sixty-six. The net gain was sixty-three, since three seats went the other way.
24. Or got a free ride. The other three were Rick Berg (ND), who ran for the Senate and lost; Sandy Adams (FL), who lost a throw-in primary against another (nonfreshman) Republican incumbent; and Jeff Landry (LA), who faced another (nonfreshman) Republican incumbent on the November ballot in a contest not decided at that juncture.
25. These categories may seem clear enough, but in practice there is some messiness. Other classifications are possible. It is important to inspect and appreciate the details.
26. For thirty-one of the states, the allocations into redistricting categories are specified in the notes of Table 9.2. For the record, the additional allocations (that is, for states that lacked representation in the set of the sixty-three Republican freshmen) are as follows. Republican-controlled: Louisiana, Oklahoma, Utah. Democratic-controlled: Massachusetts. The rest (including the one-district states, which harbor a total of seven districts—that figure including South Dakota which was already accommodated in Table 9.2): Alaska, California, Connecticut, Delaware, Hawaii, Iowa, Kentucky, Maine, Montana, Nebraska, North Dakota, Oregon, Rhode Island, Vermont, Wyoming.
27. It will come as no surprise that the Republican-controlled states are terrain where, generally speaking, Republican candidates tend to have the best luck. Likewise for the Democrats. Those tendencies will obtain, redistricting or no redistricting.
28. To help explain the House outcome disparity of 2012—the Republican edge in seats but not popular voles—another line of analysis may be mentioned. In the sixteen presidential elections from World War II through 2008, the Republicans enjoyed what might be considered a slight, continuing bonus in both the House and Senate electoral universes. Here is the analytic wedge: For any presidential election, calculate the Democratic share of the two-party presidential vote cast nationwide. Then calculate the share of that same statistic (the presidential vote) cast in the median House district—that is, the 218th District if the 435 districts are arrayed according to their presidential vote share. Additionally, calculate that presidential-vote statistic for the median Senate district (that is, state; the result will always be an average for two adjoining states since the chamber's membership is an even number). The results are as follows: The median on the House side is on average 1.1 percent lower than the pure Democratic share of the presidential vote calculated nationwide. That seems to be because Democratic voters tend to concentrate geographically more than do Republicans, thus "wasting votes" in a subsidiary scheme of single-member districts. The median on the Senate side is on average 1.3 percent lower. That is because the smaller-population states are a tad—notably, just a tad—more Republican. There is no apparent time trend in either the House or the Senate statistics. (These statistics are not calculable yet for the 2012 election.) Possibly these slight gaps have rendered both chambers on average just a bit more conservative than the presidency (this is in principle regardless of the formal statistics of party holdings; consider the Blue Dog Democrats of the House). But it is not clear that

this analysis can throw much light on the particular disparity in election results for the House in 2012. Other factors can and do intrude into elections. Note that the Democrats have had no trouble winning and keeping the Senate lately. Personal incumbency advantage, for one thing, can infuse both Senate and House elections. In the 1980s, the marvel of the national election universe was the Democrats' outlier success in winning the House. It is a plausible bet that that continuing success owed a good deal to personal incumbency advantage stacked up on that era's Democratic House incumbents. It is interesting that since World War II the Democrats have won the House more often than either the presidency (by a wide margin) or the Senate (by a margin of one instance). In process terms, today's election success of the House Republicans under Speaker John Boehner, featuring personal incumbency advantage as it apparently does, seems a cousin to yesterday's success of the House Democrats in the 1980s under Speaker Tip O'Neill. The source of the analysis generating the statistics of 1.1 for the House and 1.3 for the Senate: David R. Mayhew, *Partisan Balance: Why Political Parties Don't Kill the U.S. Constitutional System* (Princeton, N.J.: Princeton University Press, 2011), ch. 1.

29. For a chart showing the spectacular rise in the economy during the entirety of FDR's first term, see Gauti B. Eggertsson, "Was the New Deal Contractionary?" *American Economic Review* 102, no. 1 (February 2012): 524–535, at 527. On this period, see also D. Roderick Kiewiet and Michael Udell, "Twenty-five Years after Kramer: An Assessment of Economic Retrospective Voting Based upon Improved Estimates of Income and Unemployment," *Economics and Politics* 10 (November 1998): 219–248, at 234–249.
30. An oddity in Table 9.3 is the juncture of 2001–02. The Republicans enjoyed unified party control briefly after the clouded Bush-Gore election of 2000. But partway into 2001, after the Bush tax cuts were enacted, Republican senator James Jeffords of Vermont switched sides. He moved over to caucus with the Democrats, giving them narrow control of the Senate through December 2002.
31. On this topic, see Morris P. Fiorina, *Divided Government* (New York: Longman, 2002), pp. 11–12; Markus Prior, "The Incumbent in the Living Room," *Journal of Politics* 68 (August 2006): 657–673.
32. Person for person, in earlier days the American electorate must have been typically fresher every four years than it is now. Life expectancy used to be lower and the voter eligibility age higher.
33. Famously, this was the view of Social Democrats in Germany a century ago as the working class grew in size.
34. For some statistics on this point, see David R. Mayhew, "Understanding U.S. Presidential Elections," http://press.princeton.edu/blog/2012/04/02/understanding-u-s-presidential-elections/; of course, the Federalists and Whigs did not finally adapt, but the Democrats and Republicans have been going at it for more than a century and a half.
35. Daniel J. Tichenor, *Dividing Lines: The Politics of Immigration Control in America* (Princeton, N.J.: Princeton University Press, 2002), pp. 73–75. For that era, which brought similar antirestrictionist positioning on immigration by Republican House Speaker Joseph Cannon, see also pp. 81–83, 116, 124–128.
36. The Pew Research Center for the People and the Press, *Partisan Polarization Surges in Bush, Obama Years: Trends in American Values: 1987–2012,* June 4, 2012, www.people-press.org/2012/06/04/partisan-polarization-surges-in-bush-obama-years/.
37. The relevant information is at *Partisan Polarization Surges,* Overview, pp. 3–6; Section 4, pp. 2–3; Section 5, pp. 2–5; Section 8, pp. 2–4.
38. Actually, the much-despised $2.1 trillion deficit-reduction plan finally enacted under Obama after the showdown wrangling in August 2011, including its

complex rescission design, seems to have offered bigger money than the sum of the Bush-led plan of 1990 and the similar deficit-reduction plan engineered by Clinton under unified Democratic control in 1993. But in 2011 the problems were much greater.

39. See Robert A. Dahl, "Myth of the Presidential Mandate," *Political Science Quarterly* 105, no. 3 (Autumn 1990): 355–372.
40. Although the slate is not bare: Consider the Fair Labor Standards Act of 1938, the Housing Act of 1949 (if Truman can be said to have had a second term), the Civil Rights Act of 1957, the Tax Reform act of 1986, the Children's Health Insurance Program in 1997, and, for that matter, the many enactments passed by Democratic Congresses under Nixon and Ford during 1973–76 that were not White House measures. Still, presidents are higher legislative performers during their first terms.